Inventing Stanley Park

The Nature | History | Society series is devoted to the publication of high-quality scholarship in environmental history and allied fields. Its broad compass is signalled by its title: *nature* because it takes the natural world seriously; *history* because it aims to foster work that has temporal depth; and *society* because its essential concern is with the interface between nature and society, broadly conceived. The series is avowedly interdisciplinary and is open to the work of anthropologists, ecologists, historians, geographers, literary scholars, political scientists, sociologists, and others whose interests resonate with its mandate. It offers a timely outlet for lively, innovative, and well-written work on the interaction of people and nature through time in North America.

General Editor: Graeme Wynn, University of British Columbia

A list of titles in the series appears at the end of the book.

NATURE | HISTORY | SOCIETY

Sean Kheraj

Inventing Stanley Park
An Environmental History

Foreword by Graeme Wynn

UBCPress · Vancouver · Toronto

21 20 19 18 17 16 15 14 13   5 4 3 2 1

Printed in Canada on FSC-certified ancient-forest-free paper
(100% post-consumer recycled) that is processed chlorine- and acid-free.

Library and Archives Canada Cataloguing in Publication

Kheraj, Sean
    Inventing Stanley Park : an environmental history / Sean Kheraj ; foreword by Graeme Wynn.

(Nature, history, society, ISSN 1713-6687)
Includes bibliographical references and index.
Issued also in electronic format.
ISBN 978-0-7748-2424-8 (bound); ISBN 978-0-7748-2425-5 (pbk.)

    1. Stanley Park (Vancouver, B.C.) – History. 2. Human ecology – British Columbia – Vancouver – History. 3. Nature – Effect of human beings on – British Columbia – Vancouver. 4. Parks – Government policy – British Columbia – Vancouver. I. Title. II. Series: Nature, history, society

FC3847.65.K44 2013   971.1'33   C2013-901329-6

Canada

UBC Press gratefully acknowledges the financial support for our publishing program of the Government of Canada (through the Canada Book Fund), the Canada Council for the Arts, and the British Columbia Arts Council.

This book has been published with the help of a grant from the Canadian Federation for the Humanities and Social Sciences, through the Awards to Scholarly Publications Program, using funds provided by the Social Sciences and Humanities Research Council of Canada, and with the help of the University of British Columbia through the K.D. Srivastava Fund.

UBC Press
The University of British Columbia
2029 West Mall
Vancouver, BC V6T 1Z2
www.ubcpress.ca

Contents

Illustrations

Foreword
Between Art and Nature
Graeme Wynn

One of my favourite episodes in the history of Vancouver is the visit (mentioned on p. 109 of this book) of English landscape architect Thomas H. Mawson to the city late in March 1912. The record of this fleeting moment is relatively thin, but it is nonetheless fascinating. Mawson was in Vancouver for but a few days (although he returned several times in 1912 and 1913, and his firm ran a Canadian office in the Rogers Building on Granville Street for some years).[1] Invited, as Kheraj notes, by civic officials anxious to have his advice about the development of their city, Mawson must have cut quite a figure in this fast-growing, still somewhat rough-and-ready frontier town of barely 110,000 people.[2] Generally pictured in a stylish three-piece suit, often wearing the high starched shirt collars fashionable in Edwardian England, and sporting a luxuriant moustache, Mawson was no shrinking violet.[3] Although his reputation "as perhaps the greatest living authority on city planning" preceded him, he made a point of telling members of the Canadian Club gathered to hear his thoughts on "Civic Art and Vancouver's Opportunity" that he was "probably a greater student of this subject than any man living." By his own account, he also set out shortly after his arrival in the city to take the measure of this "most marvelous creation of twenty-five years." Seeking to discover what local residents thought "about Art and Nature," he pursued his research in "every place – clubs, hotels and even churches." On the basis of the conversations he had in these places, he quickly concluded that the people of Vancouver fell into two camps: those who loved Nature so unreservedly that "they can never imagine that Nature cannot always be at her best" and a second group "interested only in commercial pursuits, with no idea or imagination that ever rises above that level." Lacking the "reverent soul" and unable to hear "the music of the spheres," members of this latter group "would do anything to destroy Nature."[4]

Born in decidedly modest circumstances in Lancashire, England, in 1861, Mawson had left school at the age of twelve and worked in the building trades and a plant nursery before branching out into garden design in the 1880s.[5] In the following decade, he sharpened and refined his ideas through several estate commissions. Executing these, he effectively resolved the battle of horticultural styles – which pitted proponents of wild gardens against those who favoured formal spaces – by including formal elements normally associated with the house in the surrounding landscape and even more distant (and often artfully enhanced) woodland. As historian Edward Hyams described them, these fin de siècle years saw the reconciliation of picturesque, Italianate, and architectural principles with plantsmanship in the English garden, and Mawson was near the centre of these developments.[6] In 1900, he published *The Art and Craft of Garden Making*, signalling his indebtedness to the ideas of William Morris, John Ruskin, and the Arts and Crafts movement.[7] Links with the Scotsman Patrick Geddes led him in the first years of the twentieth century to the forefront of the emergent town-planning movement where he advocated what he termed *civic art*. Strongly influenced, initially, by ideas emanating from the École des Beaux-Arts in Paris and, latterly, by the American City Beautiful movement, Mawson's civic art was a mixture of town planning and park building that emphasized the aesthetic rather than the practical (e.g., sewage and water supply) elements of urban design.

A decade or so into the twentieth century, Mawson's star was high; he had completed important commissions for Lord Leverhulme in England, been chosen to design the gardens of the Andrew Carnegie–funded Peace Palace in The Hague, and undertaken a lecture tour that encompassed several cities in the eastern United States and included visits to Harvard, Cornell, and Yale Universities, as well as to the governor general in Ottawa. Looking back on this 1910 trip, he reflected with typical immodesty: "I had now, metaphorically speaking, annexed America, and made this vast continent a part of my sphere of influence."[8] A year later, he published *Civic Art: Studies in Town Planning, Parks, Boulevards, and Open Spaces,* and early in 1912 he was invited back to Canada to consult on a park at Niagara Falls and the replanning of Ottawa.[9] When these plans fell through, he arranged to give lectures on city planning in a dozen centres from Halifax to Victoria, including Vancouver. These contacts led to a virtual reprise of this itinerary in the fall, a three-month trip that "constituted the biggest bustle of ... [his] life."[10] In Vancouver a second time, Mawson was beset by newspapermen, people interested in town planning, and citizens concerned about social problems, but he insisted that his business in the city on this visit was "limited to the improvement of Coal Harbour and the famous Stanley Park."[11] In a brief stay, he worked up a preliminary report for the Park Board and was instructed to develop alternative schemes for these purposes. These were further refined during a six-week visit to Canada in April-May 1913 and submitted in person on another visit in December of that year.[12]

Accepted but never implemented, these plans mapped an unbuilt land-scape, part of a city that might have been.[13] Yet they warrant some atten-tion, because they reflected well-established principles of Mawson's design practice as well as the insights he derived from his quick assessment of the city and its inhabitants' attitudes toward nature on his first visit in 1912. They are also an engaging starting point for thinking about the en-vironmental history of Vancouver, the place of Stanley Park in the city, and the tensions between Art and Nature (or perhaps even God and Mammon) in the developing metropolis. They serve, in other words, as a convenient springboard from which to contemplate the arguments and achievements of *Inventing Stanley Park*.

In his address to the Canadian Club, Mawson left no room for doubt about the importance of Stanley Park to the city.[14] It was Vancouver's greatest asset, known (he claimed) "to every schoolboy in the Old Country" and something akin to a great work of art in the possession of a collector, over which Vancouverites had custody on behalf of "the whole English-speaking race." This valuable place HAD to be saved from those second-order denizens of the city's clubs and hotels who "would do anything to destroy Nature." Heed the powerful import of Ruskin's rhetorical question, he implored his listeners: "What shall it profit you if you turn the whole world into a gasometer and lose your own souls?" But it was not sufficient to treasure Nature as it was. Nature sometimes dropped a word or missed a note in the composition of her poetic lyrics or the performance of her magnificent tune. Human intervention was necessary to realize Nature's full potential. In a park or garden, the basic "features are supplied by Nature," but they required an artist – "he who can combine and co-operate what Nature gives ... with the suggestions of Art clothing our needs."

More than this, Mawson insisted, Vancouver was distinguished by the juxtaposition of the city, "a purely artificial creation," and Stanley Park, "which is a work of Nature." Art was inherent in neither, but it had the capacity to unite the two and provide a "perfect orchestration."[15] Here, he outlined the essence of the plans that he would submit to the Park Board in December 1913, with Georgia Street as the prime axis (the "Champs-Elysées of Vancouver") of a design intended to make Coal Harbour "the great social centre" of the city. But he also embarked on a flight of fancy that – perhaps mercifully – substantially disappeared from his later designs. Between the artificial city ("where Art plays first fiddle and Nature a muted string") and the natural park (where these roles were reversed), he insisted that there should be a progression allowing citizens to "pass by gradual degrees from that which is purely artificial to that where Nature has full sway." This, he suggested, could be realized along Georgia Street by creating a purely architectural civic square in the centre of the city. "Belts of grass and a few trees" would be planted to adorn the architecture after the street left the plaza; a little farther along, the trees would be "clipped into the shapes of birds and beasts"; then they would be allowed to grow wilder and freer, until "in the far distance," Nature would be left "to tell her own story." Clearly, this distance was well beyond Coal Harbour, which was to be converted into a Vancouver version of Paris's Grande Ronde Pond, surrounded by a promenade, carriageways, playgrounds, and an imposing neoclassical building to house a natural history museum. Here, "Art, Nature and Science ... [would] meet and arrange terms." In Mawson's analogical telling, the park beyond would be "the Tuilieries, only not humanised" – but even this did not mean "free of human interference" because Mawson offered his listeners advice on the style of buildings to be erected there ("if you require a bandstand, let it be worthy of a Temple of Music") and advocated banishing "absolutely every exotic, whether plant, tree or animal."

Delivered with verve, these sometimes rather rambling remarks were received with great enthusiasm. In Vancouver, Mawson was, of course, something of an "exotic" himself, a *rara avis* with an international reputation who worked and walked and talked with members of the landed gentry, high government officials, business leaders, important public figures, and major philanthropists. This alone probably guaranteed him a rousing reception in frontier British Columbia. But Mawson's clever incorporation of local "research" into his speech also won him favour. Although his half-formed plans for Coal Harbour and Stanley Park, with their roots in European and British debates about architecture and landscape design, may have been as grandiose as his address was grandiloquent, they also struck a chord, as Mawson's biographer Janet Waymark has noted, with those who "either admired or were intensely patriotic to Empire and its roots in the Crown."[16] Perhaps most tellingly, however, his recommendations and remarks resonated with local convictions in their boosterish tone, and in their strong sense of people's capacity and responsibility to alter and improve the world. In the end, Mawson's call to unite art with nature in Stanley Park essentially echoed Mayor David Oppenheimer's remarks at the opening of the park, although his arguments for this approach were both more elaborate and better undergirded, intellectually, than was the mayor's 1888 call to improve the area through the combination of human artifice with natural scenery (see p. 92).

As Kheraj shows in the pages that follow, there were numerous efforts to improve upon Stanley Park nature in the decades before and after Mawson's visits to Vancouver. In the quarter century after the establishment of the park, many of these initiatives drew their inspiration from the American school of park designers and landscape architects. Use of the word *school* in this context suggests a movement, and it is worth recalling that the creation of urban parks was something of a fad in the late nineteenth and early twentieth centuries. Indeed, park historian and geographer Terence Young has pointed out that no municipality in the United States had a developed public park in 1850 but that only one of the 157 American cities with more than thirty thousand residents was without one in 1908.[17] Many of these parks were designed by or followed ideas promulgated by Andrew Jackson Downing, Frederick Law Olmsted, and Calvert Vaux, whose approach historian Anne Whiston Spirn has termed *naturalistic constructivism*.[18] That is to say that these designers "sought to disguise anthropogenic interventions to make park spaces appear more natural" even as they made them more accessible (see p. 94). In effect, human artifice was employed to hide signs of human disturbance by the artful construction of curvilinear roads and pathways and the careful planting and management of vegetation. Similar strategies continued well into the twentieth century as park officials employed the techniques of facade management "to mask or minimize" the impact of such intrusions as roadways, water pipelines, reservoirs, and sewer lines (see p. 137).[19] Although often described and long cherished as a "wilderness" or ancient forest, Stanley Park was and is a profoundly humanized landscape.

To write of the "invention" of Stanley Park is to emphasize this disjunction, to argue that the park has been made not given, and to point to the complexities embedded in the process of creating and re-presenting such a space. Kheraj tackles these tasks in a handful of thematic chapters in which he traces the pre-park history of the peninsula that became the park, the legal and social processes involved in making this a public space, the various efforts to remake park nature, the impacts of the city upon the park, and the ways in which efforts at environmental restoration after severe disturbances in the 1930s and the 1960s both reflected popular perceptions of nature and reinforced the view that the much-altered park was untouched.

Summarized thus, *Inventing Stanley Park* might be perceived either as simply another addition to the very substantial pile of books and articles treating North American parks or as a micro study adding details to the already reasonably well-known story of some four hundred hectares of land in the city of Vancouver. It is, after all, now widely accepted that the idea of wilderness is a social construction and that bounding spaces and conferring a particular status on them (by declaring them parks, for example) has shifting and ramifying consequences, depending on what the status entails (or what people take a park to be) at different points in time.[20] Similarly, those familiar with Vancouver's past might feel that several of the stories in this book have been adumbrated in earlier work. So they might point, for example, to Robert McDonald's discussion of competing perceptions of Stanley Park as a "holy retreat" or "practical breathing spot" as a reflection of class divisions in the city; or to Jean Barman's exploration of the displacement and dispossession of the indigenous inhabitants of the park peninsula; or to a couple of master's theses written in the 1970s that trace the history of Vancouver parks.[21] One of these, by planning student Diane Beverley Hinds, examines park design ideas in pre–First World War Vancouver and concludes (broadly congruently with *Inventing Stanley Park*) that they were largely influenced by the attitudes of Vancouver residents, by ideas and influences from other places, especially Britain and the American West Coast, and by "various civic associations and ratepayers groups who asserted themselves in the decision making process."

To stop at these observations would, though, do Kheraj's alluring and magnificently illustrated work a very considerable injustice. All scholarship is cumulative. The value of historical studies is measured in their details, in the acuity of their critical analysis, and in the veracity and pertinence of the stories they tell rather than in the sorts of "detachable conclusions" drawn from Hinds's extended essay. Looked at in this light, *Inventing Stanley Park* works, in often-understated ways, to make several contributions. In sum, it adds to and revises established interpretations of the processes of urban park creation in North America, offers fresh insight into the development of Stanley Park, and brings a distinct perspective to understanding the park, the city that encompasses it, and the changing society that shaped it.

In his fine and important study of San Francisco's parks, Terence Young argues that American park advocates saw the creation of parks as a form of social reform intended to realize four virtues – public health, prosperity, democratic equality, and social coherence – but that "their understanding of *how* parks fostered the good society" changed with time.[22] In this telling, an earlier romantic view of parks that saw nature as God's handiwork and conceived of parks as places for visitors to contemplate "the beauty of the larger landscape scene," gave way, as society grew more specialized (in the 1880s in San Francisco but earlier and later elsewhere), to a rationalistic vision that saw parks as settings for organized leisure activities. In essence, Young argues that a "Darwinian, mechanistic view of nature replaced a romantic teleological one," and nature came to be seen as external to rather than inclusive of humanity even as he acknowledges that the rationalists' "new vision of the nature-society connection was both figuratively and literally built out, of, upon, and beside the existing, romantic one." Kheraj draws upon Young's work, but to my mind his study suggests that conceptions of park design, in Vancouver at least, were both more complicated and more entangled than Young's dichotomized interpretation implies. Here, *Inventing Stanley Park* begs an implicit question about (and points, perhaps, to the need for further work exploring) the extent to which the trajectory of urban park development in Canada differed from that in the United States.

As a contribution to scholarship on British Columbia, Kheraj's study makes a particular mark by viewing the creation of Stanley Park from a perspective shaped by the venerable political-economy tradition in Canadian scholarship. So he describes the park as "founded on speculation and ambition." So the eviction of indigenous people from the park had "more to do with private property rights and Aboriginal land claims" than any desire to make the space of the park appear "natural"; families were banished from long-occupied residential sites "because they challenged the very notion of a public park by possessing private homes within it" (p. 57 and 82). So the law is recognized as instrumental in producing Stanley Park as public space and reshaping Vancouverites' relations with nature within its bounds.

With sensitivities heightened by insights drawn from that important body of scholarship loosely known as subaltern studies, Kheraj adds to all of this an awareness of the importance of protest and resistance to the story of Stanley Park's development. Parks may be for people, but recent scholarship has demonstrated that the notion of "the people" is far from inclusive and that generally some are more welcome, more able, or more entitled than others to use, and benefit from, parks, even when these places are ostensibly dedicated "to the use and enjoyment of peoples of all colours, creeds, and customs, for all time" (p. 63). In Vancouver, the legal regime that created the park allowed the displacement of its indigenous inhabitants, even though they did not go meekly into the good night. Settlers who had foraged in the peninsula and come to regard it as a commons were prohibited from continuing this practice once the land became a park. And although the story of this park is inevitably and substantially the story of what was done, and what was made, Kheraj marks the fact that the decisions that produced these outcomes were often contested. By noting several instances of resistance to the agenda for the park promulgated by city officials and others – by those who perceived extensions to the park road network as "the destruction of nature rather than an improvement," for example – he reminds us that things might have turned out differently, that history is contingent, and that (like that of true love) the course of development rarely runs smooth (quote from p. 102). To recognize as much is to begin to realize something of the contribution that good humanistic scholarship can make to understanding the human condition.

Finally, *Inventing Stanley Park* makes an explicit contribution to the fast-developing field of Canadian environmental history. This is where Kheraj finds the uniqueness of his book. He presents Stanley Park as "a hybrid produced by a confluence of natural and cultural forces" and argues that his environmental historical approach to its development enables us "to determine the relationship between humans and the rest of nature that is reflected in the landscape" of the park (p. 204). Here, the author's aim is to demonstrate the interdependence of nature and culture by acknowledging the power of nature's agency and recognizing the limits of human intention. So, for instance, he notes, "erosion, fire, insects, animals, drainage, and other natural features impeded improvement projects such as road construction and forest preservation ... [which] were often a struggle *against* the autonomy of nature" (p. 195). There is a good deal, then, in these pages about geology and hydrology, and because foresters, engineers, and entomologists were enrolled in one way or another in the task of managing the park – becoming in the process instruments of a landscape art designed to balance popular cultural expectations with the ecology of the peninsula – about the science they practised.

These discussions are given contemporary salience by Kheraj's examination of the efforts to restore Stanley Park nature after particularly destructive windstorms in 1934 and 1962, of the debates (running into the 1970s) over plans for new bridges and freeways that would have impinged on the park, and of a scheme to remake the park forest in the image of its purported 1888 condition – all of which play against the book's opening description of the powerful December storm of 2006 that felled ten thousand trees in the park and fuelled an outpouring of despair at the damage done to Vancouver's "Crown jewel." Time and again, public reactions to the devastation of 2006 revealed that they were grounded in what Kheraj's book shows to have been "an illusory vision of an unchanging forest" (p. 3). In the 125 years since its creation, the park had become "a temple of atonement for the environmental destruction that was necessary to build the city and the province" (p. 190). Even though a consequence of "the forces of nature," the dramatic alteration of even a small part (no more than 10 percent) of what was widely regarded as ancient unspoiled forest was considered a desecration. People had forgotten, or perhaps they never knew, what the park superintendent had admitted in an unguarded moment in the early 1950s: that "it takes a considerable amount of work to keep a forest area looking as though it were just as nature intended" and that – as he noted three years earlier – "a lack of such work allows the forest to get into a messy and untidy condition" (p. 180). In his somewhat idiosyncratic, Edwardian way, Thomas Mawson understood full well the myriad entanglements of art and nature, but it is Kheraj's achievement to remind us that decades of natural constructivism and facade management combined in Vancouver with the widespread disposition to set humans and nature asunder to produce what he calls "the fiction of Stanley Park" – that "no one worked there" (p. 180).

Acknowledgments

I have always thought of historical scholarship as the product of a community. Historians work in conversation with other researchers, archivists, editors, and, of course, their subjects of study. This book is no exception. I owe a great debt of gratitude to many people. *Inventing Stanley Park* benefitted from the generous support of colleagues, friends, and family. All its flaws are my own, but where it shines it does so because of the thoughtful effort of others whom I must thank.

This book was funded by a number of organizations, including the Social Sciences and Humanities Research Council of Canada, the Canadian Union of Public Employees Local 3903, the Faculty of Graduate Studies at York University, the Graduate Program in History at York, and the Federation for the Humanities and Social Sciences' Awards to Scholarly Publications Program. Without the support of such bodies, Canadians would be culturally impoverished, and knowledge of Canada's past would be severely restricted. Their generous funding allowed me to conduct many months of research at archives in Vancouver, Victoria, and Ottawa, and it supported the final publication of this book. I also gratefully acknowledge permission to use materials previously published in the *Canadian Historical Review, BC Studies,* and *Environment and History.**

---

* These include the following articles: Sean Kheraj, "Restoring Nature: Ecology, Memory, and the Storm History of Vancouver's Stanley Park," *Canadian Historical Review* 88, 4 (2007): 577-612; Sean Kheraj, "Improving Nature: Remaking Stanley Park's Forest, 1888-1931," *BC Studies* 158 (2008): 63-90; and Sean Kheraj, "Demonstration Wildlife: Negotiating the Animal Landscape of Vancouver's Stanley Park, 1888-1996," *Environment and History* 18, 4 (2012): 1-31.

For his support, astute observations, and gentle guidance, I must thank H.V. Nelles. The subtlety with which he directed my research provided me with great intellectual liberty while simultaneously keeping it from spilling aimlessly in all directions. More than once, an apparently inscrutable remark on a draft ended up reshaping an entire chapter. Similarly, I am thankful for the support of Kathryn McPherson and Myra Rutherdale, who exercised great care and patience as I toiled on this research during my years in Vancouver.

The revisions for this book were improved by the insightful comments of other watchful readers along the way, including Jean Barman, Victor Guerin, and Delbert Victor Guerin, who provided invaluable insights into the pre-contact Coast Salish histories of the Stanley Park peninsula. Patricia Thompson and Robyn Worcester from the Stanley Park Ecology Society and Bill Stephen, urban forestry technician from the Vancouver Park Board, helped me better understand the public policy implications of my research. Richard Hoffman, Alan MacEachern, and Anders Sandberg provided critical feedback that aided in the creation of a focused manuscript. I also received ample assistance from Tina Loo and my other colleagues and friends at the University of British Columbia, including Michel Ducharme, Matthew Evenden, Bob McDonald, and Jocelyn Thorpe. I benefitted from great professional support in my earliest years as a professor from all my colleagues at Trent University, Mount Royal University, and now back at York University. Graeme Wynn, Randy Schmidt, the staff at UBC Press, and the anonymous reviewers of this book all played crucial parts in its publication, for which I am grateful.

Like all historians, I relied on the professionalism and skill of several archivists and librarians. I would especially like to thank the archivists and staff at the City of Vancouver Archives, including Megan Schlase and Chak Yung, who helped me unearth important records. With each new discovery, they made the days at Vanier Park more productive and, at times, exhilarating. I am also grateful for the assistance of the archivists and staff at the British Columbia Archives, Library and Archives Canada, and the University of British Columbia Special Collections.

I will never forget the moral and critical support of numerous friends and colleagues, each of whom helped me along the path to publication. These include Kristine Alexander, Uttam Bajwa, Cynthia Belaskie, Tarah Brookfield, Jodi Burkett, Jenny Ellison, Sarah Glassford, Laura Godsoe, Christine Grandy, Dan Horner, Colin McCullough, Susana Miranda, Liza Piper, Victoria Pitkin, Lee Slinger, and Teresa Welsh. For his hospitality, generosity, and cooking skills, I thank my friend Mark Abraham. I owe special thanks to Michael Harris, a close friend and talented writer, for spending many weeks reading through draft chapters and offering important feedback over coffee in the West End. His careful eye and editing skills made this a better piece of writing.

For their support and understanding as I leapfrogged across the country (from Toronto to Vancouver to Peterborough to Calgary and back to Toronto), I must thank my family, including all the Kherajs (Rizwan, Fatima, Evaan, Stefan, Nara, Tuvok, and Spock). I must also thank the Gills, including Jim, Kathy, Oliver, Cleo, Libby, and Hobbes. Except for myself, no one has lived longer with this book than my partner, Andrea Gill. She read drafts, offered feedback, and suffered through what probably felt like an endless number of unsolicited conversations about the history of Stanley Park. For that, and so much more, I am forever indebted. For two years, we were fortunate enough to live in Vancouver's West End on the doorstep of Stanley Park, where we ran along the seawall in the mornings, spotted wildlife at Lost Lagoon (including a beaver!), and huddled under the lighted conifers, sipping hot chocolate in the rain while waiting our turn to ride the Christmas train. Although we no longer live in Vancouver, it will always be our home, and Stanley Park will continue to be the site of many of our best memories.

Inventing Stanley Park

Introduction
Knowing Nature through History

It struck the city overnight. A ferocious tempest tore through Vancouver and the surrounding area, shattering glass, downing telephone poles, and toppling power lines. In the early hours of 15 December 2006, the Point Atkinson weather station in West Vancouver recorded winds of 119 kilometres per hour. By daybreak, more than 250,000 households on Vancouver Island and the Lower Mainland had lost power. In the light of dawn, as BC Hydro crews worked tirelessly to restore electricity to thousands of homes, Vancouverites awoke to discover that the city's treasured landmark had been transformed into a tangle of splintered, fallen, and uprooted trees.[1]

During that tumultuous winter, three separate windstorms ripped through Stanley Park. According to surveys by Vancouver Park Board staff, they felled more than ten thousand trees, approximately 5 to 10 percent of the forest. About thirty hectares of the four-hundred-hectare peninsula were severely affected, and another fifty experienced light to moderate damage. In addition, the storms destroyed large portions of the seawall between Prospect Point and Third Beach. Roadways and trails were closed for several weeks as foresters worked to clear the debris and repair damage to park infrastructure.[2]

In the following weeks, Vancouverites toured Stanley Park, like a procession of mourners at a funeral. The *Vancouver Sun* claimed that "our jewel, the gem in the heart of the city had been damaged and we felt it as deeply as the bite of a saw." People who had not even seen the damage claimed that the mere description of it caused them tremendous emotional pain.

This reaction was deeply rooted in memories of the park – personal histories. Long-time visitors struggled, according to one reporter, "to take in the drastic alteration to the happy memories and images of the park built over a lifetime." Vancouver billionaire Jim Pattison was moved to pledge up to $1 million of matching funds in a local drive to raise money for the park's restoration. The popular sentiment in the wake of the storm was for immediate restoration, "to make the hurting stop." All this anguish revealed not simply an attachment to the memory of a park but to a vision of a timeless and unchanging natural space – an elusive quest for a stable "balance of nature." Yet nature rarely provides such stability.[3]

Stanley Park is synonymous with Vancouver, like Central Park to New York City or Golden Gate Park to San Francisco, and thus it holds great cultural value. According to local historian Richard M. Steele, this peninsula, adjacent to Vancouver's downtown, is "the foremost symbol of Canada's most beautiful city."[4] Unquestionably among Canada's best-known parks, it is one of the largest and oldest urban parks in North America. As has been stated repeatedly for more than a century to the point of cliché, Stanley Park is the "jewel" of Vancouver.[5] It holds such tremendous symbolic significance, and Vancouverites guard it so jealously, that it has become "a fetish of untouchability," as one newspaper editorial remarked years ago. Despite the deep interdependence of nature and human culture in the history of this park, the public often recoils at the prospect of overt human interventions in it and laments natural disturbances such as windstorms. By the late twentieth century, this popular stance had come to shape the policies of the elected Park Board. For instance, in the late 1990s, the board became embroiled in a prolonged debate with the provincial government regarding widening the Stanley Park causeway connector, which cuts through the park and connects downtown Vancouver to Lions Gate Bridge. With substantial public support, the board resisted Victoria's efforts to gain approval for the plan, expressing a preference for "the elimination of vehicular traffic through Stanley Park" and stipulating that "no trees be removed as a result of this project." The bitter fight over the connector illustrates the power of Vancouver's affection for the park.[6]

How do we account for such a strong attachment? Current tourist publications suggest two main explanations. First, Vancouverites perceive the park as a natural marvel made all the more miraculous by its proximity to a densely populated city. "So close to a large population," the Vancouver Natural History Society's 2006 guide *Wilderness on the Doorstep* reads, "it provides hundreds of hectares of BC coastal forest, many kilometres of accessible seashore, two very beautiful lakes and hectares of ornamental gardens." Second, according to the same book, "it is Stanley Park's forest, especially its large old cedars and Douglas-firs, that gives the park its international reputation." Nature in the park is precious because most visitors believe it to be old and unspoiled. Since the park opened to the public in 1888, its advocates have regularly described its forest as "impenetrable," "unbroken," "primeval," "a jungle," "virginal," "untouched," and "pristine." For instance, a 1936 tourist brochure claimed that it "remains today as it was at the time the 'white man' came ... a virgin forest, and just a short walk from the shopping section of the city." A 1980 guidebook to Vancouver asks, "Where in the world could 1,000 acres of ancient forest reside in the heart of a major city? Vancouver – naturally. Literally within minutes of downtown, the huge expanse of Stanley Park harks back to the hospitable virgin wood that once sheltered the coast's native people." A more recent publication, *The Stanley Park Companion,* notes that just minutes from the city, "you're in the calm, green heart of an *ancient* forest," a comment contradicted by its admission that "Stanley Park is no pristine example of first-growth forest." Of course, the meaning of wilderness and nature has changed over time, as this book will explore, but the popular perception that Stanley Park is old and undamaged has come to influence contemporary park policy. Many Vancouverites value the park for its perceived sense of naturalness, its proximity to a highly urbanized environment, and its imagined connection to a pre-colonial past.[7]

The ubiquity of this view was most vividly demonstrated in the outpouring of grief following the windstorms of 2006 and 2007, as many Canadians expressed a profound sense of loss. The storms blew down thousands of trees, "ruining" the image of the unbroken forest. Eric Meagher, park supervisor of maintenance, admitted in a special issue of *British Columbia Magazine* that "it hurts, really hurts. There were some nights I went home and would just sort of sit in quiet reflection and just want to start crying because of what I'd seen." Although his confession illustrates a remarkable emotional attachment to the park, it is grounded in an illusory vision of an unchanging forest.[8]

The most remarkable aspect of this perception is the disjuncture between public memory and the peninsula's environmental history, which belies the popular narrative that Stanley Park is a preserved "ancient" wilderness. On a geological timescale, this landform has undergone a continuous series of dramatic changes by powerful natural forces. Responding to varying climatic conditions of the past thirteen thousand years, the vegetation has altered in numerous ways, and by the time it began to resemble a modern Northwest Coast coniferous forest, humans had already exploited its resources and transformed the landscape. When the first European navigators charted the waters of Burrard Inlet during the late eighteenth century, they mistakenly believed they were in a virgin wilderness untouched by human hands. They extracted the wealth of nature from the resources of the region and eventually settled the land, further transforming what was already an anthropogenic (human altered) landscape. The creation of Stanley Park imposed a new set of ideas and values, but far from eliminating the human presence in the peninsula, it required a massive human effort. Regulations governed the use of the park and changed human relations with nature. In the late nineteenth and early twentieth centuries, advocates called for both protecting the park from human intervention and *improving* it via the same means. And despite the seemingly stark contrast between the park and the city, Stanley Park was woven into the infrastructure of Vancouver's urban environment. This is most obviously illustrated by the causeway connector – a three-lane highway that runs through the centre of the park. In addition to these human modifications, natural forces have continued to reshape the landscape. Fire, animals, insects, climate, rain, and windstorms have unceasingly altered the forest and ecology. Throughout this history, nature has constantly been an agent of change.

Stanley Park has become a symbol of an imagined past, a static portrait of a pre-colonial wilderness that never existed. Yet this myth is a relatively recent phenomenon, one common to many other large North American parks. As *Inventing Stanley Park* will show, humans have engaged with this peninsula in a number of different ways over time. By necessity, then, this book deals with the changing meanings of parks, nature, and wilderness as social and cultural constructs.[9] The region's first inhabitants occupied the peninsula as a living space; colonial entrepreneurs saw opportunities for natural resource exploitation; and the first park advocates of the late nineteenth century sought to improve the landscape through human intervention. The idea that the park is an inviolable wilderness did not materialize until the second half of the twentieth century. Not until the 1960s did Vancouverites begin vigorously to resist all types of disturbance in the park, including both human and non-human interventions. Although changing ideas about ecology and humanity's relationship to the environment played a role in this shift, popular memory and the sense that the park represented part of Vancouver's past proved to be more crucial factors in guiding park policy. The anti-disturbance approach was best symbolized by the completion of the seawall in 1971. Designed to protect the shoreline from erosion, the wall would, in effect, preserve the landform from natural change. Symbolically, the encasement of the park in stone represented the public's desire to maintain what was considered a valuable historic landmark rather than a vulnerable ecosystem. This perception of the park as historically significant was formalized in 1988 when the Historic Sites and Monuments Board of Canada recommended its commemoration as a national historic site. Why, then, contrary to historical evidence, do many Canadians believe that nature in Stanley Park is pristine and ancient?[10]

This book offers three main explanations. The first, which focuses on the role of people, argues that though humans have always interacted with nature on the peninsula, their role in reshaping its landscape and ecology was greatest *after* its designation as a park. A park is an idea imposed upon the land. Therefore, the creation of the park and the subsequent ecological changes were grounded in human intervention. The park encompasses an ever-varying environment that has never been free from human use and modification. From its use as a Coast Salish village prior to European colonization to its transformation into an urban park, its landscape and ecology have been hybrids of natural and cultural forces. This, of course, is true of all parks and all landscapes, according to Carl O. Sauer's foundation for understanding landscape as the product of the interrelationship between humans and the environment, "an area made up of a distinct association of forms, both physical and cultural." This history underlines the ways in which shifting human ideas about how to exploit the material space and the concept of the public park were significant agents of environmental change.[11]

The second argument examines the role of nature and the limits of human agency. Although a park is an idea, it is realized in relationship to the material world. The history of the urban parks movement in North America has focused largely on political and social influences on the production of landscape and ecological change. This perspective – most evident in Galen Cranz's influential work *The Politics of Park Design* – deals solely with human-induced change.[12] *Inventing Stanley Park* reinterprets this history and the politics of preservation by considering the agency of non-human actors. To fully appreciate the development of urban park design and understand the often politically contentious controversies over culturally significant landmarks such as Stanley Park, we must contemplate not only the ways in which human ideas and actions have influenced park policy but also the role of nature. Indeed, nature placed constraints on the design of the park: animals, insects, vegetation, and weather reshaped both its landscape and its ecology as well as human relations with the peninsula. The social, political, and cultural influences on Park Board landscape policies cannot be understood outside of biophysical and ecological materiality.

The third argument focuses on the relationship between popular memory of nature in Stanley Park, Park Board landscape policies, and the volatile and unpredictable condition of complex ecosystems. This history shows that the contemporary shift in public thinking and policy in favour of strict preservation was produced through a relationship between popular concepts of the idealized wilderness, Park Board landscape policies, and tourist promotion in the twentieth century. This conjunction reinforced the image of the park as an ancient forest and shaped public memory of its past. The board's policies continuously interacted with powerful and capricious natural forces, characteristic of the peninsula's complicated ecology, that were the agents of change. For over a century, the board struggled to reconstruct the landscape, masking evidence of human and non-human disturbances in order to produce a more naturalistic appearance, a strategy commonly adopted in large North American parks throughout the nineteenth and twentieth centuries.[13] The case of Stanley Park demonstrates that such landscape effects have the capacity to influence public memory and make the park seem like a timeless place.

In his work on the Spanish influenza epidemic of 1918, Alfred Crosby found that "historians and people in general can overlook subjects of colossal importance," especially when they are thought to be inconsequential. Without proper consideration of such seemingly insignificant factors as insects, fire, vegetation, and wind, historians cannot fully explain the politics of park design and the changing popular perception of wilderness in parks. Because nature limits human actions, Donald Worster has called upon historians to reject "the conventional assumption that human experience has been exempt from natural constraints" and to critically rethink the notion of agency. Historians have traditionally relied too heavily on a Kantian sense of autonomy, which emphasizes intentionality and moral choice, an understanding of agency that overlooks the crucial role of unintentional consequences in history. Non-human forces, such as earthquakes and hurricanes, may lack a sense of moral choice or purpose, but their impact unquestionably has repercussions for human societies. As well, human actions always produce unintended results, especially in relation to competing autonomous forces. Consequently, the criterion of intentionality does not adequately define agency in this case. By considering the limits of human agency and the role of nature in Stanley Park, this book brings the interdependence of nature and culture into sharper focus.[14]

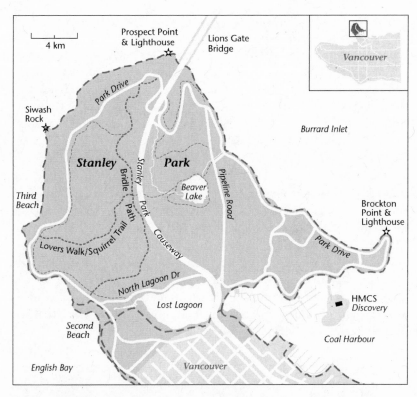

Map 1 Official Park Board map, Stanley Park, 2007. Vancouver Board of Parks and Recreation

Stanley Park in Park History

Surrounded by the waters of Coal Harbour, Burrard Inlet, and English Bay, Stanley Park lies adjacent to Vancouver's downtown core (Map 1). Its use as a public park was granted to the City of Vancouver by the federal government in 1887. Prior to this, the peninsula was a government reserve, which had been set aside in 1859. And for centuries before the arrival of Europeans, it was the site of a large Coast Salish village called Whoi Whoi (located near the present-day Lumbermen's Arch).

Stanley Park emerged as part of a larger urban parks movement in the United States and Canada that began during the mid-nineteenth century.[15] The movement's first notable example, New York City's Central Park, was established in the 1850s. Before its creation, the inhabitants of many large

American towns visited landscaped rural cemeteries in search of a scenic natural space for reprieve from the congested streets of the city. Burgeoning urban populations and their emergent desire for open spaces within the city placed pressure on public officials to create parks. Aware of this trend, and inspired by the urban parks and squares of Europe, Frederick Law Olmsted became a leading advocate for the creation of city parks in North America and the most influential landscape architect in the American parks movement. Olmsted designed parks in several American and Canadian towns, including New York City, Brooklyn, Boston, Buffalo, San Francisco, and Montreal. His collaboration with Calvert Vaux influenced the development of the profession of landscape architecture and informed the work of other park builders, including Horace W.S. Cleveland, Hammond Hall, Frederick Law Olmsted Jr., John Olmsted, Thomas Mawson, James C. Sidney, and Frederick G. Todd.[16]

Park advocates in the nineteenth century believed that large urban parks were necessary for the growth and development of cities. They also believed that a natural retreat within the artificial confines of a city could cure many of the problems caused by the urban environment. These ideas were part of an influential social and intellectual movement, known today as anti-modernism, in which middle-class men and women sought refuge from the sterility and stifling effects of urban life. The anti-modern movement led to the creation of national, state, and provincial parks throughout North America, where city-dwellers could enjoy an authentic experience with wild nature, but it also inspired the creation of pockets of nature inside the city, the most ostentatious Canadian example being Stanley Park.[17]

Geographer Terence Young identifies four main benefits, or virtues, associated with the creation of parks, which American park advocates and reformers promoted in their campaigns. First, parks were a necessary measure in counteracting the negative health effects of urban areas. Cholera scares in the 1830s inspired many reformers to call for the creation of natural spaces in the city to cleanse the air of the "miasmas" that were thought to cause disease. On the grounds of public health, and in the belief that trees and other plant life purified water, authorities established Philadelphia's Fairmount Park near the city waterworks and principal water supply, the Schuylkill River. Second, parks brought prosperity to cities by increasing real estate values and tourism. Following the creation of Central Park, nearby real estate quickly rose in price, leading other cities to emulate this kind of real estate boom. By the late nineteenth century, civic boosters argued that all notable cities in North America needed a large park to draw tourists and potential investors. The third virtue associated with parks was the notion that they were social levellers, which promoted democratic equality. Unlike the royal gardens of Europe, American city parks were intended to be symbols of democratic ideals; they were the property of the people rather than the elite, and reformers hoped that they would uplift the lower classes. The final virtue was that the levelling effect of parks would lead to greater social cohesion.[18]

The leaders of the American urban parks movement, who subscribed to the four virtues mentioned above, tended to come from the wealthy class. In most North American cities, a small elite group of influential men controlled park commissions and determined the direction of park development in the nineteenth and twentieth centuries. These men were also likely to profit from the real estate and tourism benefits of parks. They shaped the emergence of many large urban parks in North America and moulded their landscapes according to particular values and understandings of nature, which historians have associated with a romantic period in park development.[19]

Most historians divide the early urban parks movement into two distinct periods: a romantic phase lasting from the 1850s until 1900, and a reform, or rationalistic, era that began in the late nineteenth century and continued until the 1930s. During the romantic period, promoters saw parks as places for quiet contemplation and rejuvenation through passive interaction with nature. They viewed parks as the antithesis of the city and an antidote to stress and nervous exhaustion. Landscape architects such as Olmsted were influenced by this romantic ideal of nature and strove to construct parks along its lines. Olmsted's design for Central Park is a case in point: he orchestrated the complete transformation of the site from a swampy, treeless property to a manicured pastoral landscape. The romantic view of parks as naturalistic landscapes for passive leisure, separate but within the urban environment, dominated North America from 1850 to 1900.[20]

In the second phase, a new group of advocates challenged the elite view of nature in urban parks and called for more useable spaces for active leisure and recreation. This development is associated with the emergence of the American playground movement. New neighbourhood parks were established on small plots of land and scattered throughout town to provide useable recreation space for working-class people, who were often unable to access the larger urban parks, which were located at a great distance from the more populated areas of the city. These new parks included more space for sports, playgrounds, and other active leisure pursuits. Some historians argue that the reform phase was associated with working-class views of leisure and recreation, whereas others suggest that urban reformers sought to uplift working-class children through supervised play in the new parks. During this phase, the large landscaped urban parks of the romantic period were modified to meet the demands of the reform park. However, most of the large parks were divided into distinct areas for active and passive leisure, and most retained their romantic qualities.[21]

Most of these American trends directly influenced the development of Stanley Park. The Vancouver Park Board was an active member of the International Association of Park Commissioners of the Pacific Coast, an organization of park commissioners and superintendents from Canada and the United States that met annually to discuss various matters relating to urban parks. On numerous occasions, Vancouver's park commissioners and superintendents consulted with their counterparts in various American and Canadian cities.

Vancouver was also affected by the transition from the romantic phase to the reform phase. Robert A.J. McDonald effectively demonstrates that, in Vancouver, class and class perceptions were aligned with these two approaches to park design, just as they were elsewhere in North America. He reveals that an elite group, which had been influential in the creation of Stanley Park, had lost its grip on the Park Board by 1913 and was no longer able to impose its romantic vision. At the same time, a reform-minded board was able to pursue some of the trends that Galen Cranz and others have noted in reform parks. W.C. McKee shows how the playground movement and other aspects of the rationalistic phase influenced the expansion of Vancouver's park system in the early twentieth century.[22]

Stanley Park must also be considered in relationship with the national park movements in Canada and the United States, which played a significant role in its genesis. Because it was so large and was perceived as a preserved wilderness, it was seen, in some respects, as an urban national park distinct from the manicured city landscapes like Central Park. Canadian Pacific Railway (CPR) promoters in the mid-1880s envisioned the creation of Stanley Park as a logical complement to the construction of the transcontinental railway. Like Rocky Mountains Park (later renamed Banff National Park) – founded just two years earlier – it would draw people to Vancouver and increase tourist traffic on the CPR. In the United States, railway corporations helped create national parks for some of the same reasons, particularly in the case of Yellowstone Park in 1872.[23]

Of course, the profit incentive of railway executives does not adequately explain the emergence of national parks (or of Stanley Park for that matter). Historians who have scrutinized the complicated motives for the creation of North America's grand wilderness retreats struggle to reconcile the seemingly intractable paradox of national parks: the dual mandate of preservation and use. Environmental historian Alan MacEachern describes the dual mandate as the "unresolved problem at the heart of park history." It is indisputable that parks were created with the intention of deriving economic benefit from tourism and other activities, but there were aesthetic, cultural, and social motivations as well. The dual mandate of permitting human use and enjoyment while simultaneously preserving nature for future generations must not be seen as entirely contradictory; in some ways, the two strands are complementary. The Vancouver Park Board struggled with the tension between preservation and use in much the same way as authorities for national parks in North America.[24]

What follows, then, is a chronological account of the environmental history of Stanley Park, with a thematic focus for each chapter. Although hydrology, animals, insects, and geology are discussed, this book necessarily devotes much of its attention to changes in the park's forest, the most prominent feature of the landscape and the predominant component of its ecology. Beginning with an overview of geological history, Chapter 1 looks at the many ways in which humans used the forested peninsula that emerged after the final retreat of the glaciers. The first human inhabitants, ancestors of the modern Coast Salish, occupied the peninsula more than three thousand years ago. European colonization introduced new ideas along with new microbes, plants, and animals that transformed its ecology before its designation as a public park.

The next two chapters examine the process of park creation, or "emparkment," in the late nineteenth and early twentieth centuries. Chapter 2 looks at the legal genesis of Stanley Park from the late 1880s until the 1930s. It explores the ways in which the park was invented as a legal entity according to a new environmental ethic, which sought to exclude consumptive uses of nature. In particular, the regulations that governed it were designed to eliminate practices that were common during the colonial period and to ensure that it remained within the public realm for nonconsumptive use. Chapter 3 discusses a series of improvements launched during the same time period. In the late nineteenth and early twentieth centuries, park creation required massive human interventions in nature, a fact that was not incongruent with public perceptions of wilderness in Stanley Park during this time. Indeed, the public sometimes endorsed the Park Board's highly intrusive activities. But wherever the board sought to improve nature, it hid its tracks, employing landscaping techniques designed to conceal the human footprint. In addition, nature itself played a prominent role as an uncooperative partner in this venture. Often, the improvements were acts of resistance against autonomous natural forces.

The fourth chapter focuses on the integration of Stanley Park into the urban environment of Vancouver during the 1930s and 1940s. Various government authorities used the park for a variety of infrastructure projects, including a water pipeline, reservoir, sewer, highway, and coastal defence gun emplacements. The social and economic conditions of Vancouver determined when the urban environment intruded into the park. Chapter 5 looks at the role of environmental restoration in the park, following the severe windstorms of 1934 and 1962. By the 1930s, the Park Board had moved beyond the simple management of nature via judicious improvements and turned toward active restoration of past landscapes through extensive reforestation. This effort was informed by popular perceptions of nature, which envisioned wilderness as a climax coniferous forest. The restoration policies reinforced the prevailing sense that the park was untouched, with the result that by 1962, when Typhoon Freda devastated the peninsula, the public had largely forgotten its very long history of change by natural forces. In the wake of Freda, the board and the public became more vigorous in their resistance to encroachments, particularly to proposals for a third crossing of Burrard Inlet in the late 1960s and early 1970s, an anti-disturbance approach that became entrenched.

The 2006 and 2007 storms revived the 1960s debates surrounding environmental restoration. To a considerable extent, the perception of Stanley Park as an untouched wilderness emerged because of policies that sought to fulfill this expectation. In erasing evidence of past disturbance by human and non-human agents, Park Board policy clouded the public memory of the park. Rather than reconciling dynamic, entropic non-human forces with the human role in nature, these policies have repeatedly reinvented an imagined portrait of the park's past.

1

Before Stanley Park

The construction of the seawall was a battle against nature and an effort to stall processes that had been at work for thousands of years before there was a Stanley Park. It was, as *Vancouver Sun* staff reporter Al Birnie plainly wrote in 1964, an urgent "fight to push the sea from the base of Stanley Park."[1] It is difficult to imagine the park without its famed 8.8-kilometre perimeter seawall, but prior to 1971 its forest stood at the shores of Burrard Inlet (Figure 1.1). For more than fifty years, park employees, many of whom were temporary relief workers, struggled to defeat the persistent tides that wore away the edges of the park and sharpened its cliffs. The seawall, now one of Vancouver's most popular tourist attractions, began in 1914 as a project to halt shoreline erosion and prevent the reclamation of Stanley Park by the sea. What was then referred to as the "rip rap wall" for the Brockton Point lighthouse improvement plan was the beginning of a joint project of the Vancouver Park Board and the federal government to encircle the park in stone. One year later, park engineer Allen Shakespeare Wootton called attention to the erosion of the sandstone cliffs near the bathing area at Second Beach and the need for "rough walls constructed of Beach rock" to protect them. The seawall project then began from opposite sides of the park during the Great War and met over a half century later near Third Beach in 1971.[2]

From the early twentieth century to the 1970s, Park Board records clearly indicate that the purpose of the wall was to intervene in the sea-wave erosion that had been diminishing the peninsula for millennia. Its recreational uses were of secondary importance. The erosion problem became especially

LOOKING TOWARD ENGLISH BAY FROM SIWASH ROCK STANLEY PARK

Figure 1.1 View from Siwash Rock toward English Bay in 1905, before the construction of the seawall. Major Matthews Photograph Collection, St Pk N134, City of Vancouver Archives

acute in the 1920s as shipping traffic accelerated wave action in the harbour. Park engineers alerted the board to increasing instability near Second Beach, where erosion was "causing a constant slide of soil and rock from the high bank East of the Beach," and at the north shore at First Narrows,

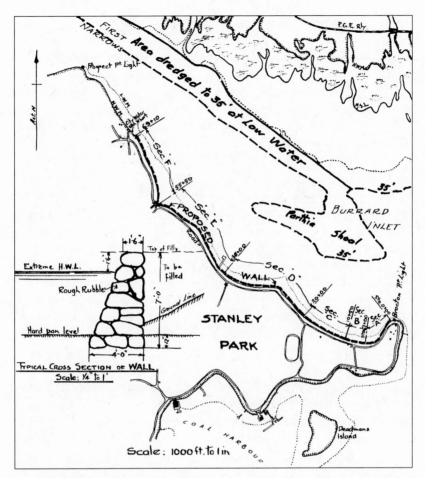

Figure 1.2 Blueprint plans from 1921 for the construction of a protective seawall along the First Narrows shore of Stanley Park. Correspondence, Stanley Park, 1922, Board of Parks and Recreation fonds, 49-C-5, file 2, City of Vancouver Archives

where parts of the road had "already washed away" (Figure 1.2). Upon further inspection, the secretary of the Vancouver Harbour Commission found that the damage was "due to natural causes – scour of tide, and the effects of wind and weather, the wash from passing vessels being, at high tide, a contributory cause to some extent." Alarmed, the Park Board cemented a deal with Ottawa to fund the construction of a seawall around the entire peninsula.[3]

This became the life work of James Cunningham, the master stonemason and later foreman for the seawall project from 1931 until his sudden death in 1963. According to the *Vancouver Province*, he and many other men exerted considerable effort to fortify the shoreline to "protect the precious soil of Stanley Park from erosion." Their labour was a reworking of geology, which shifted massive quantities of rock and earth. At times, they even used materials from the park itself to guard its shore. For instance, soil from the excavation of the outfall sewers that run beneath the eastern portion of the park was used as backfill to support the emerging seawall. Cunningham and his staff were geological agents, pushing against the forces of erosion that had been at work long before any human set foot on the peninsula.[4]

The creation of the seawall vividly illustrates the power of the human impact on the peninsula and the cultural significance of parks. As Mike Davis and other scholars argue, human forces can be characterized as a "geological drama" on par with their natural counterparts. In the case of the wall, humans exerted an enormous effort to counteract commanding geological processes to preserve a valued landform, a fact that shows the tremendous influence of human ideas and perceptions of space on ecology and landscape. As Christopher Armstrong, Matthew Evenden, and H.V. Nelles found in the case of the Bow River, "the power of an idea linked to perceived group interests is one of the most potent driving forces in history." That Cunningham and his compatriots would go to such lengths to halt shoreline erosion says a lot about the potency of the idea of parks.[5]

Of course, human perceptions of this space have altered over time, often in confluence with or in response to environmental changes. The story of the park begins with profound geological and climatic transformations on a scale that dwarfs human history. Global warming created Stanley Park. The landscape we know today was fashioned by the retreat of the Cordilleran Ice Sheet between twenty thousand and eleven thousand years ago as the Earth warmed following a prolonged period of glaciation, producing conditions for the spread of vegetation from the south and the establishment of habitable terrain for human beings. The first people to arrive on the peninsula used it as a living space, and archaeological evidence has revealed more than three thousand years of occupation during which humans exploited its resources, modified the surrounding area, and adapted to and altered its ecology. The arrival of Europeans during the late eighteenth century introduced new ideas and values, along with new microbes, plants, and animals, all of which played a transformative role. The ecological consequences of European colonization further changed the landscape and altered human relations with nature as the peninsula became a logging camp, a settler village, and grazing land. Prior to the opening of

Stanley Park in 1888, a heterogeneous mix of values reshaped this space, altering it long before a preservationist impulse drove people to protect it. Before Stanley Park, this place was many other places.[6]

The Geomorphology of Stanley Park

Environmental change in the Stanley Park peninsula began long before any human beings arrived there. Indeed, Vancouverites owe a debt to millions of years of geomorphic processes, rather than to a small group of aldermen and Canadian Pacific Railway officials in the 1880s, for the creation of Stanley Park. Its geological inheritance consists of numerous layers of rock, including metamorphic and volcanic bedrock, sedimentary sandstone and shale, and glacial drift. A combination of diastrophism (the process of deformation of the Earth's crust that produces continents and ocean basins), sedimentation, volcanic intrusion, glaciation, and mass wasting has produced the peninsula. From a geological perspective, it has undergone tremendous change during the past 200 million years.

The deepest bedrock is composed of plutonic rocks, such as granites, formed over 140 million years ago from the cooled magma of volcanic islands that pushed their way to the surface. This ancient volcanic activity, caused by the subduction of the Juan de Fuca plate beneath the North American continental plate, produced the geological bedrock of Vancouver and Stanley Park. Most of the park peninsula, however, consists of sedimentary rock, some of which dates from 70 million years ago. Rock, sand, mud, and plant debris from the mountains to the north were eroded by stream water and deposited in a vast freshwater lake that once filled the Georgia Basin, itself bordered by the Coast and Cascade Mountains. Debris accumulation created the major landforms of the Burrard uplands, including the Stanley Park peninsula. Some of the plant debris transformed into thin seams of coal, which attracted the attention of mid-nineteenth-century European colonists, who noted these deposits in the first surveys of Burrard Inlet and Coal Harbour.[7]

About 32 million years ago, an intrusion of basalt erupted as a sheet of volcanic material between what are now Prospect Point and Siwash Rock. Over thousands of years, as sea waves washed away the sandstone to the northwest of it, it became exposed, forming a dramatic cliff and acting as a dike to protect the land mass to the south, a role that the seawall would mimic many years later. Indeed, some geologists argue that "Stanley Park peninsula likely owes its present size to this resistant northern tip of volcanic rock. Without it, storm waves might have long ago eroded away the

Figure 1.3 An early postcard of Siwash Rock. F. Gowen, "Siwash Rock, Stanley Park, Vancouver, BC," 1916. Author's collection

soft sandstone." This remarkable curtain of basalt, which rises 60 metres above sea level and is 30 metres deep at its base, extends to about 1,200 metres south of Siwash Rock. Siwash Rock itself was originally part of the cliff, but erosion eventually separated it, creating one of the few examples of a sea stack on the BC coast (Figure 1.3). This geological oddity has since become an important spiritual landmark for the Coast Salish and a favoured tourist attraction.[8]

The sedimentary rocks lying beneath Stanley Park and the enormous volcanic intrusion on its northwest tip provided a geological foundation that was reshaped by climate change and the Pleistocene glaciations. John Clague and Bob Turner argue that glaciation was one of the most significant occurrences in Canadian history because it altered the landscape, including its vegetation and animal life. Twelve separate ice ages arose during the Pleistocene epoch, three of which are evident in the Lower Mainland. However, the last of them, known as the Fraser Glaciation, had the most profound impact on the Vancouver area. Between 25,000 and 12,000 years ago, a vast ice sheet covered the entire Lower Mainland. The Fraser Glaciation reached its peak around sixteen thousand years ago and steadily declined as the climate warmed.[9]

The Fraser Glaciation had two important effects on the landscape. The first was produced by the sheer weight of the ice: at 1,500 metres thick, the ice sheet isostatically depressed the land until it was 250 metres below sea level. At the same time, the sea level dropped as massive quantities of water were stored in continental ice sheets. As the glaciers retreated between 13,000 and 11,000 years ago, the Stanley Park peninsula was submerged beneath the ocean. In fact, it has spent more time underwater than it has above. Over several thousand years, the weight of the Fraser Valley glacier diminished, permitting the land to isostatically rebound. Although the melting ice contributed to the eustatic rebound (increase in ocean depth due to ice melt), the rate of isostatic rebound outstripped that of the rising ocean. It was so rapid that the drop in sea level averaged one metre every ten years, or ten centimetres annually, from 13,000 to 12,000 years ago. This enormous change would probably have resulted in an unstable environment disturbed by a constant series of severe earthquakes. That the land was rapidly rising out of the sea would have been evident to early human inhabitants. From 9,000 to 7,000 years ago, the sea was roughly five metres below its present level and did not stabilize at its current state until around 4,500 years ago. Because the elevation of Stanley Park is so much higher than that of Vancouver's downtown core, it probably emerged from the water as an island around 11,000 years ago.[10] Second, the glaciers left a layer of sedimentary deposits, blanketing the peninsula with glacial drift, a loose conglomerate of rocks, sands, and silt. Hidden just beneath the trees, grass, and picnic tables, these glacial sediments form the surface layer of the peninsula.[11]

Stanley Park lies within the Coastal Western Hemlock Biogeoclimatic Zone, which is characterized by a temperate climate and dense coniferous forests. Dominated by a mature conifer forest, mainly of western red cedar *(Thuja plicata)*, Douglas fir *(Pseudotsuga menziesii)*, and western hemlock *(Tsuga heterophylla)*, the peninsula also hosts a variety of trees influenced by disturbances and patterns of ecological succession. These include deciduous species such as the red alder *(Alnus rubra)*, which is often the first tree to colonize recently disturbed areas. Windthrow from coastal storms is the most persistent non-human disturbance agent, but less common lighting-ignited fires, landslides, and earthquakes also play a role. Although conifer and deciduous species have flourished on the peninsula since its modern climatic and vegetative regime was established between four and two thousand years ago, the mature stands of conifers became predominant, creating habitat for birds and animals, and providing primary natural resources for the material culture of the Coast Salish.[12]

As the forest emerged, new animal life appeared, taking advantage of the altered environment. Terrestrial mammals, including deer, elk, bears, and cougars, occupied parts of the Lower Mainland and became important resources for later human inhabitants. The abundant marine species that characterize much of the Northwest Coast were the most essential food supply for the first peoples, following the retreat of the glaciers. The various types of Pacific salmon predominated, but other significant marine species included cod, halibut, herring, rockfish, and shellfish, many of which were readily accessible from the shores of the Stanley Park peninsula.[13]

The retreat of the glaciers and the warming climate gave birth to the modern environment of Stanley Park. But as the land emerged from the sea, it was a place without people. Dramatic and transformative events occurred long before the very short time that humans have interacted with it. These geological and climatic processes created the stage upon which the human history of Stanley Park would play out. Global warming released the drowned peninsula and its surrounding region from the inhospitable glacial environment and produced ecological conditions that could sustain human settlement. In turn, these ecological conditions would be reshaped by shifting human ideas and uses of nature.

People and the Peninsula

The human history of the Stanley Park peninsula is ancient. Humans have inhabited the Lower Mainland for more than ten thousand years, and the earliest archaeological evidence shows that the peninsula was occupied more than three thousand years ago. The settlement of the first human migrants coincided with the enormous ecological transformation brought by the warming climate and deglaciation. As the natural environment changed, these early inhabitants adapted to their surroundings and exploited the plant and animal life to develop some of the most complex, populous societies in North America prior to contact with Europeans. Over several millennia, these indigenous groups reshaped the natural environment, including that of the Stanley Park peninsula.[14]

A wealth of archaeological research provides a rough image of the so-called prehistory of the Lower Mainland and affirms the ancient presence of human beings in the region.[15] Poor colonial records and early epidemic disease outbreaks make it difficult to estimate the pre-contact population of the Northwest Coast. Robert Boyd offers a conservative figure of approximately 183,000 people for the coastal area from northern California to Yakutat Bay, Alaska.[16] The pre-contact population of the Lower Mainland is even more difficult to determine. By methods of settlement site extrapolation, researchers can estimate population based on the number and size of archaeological settlement sites. Depending on whether or not there was a modest population rebound following late-eighteenth-century smallpox epidemics, researchers estimate the pre-contact population of the Lower Mainland to range from 20,860 to 62,580 people.[17]

In spite of the ancient presence of humans, contemporary popular memory of the peninsula's Aboriginal history (both pre- and post-contact) is unclear. As Randy Shore recently wrote in the *Vancouver Sun*, "much of the native history of the park is shrouded in the mists of time." Much of that mist, however, was produced by twentieth-century tourist promotion and Euro-Canadian resistance to First Nations land claims. Although the peninsula was home to one of the Lower Mainland's largest Aboriginal villages in the mid-nineteenth century, the history of the Aboriginal presence has been lost in a tangle of tourist literature that sought to entertain visitors with "Indian legends" while obfuscating both the modern and ancient Coast Salish histories of this space.[18]

The tourist tradition of associating Stanley Park with an imagined or symbolic Aboriginal presence began in the 1920s with the work of the Art,

Historical, and Scientific Association of Vancouver (AHSA), an organization established in 1889. Dedicated to historical preservation and scientific research about Vancouver and its region, the AHSA had an interest
in showcasing the cultural artifacts of the Northwest Coast indigenous
peoples, particularly totem poles. In the 1920s, the AHSA established the
first display of totem poles in Stanley Park. Raising funds from prominent
members of Vancouver's business class, including W.C. Shelly, Jonathan
Rogers, and W.H. Malkin, the association strove to create a site of both
"great historical value" and "a strong attraction to tourists." In a 1920s tourist
pamphlet, AHSA member John C. Goodfellow wrote that the project was
intended "to give to the present and succeeding generations an adequate
conception of the work and social life of the aborigines before the advent
of the white man." This display originally consisted of two totem poles and
two house posts, all of which were acquired from Kwakwaka'wakw elders
from Alert Bay on northern Vancouver Island. In 1924, a woman from
Harrison River donated what she claimed to be "an Indian canoe" of the
Nuu-Chah-Nulth First Nation that she had kept sheltered in a barn for
forty years. Later, with the further financial backing of W.C. Shelly and
the support of Dominion Archaeologist Harlan I. Smith, the AHSA added
a petroglyph boulder from the indigenous territory of the Stswecem'c
Xgat'tem First Nation in the Cariboo region along the upper Fraser River.
By 1936, the Park Board had added three more totem poles to the growing
display.[19]

   In an updated 1937 pamphlet, George H. Raley clearly articulated the
cultural salvage motivations that lay behind the effort to preserve the
Aboriginal artifacts (or "curios" as they were sometimes called) in Stanley
Park, referring to them as evidence of "a vanishing civilization." Raley
hubristically hoped that "perhaps the shades of a forgotten people crowd
around us and maybe their totem spirits are not far away," when tourists
gazed upon the transplanted poles. The irony, of course, was that most of
the exhibited Aboriginal art and culture was not associated with the First
Nations of the peninsula, including the Squamish, the Musqueam, and
the Tsleil Waututh.[20]

   Recent scholarly research by Susan Mather, Jean Barman, and Renisa
Mawani has unearthed what Barman refers to as "Stanley Park's secret"
– that it was inhabited by First Nations for millennia, during which they
regularly interacted with its environment. Of course, this fact has been a
secret only for the contemporary non-Aboriginal population of the Lower
Mainland. It is preserved in the oral traditions of local First Nations, and
it was well known to the first European colonists. Furthermore, the BC

Archaeology Branch's most recent archaeological resource management report for the peninsula reveals a depth of historical human land use far greater than what historians have yet documented.[21]

Information for the peninsula's prehistoric period is scarce, but considerable oral history and some archaeological evidence confirms early human settlement there. In 1932, Vancouver's city archivist James Skitt Matthews conducted interviews with Squamish and Musqueam people, along with early European settlers (including anthropologist Charles Hill-Tout and Methodist missionary C.M. Tate) to record the Aboriginal place names and past land uses of Vancouver and its region. Using his own spelling, Matthews identified nine Aboriginal site names on the Stanley Park peninsula. Although no sustained, comprehensive archaeological studies have been conducted there, Matthews's oral history evidence has been borne out by a handful of small site studies. These sites were used for a variety of purposes, from village settlements to natural resource harvesting to spiritual worship and ceremony, demonstrating a multiplicity of human uses and modifications of the environment prior to European colonization.[22]

Although the evidence for both an ancient and a historical Aboriginal presence in Stanley Park is undeniable, the ancestral connections to it have not always been so clearly defined. Andrew Paull (known among the Squamish people as Quoitchequoi) was a principal source for J.S. Matthews's oral history research. He was also secretary of the Squamish Indian Council in 1932 and a leading figure in British Columbia's early Aboriginal land rights movement.[23] He sometimes spoke and wrote inaccurately about the park, referring to it as exclusively Squamish territory. For instance, he claimed in a 1938 *Vancouver Sun* article that "the area we know as Stanley Park was officially and legally conveyed by the Squamish Indians [to the British Admiralty], through Chief Capilano, in a brief ceremony on the north shore of the First Narrows about the year 1812." By writing in a major city newspaper that "long before the white men came, thousands of Squamish Indians lived on the shores of Stanley Park," Paull was attempting to affirm the broader movement for Aboriginal land rights for the Squamish Indian Council. "Paull was a prolific writer of letters, pamphlets, and newspaper columns," according to historian Brendan Edwards, "through which he (often successfully) sought to reach out to the Euro-Canadian governments and public at large and to influence positive change on behalf of the Squamish people and First Nations throughout Canada." However, his statements disguised the complexities of the situation: the Stanley Park peninsula was shared between Coast Salish groups of a common language and culture, including the Squamish,

the Musqueam, and the Tsleil Waututh. Their relationship was far more
fluid than Paull's public assertions of the 1930s suggested. For instance,
August Jack Khatsalano, an Aboriginal longshoreman and logger who lived
on the peninsula as a child in the 1870s and 1880s, was the son of a Squamish
man named Khaytulk, or "Supple Jack," and a Squamish mother named
Qwy-what. August Jack's uncle Kee-olst, however, was married to a
Musqueam woman, and he was buried at the Musqueam reserve. Even
Chief Capilano, to whom Paull referred in his 1938 article, said to have
lived on the peninsula and met with Captain George Vancouver in 1792,
had familial connections to both the Squamish and the Musqueam. Frank
Charlie, a Musqueam man who spoke with Matthews in 1932, confidently
asserted that "Capilano [is] a Musqueam name, not a Squamish name."
And in conversation with Matthews, Paull himself freely admitted that
"the Capilanos of Capilano River and Frank Charlie of Musqueam both
acknowledge descent from the same blood." On the basis of his interviews,
Matthews concluded that prior to European colonization, "the two tribes
at Musqueam and Squamish were mostly friendly; intermarried and so
on." In short, the distinctions between Coast Salish groups of the Lower
Mainland did not sharpen until the establishment of Indian reserves (including the Squamish, Musqueam, and Tsleil Waututh reserves), which
had the effect of politically separating them. The Stanley Park peninsula,
then, was probably inhabited by several Coast Salish groups, and according
to Barman, "some people went there on a seasonal basis; others remained
for longer periods of time."[24]

By far the most significant pre-contact settlement site was the village
of Whoi Whoi.[25] As Barman and others have noted, it was one of the
largest Aboriginal villages in the Lower Mainland at the time of European
resettlement. During a 1932 interview with Matthews, Andrew Paull suggested that "Whoi Whoi must have been a very large village, for it spread
from Brockton Point to Prospect Point. It must also have been a very ancient
village, none know its age, but there must have been hundreds, perhaps
thousands, living there at one time." August Jack Khatsalano also testified
that "Indians lived in large numbers at Whoi Whoi." Dick Isaacs, a
Squamish man living at the North Vancouver Indian reserve at Homul-
cheson in the 1930s, remembered that near the time of European resettlement, there was a "big settlement [of] Indians [at] Whoi Whoi." The use
of this site persisted even after European colonization. George Cary, an
early British colonist who settled near the park peninsula in the 1880s, told
J.S. Matthews that "Potlatches were held there after I came in 1885."[26]

Archaeological evidence supports the oral history regarding the longevity of the human presence at Whoi Whoi. As early as 1887, during the construction of the first park road, crews cut into an enormous ancient midden near the village. According to Charles Hill-Tout, a pioneering anthropologist who examined it, the midden was "composed mostly of calcined shells and ashes." He also found "numerous skeletons," some of which were returned to the Aboriginal families who were displaced to Indian reserves in the Vancouver area, whereas others were sent to be studied in an Ottawa museum. Unfortunately, the remainder of this valuable archaeological evidence was removed from the site and used as paving material for the road (Figure 1.4).[27] William Grafton, an early Vancouver resident who came to the city in 1887, also testified to having seen ancient human remains near Whoi Whoi at the time of the road construction:

> When I first saw that Indian graveyard, there were quite a lot of graves; not graves as we know them, but graves above ground. The canoes with bodies in them were still there; the canoes were supported about level with your face; the dead were inside the canoes. Then there were a lot of boxes; boxes with bones in them lying on the ground; Indian bones; that was the way they buried them.[28]

On the basis of these early findings, Charles Hill-Tout determined that "this ancient campsite [Whoi Whoi] formed one of the largest of the native villages of the Squamish in earlier days" and that "the shores and bays of Burrard Inlet and English Bay have been occupied by rude communities of people for a very considerable period of time."[29]

Hill-Tout's preliminary observations are sustained by subsequent archaeological findings near Whoi Whoi. For instance, a lanceolate point, discovered just south of the village in the 1960s, had a radiocarbon date of 3200 BP (before the present).[30] Since the unearthing of the Whoi Whoi midden in 1887, archaeologists have conducted several investigations of the area (known by its Borden number, DhRs-2) that provide some insights into the pre-contact natural resource uses. For example, the midden material was found to contain traces of Pacific littleneck clams *(Protothaca staminea)*, cockles *(Clinocardium nutallii)*, and blue mussels *(Mytilus edulus)*, common Northwest Coast molluscs that inhabit the sandy shores of Stanley Park.[31] August Jack's own memories support the archaeological evidence that Aboriginal people harvested clams and other sea creatures on the peninsula:

Figure 1.4 Road crews working on the park drive discovered a large midden eight feet deep consisting mainly of crushed clamshells. In the interest of fiscal prudence, the contractors used the shells to surface the road. Bailey Brothers Studio, "Deposit of Shells, 8 ft. Deep on Park Road, Vancouver, B.C.," 1888. Major Matthews Photograph Collection, St Pk P80 N50, City of Vancouver Archives

They dug clams, caught fish, for instance, octopi, under rocks, especially the huge boulder now gone. Coming at night, through the First Narrows at extreme low tide, just as it turned from ebb to flow, the pleasing spectacle presented itself in the darkness, of hundreds of tiny lights, stretching in an uncertain line into the distance, glowing in the inky dark shadow of the trees lining the shore of Stanley Park from Prospect Point to Brockton Point ... The Indians were harvesting clams from the narrow belt of beach exposed to their spades by the extreme low tide.[32]

Similarly, William Grafton also recalled witnessing this resource-gathering activity at Whoi Whoi in the 1880s:

It was a very interesting sight coming through the First Narrows at night time, when the tide was out. There, on the beach, were all the Indians with their pitch sticks alight, and digging clams; the Indians, used to go there. They used to look very pretty coming in. Being dark, you couldn't see the Indians, but you could see their pitch stick lights, and you could see their figures digging away.[33]

New archaeological studies of "wet-sites" are uncovering the extent to which the Coast Salish used woody plants, especially red cedar, to create the necessary components of their material culture. Whoi Whoi was valued for its cedar, which was used to construct houses, canoes, boxes, baskets, and other objects. According to August Jack, his grandfather settled on the peninsula "because there's lots cedar there, and he makes canoe." Because Whoi Whoi was a settlement site, several acres of trees were cleared and used for housing. The houses, August Jack told Matthews, "stood in a row above the beach, facing the water; all were of cedar slabs and big posts; all built by the Indians long ago." Andrew Paull claimed that "in bygone days my ancestors cut down many cedar trees in Stanley Park for making canoes and other purposes. You can see the evidences of their attempts to cut down trees even yet. There are many trees in Stanley Park with little holes ... some feet up from the ground."[34] In fact, numerous culturally modified trees (CMTs) – that were stripped of a portion of their bark or altered in other ways by Aboriginal people prior to European colonization – remain in the park. In 1996, the Council of the Squamish Nation hired Arcas Consulting Archaeologists to survey it for CMTs, fifteen of which were discovered near Whoi Whoi (DhRs-305), including both stumps and living trees. Some cedars showed evidence of bark-stripping techniques, a method that takes the bark without killing the tree. A 1998 Suzuki Foundation report found that "Stanley Park, in the heart of downtown Vancouver, contains numerous CMTs, although very few people are aware of the fact that native loggers used that forest long before the historic settlement and logging of Vancouver." Using stone and shell adzes, the indigenous inhabitants selectively felled trees and stripped the bark from others. Studies of the park reveal that the use of these trees dates back as far as three thousand years.[35]

Several other significant sites of Aboriginal settlement and land use exist on the peninsula. Matthews's interviewees identified the high ground at Prospect Point as an ancient settlement known as Chaythoos, which was separate from Whoi Whoi. August Jack and his family lived there during the 1870s and 1880s, but oral history and archaeological evidence reveal a much longer use of the site. August Jack's testimony suggests that at least two generations of his family lived there: when his grandfather arrived during the mid-nineteenth century, it was already an inhabited village. August Jack's father, Supple Jack, also lived at Chaythoos and was interred there in an above-ground tomb. When the first park road was built in 1887, it bisected Chaythoos, and the family was forced to move Supple Jack's remains. Archaeological resource inventories and surveys conducted in the 1980s and 1990s determined that the Chaythoos site (DhRs-79) was a prehistoric Aboriginal village. According to these reports, the size of the clearing and the "depth of deposits suggesting ethnographic and pre-historic use" indicate that, like Whoi Whoi, Chaythoos "may also be of considerable age." Again, the shellfish in the archaeological materials suggests the importance of marine resources to the inhabitants.[36]

A handful of other sites show evidence of pre-contact use. In 1955, at an area near Third Beach (DhRs-7), archaeologists found midden materials consisting of shells and fire-altered rock, indicating that "it is possible that this site represents a location used in early times as the size of deposits suggest substantial use at some time." Many of the marine resources of Burrard Inlet were probably accessible from this location. Both oral history and archaeological remains reveal that the current Canadian naval base, HMCS *Discovery* (once known as Deadman's Island and before that Squtsahs), was formerly used for Aboriginal tree burials, a practice in which bodies are interred in boxes suspended above the ground (DhRs-303). Hill-Tout claimed that in the 1890s, he "saw several tree burials, twenty or thirty feet up in the fir trees" that once covered the island. Similarly, Joseph Morton, the son of John Morton, an early landowner in Vancouver's West End, told Matthews that when his father first settled at Burrard Inlet in 1863, "he went over to Deadman's Island and found Indian coffins in the trees and also fallen to the ground." Pre-contact human remains and other archaeological materials have since been unearthed, suggesting ancient use of this island.[37]

The Coast Salish knew the Second Beach area as Stait-Wouk. According to Andrew Paull, it was not inhabited but was nonetheless useful because it supplied a particular type of mud. Paull told Matthews that the Coast Salish

> gathered the mud – I think from the bed of the creek – rolled it into loaves about the size of bread loaves, put the roll against the fire, and the mud would get as white as chalk. The white powder was used to dust upon Indian blankets, made from the mountain goat's fur, to give the blankets a white appearance.

August Jack claimed that "Indians living there; just come there to camp; kill ducks." An archaeological survey conducted in 1955 by Donald Abbott found a thin layer of shell midden at the Second Beach area (DhRs-6). However, road construction and other disturbance had dispersed most of it by 1978, leading to the conclusion that "a thin covering of midden would be highly suggestive of redeposited materials from a prehistoric location as opposed to *in situ* remains." That is to say, the spot was probably used for resource procurement rather than prolonged settlement.[38]

Matthews documented what is now called Siwash Rock as Slah-Kay-Ulsh. Neither a settlement nor a natural resource site, it had spiritual significance associated with Coast Salish transformation stories. Jim Franks, an Aboriginal man born near present-day Kitsilano Beach around 1870, told Matthews that "Siwash Rock was once a man." Passed on from Chief Joe Capilano, this transformation story was famously documented by E. Pauline Johnson in 1910, in a series of *Vancouver Daily Province* articles that were later published in 1911 as *Legends of Vancouver.* According to her story, Siwash Rock was "a warrior man ... who fought for everything that was noble and upright." A coastal deity known as Sagalie Tyee changed him into stone in recognition of his efforts to protect the life of his unborn child. According to Johnson, the geological oddity now known as Siwash Rock is "a monument of one man's fidelity to a generation yet unborn." One of the most spiritually significant transformer sites in the Lower Mainland, Slah-Kay-Ulsh was admired for many thousands of years before it became a tourist destination.[39]

Introduced Disease Epidemics

In the late eighteenth century, the ecology of the Stanley Park peninsula was changed by perhaps the first and most devastating consequence of European colonization: introduced diseases and the subsequent epidemics that struck First Nations and depopulated the region. In June 1792, as the crew of the *Discovery* and *Chatham* gently navigated the waters of what their captain would later name Burrard's Canal, they marvelled at the seemingly impenetrable forests that stood where ocean met land. While passing through First Narrows, Captain George Vancouver saw what he believed to be an island (Stanley Park), which he recorded in his meticulous survey of the coast (Map 2).[40] One of Vancouver's lieutenants, Peter Puget, noticed Aboriginal villagers on the island, who soon approached in canoes and offered the strangers an assortment of fish in

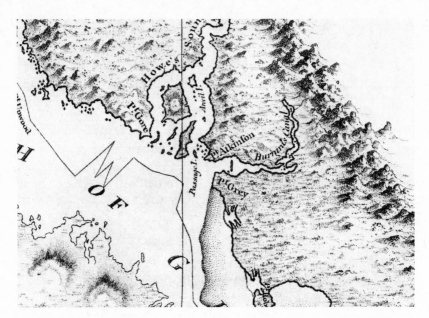

Map 2 Vancouver's 1798 chart of Burrard Inlet shows Stanley Park as an island. George Vancouver, *The Coast of N.W. America* (London: G.G. and J. Robinson, 1798), David Rumsey Historical Map Collection

exchange for pieces of iron and other goods. Confident that the villagers had not encountered Europeans or Americans, Vancouver concluded that he and his crew must be the first "people from a civilized country they had yet seen." Nonetheless, he knew that something was amiss in the Strait of Georgia. Throughout his journey northward, he had seen abandoned villages, skeleton-ridden shores, and other hallmarks of rapid depopulation. He speculated about causes, not unaware of the ubiquitous presence of smallpox among the Aboriginal people whom he encountered. What Vancouver did not fully realize was that – if they had not done so already – the people of Burrard Inlet would soon experience the first and deadliest result of contact.[41]

The destruction of indigenous New World populations by introduced Old World diseases was one of the most significant biological consequences of colonization. As Alfred Crosby and others have noted, in 1492, "the two worlds, which God had cast asunder, were reunited, and the two worlds, which were so very different, began on that day to become alike." Part of that process involved the exchange of microbes. With brutal and unimaginable mortality, the epidemiological isolation of the New World quickly

broke down. The two branches of the human family had finally circum-
navigated the Earth and met in 1492 (exempting, of course, the early Norse
voyages), beginning what Crosby calls the Columbian Exchange, a transfer
of biota between the Old and New Worlds. One of the most tragic aspects
of this was the transmission of diseases to indigenous populations that
were immunologically defenceless.[42]

As in the sixteenth-century epidemics that followed the Spanish
invasion of the New World, microbes played a significant role in the
eighteenth- and nineteenth-century depopulation of the Northwest
Coast. Its Aboriginal people suffered incredible losses in a series of epidemics as the global pattern of human disease development continued
the process of inter-hemispheric exchange. Robert Boyd suggests that the
coast experienced as many as six smallpox epidemics from roughly 1775
to 1862. The timing of the earliest outbreak is uncertain (R. Cole Harris
dates it to about 1782 for the Strait of Georgia), but research shows that
the first smallpox epidemic may have killed up to 90 percent of the population. The disease reached the Strait of Georgia during the 1780s in what
was probably the deadliest introduced epidemic in the region's history. In
1782 and 1783, it spread among nearly all the peoples around Puget Sound
and Georgia Strait. According to Harris, it was so devastating that "the
Coast Salish, once the most numerous people on the Northwest Coast,
became relatively invisible in their own territory." The elimination of such
a substantial portion of the human population undoubtedly resulted in
ecological transformations.[43]

These epidemics probably depopulated the Aboriginal settlements on
the Stanley Park peninsula. Tellingly, its first census, conducted by the
Indian Reserve Commission in 1876, recorded a total of only fifty Aboriginal people there. Andrew Paull believed that "disease wiped out Whoi-
Whoi." August Jack Khatsalano affirmed the presence of smallpox at Whoi
Whoi while describing the nearby burial sites. He recalled that the village
"had a little small pox before the white man came. There's been two or
three small pox came to Squamish peoples."[44] Charles Hill-Tout's observations during the 1887 construction of the park road provide further evidence
of epidemics. Noting that "a considerable number of skeletons were dis-
interred from the midden mass during the operation," he concluded that
the interment method was not typical of the local Squamish people, and
he speculated that these were hasty burials, the result of "the presence of
some pestilence or epidemic such as their traditions speak of."[45] Squamish
myth accounts are among many on the Northwest Coast that provide
testimony of early smallpox epidemics. In his ethnographic work, one of

Hill-Tout's Squamish informants told him about a "dreadful misfortune" that struck his people long ago. The informant claimed that

> one salmon season the fish were found to be covered with running sores and blotches, which rendered them unfit for food. But as the people depended very largely upon these salmon for their winter's food supply, they were obliged to catch and cure them as best they could, and store them away for food. They put off eating them till no other food was available, and then began a terrible time of sickness and distress. A dreadful skin disease, loathsome to look upon, broke out upon all alike. None were spared. Men, women and children sickened, took the disease and died in agony by hundreds, so that when the spring arrived and fresh food was procurable, there was scarcely a person left of all their numbers to get it. Camp after camp, village after village, was left desolate.[46]

On the basis of his archaeological findings and interviews with local Squamish individuals, Hill-Tout concluded that Whoi Whoi "had been practically abandoned since the period when small pox first attacked the native people of the region. This scourge struck this village very severely, and practically depopulated it, hence its abandonment hereafter."[47]

If, as Hill-Tout and others contended, Whoi Whoi was struck by disease and its inhabitants were substantially reduced, their impact on the local ecology – through the consumption and exploitation of its natural resources – would have been affected. Moreover, this mass depopulation contributed to the prevailing notion of *terra nullius,* the European perception that the land was largely empty and therefore primed for colonization. A thickly forested landscape of virtually abandoned villages with occasional pockets of human habitation appealed to men such as George Vancouver, who wrote that "the innumerable pleasing landscapes, and the abundant fertility that unassisted nature puts forth, require only to be enriched by the industry of man with villages, mansions, cottages, and other buildings, to render it the most lovely country that can be imagined." And as Vancouver imagined a new version of Europe on the Northwest Coast, he stood in the vanguard of a powerful set of new ideas and attitudes toward nature that would change the Stanley Park peninsula.[48]

Colonizing and Consuming Commodities: Coal and Timber

European colonizers brought new ideas about the relationship between people, the land, and natural resources. The advent of industrial mining

and forestry in British Columbia redefined the meaning of landowner-
ship and the governance of the relationship between humans and nature.
British colonial authorities clumsily introduced new definitions of land-
ownership that reconstructed the regional geography to facilitate new uses
of natural resources.

Following a period of maritime and land-based fur trading in the late
eighteenth and early nineteenth centuries, an influx of gold seekers from
California and beyond prompted the British government to assume control over the former Hudson's Bay Company territory known as New
Caledonia. In August 1858, the British created the colony of British
Columbia. With an audacious imperial stroke of a pen, this enormous
territory, larger than France and Germany combined, fell under the authority of the British Crown. Fearing the possibility of US annexation due
to the rapid influx of American miners, Governor James Douglas wrote
to his superiors in London "that the stream of immigration is setting so
powerfully towards Fraser's River that it is impossible to arrest its course,
and that the population thus formed will occupy the land as squatters,
if they cannot obtain a title by legal means." Douglas's solution was to
throw the land open to settlement under his authority as governor of
the colony.[49]

The European settlement of the colony was managed through the office
of its first chief commissioner of lands and works, Colonel Richard
Clement Moody (Figure 1.5). Moody and his family arrived in Victoria in
December 1858 and soon journeyed to the Fraser River, where he selected
a spot on the north bank of the river, west of Fort Langley, as the location
for New Westminster, the new capital city. Moody chose the site in part
for its strategic advantages, as fears of a US invasion weighed heavily on
his mind. In fact, Colonial Secretary Edward Bulwer-Lytton had specifically instructed him to "regard with a military eye the best position for
such towns and cities."[50] Consulting George Vancouver's survey of Burrard
Inlet, Moody believed that his new capital could be made more secure by
protecting its rear position where "access ... would be rendered most
hazardous, by placing a work on the island which extends across [Burrard
Inlet]. There is also on that side a range of high ground, from east to west,
on which could be placed earthen works and intrenched [sic] camp,
preventing any advance."[51] The island was the Stanley Park peninsula
(Map 3).

The governor's first land proclamation granted power to Moody, as chief
commissioner of lands and works, "to reserve such portions of the unoccupied Crown Lands, and for such purposes as the Executive shall deem

Figure 1.5
Colonel Richard
Clement Moody,
1859. A-01721,
British Columbia
Archives

advisable." Thus, in December 1859, Moody exercised this power and
marked off several large parcels of land at Burrard Inlet as government
reserves, including the park peninsula. He told Douglas of his concern
that important tracts might be lost as settlers applied to pre-empt the area
around the inlet. Interestingly, despite Moody's comments on the peninsula's strategic usefulness, no record has ever been found to show that the
new reserve was intended for military purposes. F.W. Howay, who conducted extensive research on this question, described the creation of
numerous reserves around Burrard Inlet as "the land-grabbing activities
of the Colonel" and found that "the material in reference to the formation

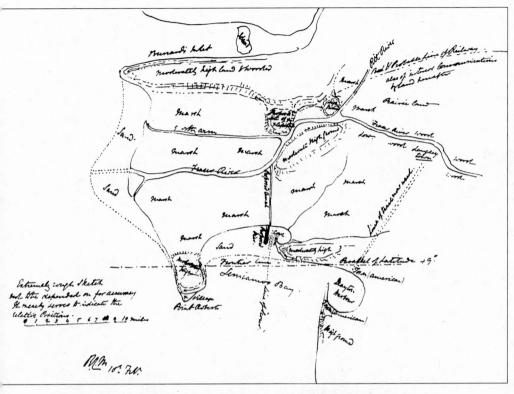

Map 3 Moody sketched this map of the Lower Mainland before detailed surveys were made of Burrard Inlet. The island at the top also appears in the maps of Captain Vancouver and Galiano. Colonel R.C. Moody to Governor James Douglas, 10 February 1859, Colonial Correspondence, 1857-1872, GR-1372, reel B01346, item 1150, British Columbia Archives

of the reserves on the inlet, whether naval, military, townsite, or Indian, is extremely vague and indefinite." Jean Barman's research confirms Howay's claim and provides evidence to suggest that the peninsula was designated as a coal reserve.[52]

Although the Colonial Office was concerned with the gold fields of the Fraser, and later, of the Cariboo, it was also interested in "the more ordinary resources of the Colony, in fisheries, in timber, in the various soils, and the extent of them, favourable to agricultural produce." It sought to engage all the potential resource wealth of the new colony. Thus, Moody was instructed to "ascertain the real value of the coal for all purposes of steam communication, both in British Columbia and Vancouver."[53] Captain George H. Richards's discovery of coal during an 1859 survey of

Burrard Inlet may have cast the fate of the Stanley Park peninsula. Because no survey of Vancouver Island and the mainland had been conducted
since George Vancouver's voyage, Governor Douglas had employed
Richards to command HMS *Plumper* to produce "a general report on the
Harbours of Vancouver Island, and the coast of British Columbia."
Richards and his crew charted Burrard Inlet in June 1859 and stumbled
upon an exciting discovery on its south shore – evidence of coal where an
"extensive vein occurred on the Southern side of the inner harbour, about
a mile and a half within the First Narrows." Richards called the site Coal
Harbour and Coal Peninsula.[54] The ship's surgeon, Charles B. Wood, who
led the examination of the seams, described several outcrops of coal along
the waterline and wrote that "sufficient evidences were thus far obtained
as to prove the presence of the true coal measures and the probability of
an extensive coal deposit." The coal was tested in *Plumper*'s furnace, and
Wood found that it "presented all the outward character of English New-
castle, it burns freely in a common furnace, and produces little smoke."
Samples were sent to New Westminster for Colonel Moody to inspect.
Richards believed that the coal would "exercise a considerable and possibly
an immediate influence on the prosperity of the new town of Queens-
borough [later renamed New Westminster]."[55]

The news of this fortuitous discovery excited Moody and his cohorts,
particularly Moody's former personal secretary Robert Burnaby, who was
anxious to capitalize on it.[56] After examining the samples that Richards
had delivered to New Westminster, Burnaby quickly organized an exped-
ition to examine possible mining sites. Led by three Aboriginal guides, he
and his crew explored the locations identified in Richards's report. They
landed and ate at Whoi Whoi among "a crowd of natives" before proceeding farther east where, according to Burnaby, he "found a stream rushing
out, and here we saw very clear indications of coal formation."[57] Burnaby
saw immense potential in the exploitation of this resource and envisioned
the accumulation of great personal wealth either by coal mining or land
speculation. He outlined his ambitions in a letter to his brother:

> We are going to prospect the whole spot, and to work the mines if things
> look well. It may turn out a most promising affair, as we have the monopoly
> if we choose, and the only bit of land probably in the outer Harbour of
> Burrards Inlet, where by steamers can go, and if ever the great Railroad comes
> near this way, we shall be in possession of the most commanding position in
> the country! A few years may do this, probably will not in the present stagnant
> condition of things, but anyhow the Coal will *pay* if worth anything.[58]

In August 1859, Burnaby and his partner Walter Moberly established a mining camp at Burrard Inlet and conducted experimental diggings to determine the potential of their site. By month's end, they had sunk three shafts and "found some Coal, but not enough yet are still *prospecting* for more."[59] They struggled to find a good, financially sustainable location and were nearly forced to abandon their venture by mid-October. Because the capital expenditures for mining were so high, Burnaby required secure access to cheap land for further prospecting. Fortunately, he had a close friend in the land office, Colonel Moody. Moody, aware that several people wished to acquire property at Coal Peninsula, decided to reserve large tracts for himself and his associates (including Burnaby), encompassing "the coal lands of Burrards Inlet," to prevent them from falling into the hands of other colonists. It is likely, then, that the peninsula became a government reserve in 1859 to protect its potential coal deposits.[60]

To officially designate the land as a reserve, Moody ordered Lance-Corporal George Turner to survey it and mark its boundaries. In April 1863, Turner surveyed the reserve and pre-emption lands of Burrard Inlet. In his survey, however, he labelled the Stanley Park peninsula as a "military reserve," a fact that would assume great significance forty years later, in a legal dispute over its ownership.[61] According to Turner, "it was generally known at the time that that was a Military Reserve; and also I must have instructions in putting all those things down; that I must have known that they were Reserves, or else I should never have put them down. I had no authority to make a Reserve myself."[62] Why Turner marked the peninsula as a military reserve is unknown, but by the completion of his survey, Colonel Moody had reserved nearly every part of the Burrard uplands, sold the remainder to well-connected friends, and secured large portions for himself. The evidence suggests that the peninsula was initially reserved to guard its coal resources but was later simply presumed to be a military reserve, due to Moody's initial reports of 1859. Coal prospecting continued until 1866, led by the British Columbia Coal Mining Company, which was granted a six-hundred-acre reserve on the south shore of English Bay in 1864 and conducted an unsuccessful five-hundred-foot test drilling at Coal Harbour in 1866.[63]

The potential for mining changed human relations with the land and its resources. Maps were drafted and surveys conducted to draw imaginary lines on the already inhabited space as land and resources were imaginatively transformed into commodities that could be sold and traded. Although the coal eventually proved too meagre for profitability, European colonizers were not deterred: they turned to the more abundant timber resources of the area.

The first sawmill operation commenced on the north shore of Burrard Inlet in July 1863, when Thomas Wilson Graham and other investors opened Pioneer Mills, informing New Westminster colonists in an advertisement that because "the quality of the timber on the Inlet is much superior to that either on the Sound [Puget] or the Lower Fraser," they could "engage to produce a better article of lumber." Ever the conscientious colonial booster, John Robson, publisher and editor of the *New Westminster British Columbian,* also trumpeted the glories of the nascent colony's forest wealth. He claimed that it was "in size the most gigantic, in quality unsurpassed, and in quantity almost boundless; it is not only invaluable for various local uses, but it is destined to be an article of export of no inconsiderable magnitude." Like many Europeans, Robson saw the forest as a commodity of limitless abundance. According to Robert A.J. McDonald, "lumbering was the industry through which Europeans placed their imprint on the landscape of Burrard Inlet." The ensuing conflicts between competing lumber businesses during the 1860s redefined the exploitation of the timber. As sawmill owners and logging camp operators fought over the resource, the government was compelled to devise new means to distribute it.[64]

Pioneer Mills continued under the ownership of Graham and McLeese until they sold out to J.O. Smith in 1864 and Sewell Prescott Moody in 1865. But major lumber exporting did not commence until Captain Edward Stamp arrived at Burrard Inlet, flush with foreign capital and intent on turning trees into dollars (Figure 1.6). Stamp had made his first foray into the lumbering business as an agent for the British firm Anderson and Company, when he established a sawmill at Alberni in 1860. With another company agent, Gilbert Malcolm Sproat, Stamp operated the mill until he left the company in 1863. Sproat then ran it until it closed in 1865. Meanwhile, Stamp returned to England, forming a new corporation known as the British Columbia and Vancouver Island Spar, Lumber and Saw Mill Company.[65]

Stamp employed two timber surveyors to explore Howe Sound and Burrard Inlet to assess the quality and extent of their lumber resources. In April 1865, after the survey was completed, he decided to construct a sawmill on Burrard Inlet. Curiously, he selected a site on the Stanley Park peninsula. He initially claimed that he was apprehensive about the location because of a lack of fresh water but changed his mind upon "the discovery of a lake on the same reserve of sufficient capacity to supply [his] wants." Stamp was probably apprised of this lucrative property by two of

Figure 1.6 Captain Edward Stamp, 1875. A-01768, British Columbia Archives

his company directors, Richard Clement Moody and Robert Burnaby. Governor Frederick Seymour was willing to grant a hundred acres of the peninsula, which had been designated as a government reserve, to Stamp "provided that the spot selected by Col. Moody for a Fort, on the South Point, shall not be included within the purchase." This decision suggests that, by 1865, the reserve was not considered a military necessity in its *entirety;* it could be divided for multiple purposes. In that same spirit, Colonial Secretary A.N. Birch unofficially informed Stamp that his company would have access to fifteen thousand acres for twenty-one years at a nominal rent as well as unrestricted use of the timber on other Burrard Inlet government reserves. Deciding to build his mill at Brockton Point, not far from Whoi Whoi, Stamp began construction in May.[66]

However, establishing a mill proved more difficult than anticipated. Sent by Birch to survey Stamp's claim, J.B. Launders found that part of the site "occurs in the centre of an Indian Village to clear which would only give the Saw Mill claim about 90 acres; by the appearance of the soil and debris this camping ground is one of the oldest in the Inlet." This was not the first time that Stamp had encountered Aboriginal people living on property that he intended to acquire; at Alberni, he had simply threatened to turn his ship's guns on their encampments, a stance that proved effective. Officials at New Westminster believed that the Aboriginal settlement consisted only of Supple Jack (August Jack Khatsalano's father) and a few of his relatives. Therefore, it would not be an impediment, and in any case, "Captain Stamp has no objection to their remaining where they are. They can be at any time removed. The ground does not belong to their tribe." Even so, Stamp probably found more Aboriginal people at Whoi Whoi than he first expected.[67]

A more immediate problem was the treacherous nautical conditions at First Narrows, which ultimately made Brockton Point an unsound site for sawmill operations. A combination of turbulent rip tides, a narrow passage, and troublesome hidden shoals impeded the construction of a wharf at the point. By mid-July, Stamp had become frustrated with the location, where he found "obstacles of so severe of nature that may compel us to abandon that particular site on which we have already gone to a considerable expense." Eventually, though a considerable area had already been cleared, he decided to abandon Brockton Point altogether. Birch acceded to his request to move the mill farther east along the south shore of Burrard Inlet, where he constructed what became known as Stamp's Mill.[68]

After a prolonged delay in shipping critical machine parts, Stamp's Mill began operation in June 1867, joining the Moodyville mill on the North Shore in processing lumber from Burrard Inlet. According to its charter, the BC and Vancouver Island Spar, Lumber and Saw Mill Company sought to take advantage of the "dense forests of most valuable timber." The charter cited Captain Richards's survey of Vancouver Island and the mainland, which had highlighted the strategic importance of the timber resource in the production of masts for the British navy. In addition, it saw great potential in the export of lumber to "the Chinese, Australian, and South American markets." At the lowest estimate, the corporation hoped to cut fifty thousand board feet per day. Lumber was sold and used locally, but it was also shipped around the world. Initially, loggers used teams of oxen to haul logs to the mills, but both mills eventually employed steam power to process lumber in greater quantities. This exploitation of trees for commercial profit proceeded at a scale and pace that far surpassed pre-contact Aboriginal wood-harvesting practices, as the Burrard Inlet sawmills of the

1860s and 1870s recruited the forest into an emerging global capitalist system with an insatiable appetite for wood.[69]

Prior to the 1870 Land Ordinance for British Columbia, timber resources were alienated along with land in the sale of private property. There was no clear policy for the disposal of BC forests, because the colonial government did not initially see timber as a valuable resource. Furs, fish, and mineral exports dominated the colonial and early provincial economy in the nineteenth century – for the government, wood ranked well below these resources. Stamp and Moody were among the first to seek access to timber through lease agreements, which would allow them to cut the trees without having to purchase the land outright. Perceiving the trees as obstacles to agricultural settlement, the government was anxious to have the two companies clear them away.[70]

Ultimately, however, the informality of the early timber and land policies resulted in conflicts during the late 1860s. In January 1867, six months before his mill came on line, Edward Stamp had secured a rather lucrative deal with the colonial government. He had spent months negotiating the terms of this agreement with Chief Commissioner of Lands and Works Joseph Trutch and Attorney General H.P.P. Crease. He was particularly concerned over his rights to the fifteen thousand acres of forest near his mill and he wanted to prevent settlers from pre-empting it. The colonial government assured him that "no pre-emption shall be allowed to be recorded without previous reference to a permission of the Governor and the Superintendent of the Mill Company and no pre-emptor shall have a right to cut timber without the permission of the Superintendent of the Company." Critically, though Stamp's original negotiations had requested free access to timber on all the government reserves at Burrard Inlet, this was never written into his lease. Nonetheless, he carried on preparations for the opening of his mill under the assumption that he had an exclusive right to log the reserves.[71]

Stamp's assumption was abruptly proved wrong in January 1867, following a dispute with one of his contract loggers, Jeremiah Rogers, who had worked with him since the Alberni days as a timber surveyor and logging camp operator. Rogers set up a logging venture on the Burrard Inlet naval reserve, located at the present-day Jericho Beach, and commenced cutting trees to be processed at Stamp's Mill once the necessary machine parts arrived from England. Stamp and Rogers became embroiled in a dispute over the price of this wood. Rather than succumb to Stamp's efforts to acquire it on the cheap, Rogers sought an exclusive right to the

timber on the naval reserve, intending to sell it for a higher price to Sewell
Moody on the North Shore. In early January 1867, H.P.P. Crease drafted
a timber lease agreement with Jeremiah Rogers.[72] When Stamp discovered
Rogers's duplicity, he was livid. In a letter to the colonial secretary, he
staked his claim to the timber on all the government reserves, reminding
the administration that

> during the many discussions that took place the right of cutting timber on
> this Reserve and the Reserve between English bay and Burrard Inlet, known
> as Col Moody Fort Reserve [Stanley Park], was frequently referred to and
> although neither of these Reserves are specially named in the lease it was
> well understood by myself and I believed also by the govt that the right of
> cutting timber was conceded to the Company.[73]

But Stamp was wrong. No one in the government, including either Crease
or Trutch, had any knowledge of this implicit agreement. Matters worsened
for Stamp when another logging camp operator decided to follow Rogers's
lead. Jonathan Miller had started selectively cutting Douglas fir on the
Stanley Park peninsula in 1866 and decided to secure an exclusive lease for
it in order to sell to the Moodyville mill.

Infuriated by the prospect that his North Shore competitor would gain
access to the timber on these two large reserves, Stamp insisted that Governor Seymour had granted him exclusive access to it through a verbal
agreement. Trutch sought to clarify matters with the governor and settle
the dispute as quickly and quietly as possible. The colonial secretary wrote
to Trutch that "on these tracts no one can claim any specific right to cut
timber." Although the governor had made an informal agreement with
Stamp in 1865, he now favoured instituting a system of timber licences.
He had the colonial secretary notify Stamp that following "some inconven-
ience having arisen from the permission verbally given to you by the
Governor to cut timber on the Crown Reserves at Burrard Inlet, I am
directed by His Excellency to inform you that he revokes such permission."
After this, logging on any government reserve at Burrard Inlet was temporarily prohibited.[74]

In defiance of this ban, both Jonathan Miller and Jeremiah Rogers
continued to log the Stanley Park peninsula and the other Burrard Inlet
reserves. Stamp made numerous complaints to Trutch until the government finally yielded to the pressure and charged the loggers with trespass
in April 1868. The Magistrate's Court at New Westminster dismissed
the charges, and the two logging camps went back to work. John Robson,

who believed that "Capt. Stamp, with his posse of spies, was at the bottom of the whole affair," was further incensed by a second attempt to prosecute "or *persecute*" Rogers and Miller in July 1868, a case that he described as a "ludicrous and disgusting farce." To Robson, Rogers and Miller were simply "industrious, sober, hard working men" who had angered Stamp by trying to cut into his monopoly over the timber lands of Burrard Inlet. He accused Stamp of making "a mere tool of the Government" in this matter.[75]

On 31 July 1868, a public meeting was held in New Westminster to discuss the timber dispute. After hearing Jeremiah Rogers and Jonathan Miller present their cases, the large crowd passed a resolution that called for the government to cease the current legal action against the two men and grant them licences to log the reserves in question. The primary concern was not the protection of the trees but the preservation of private rights to the natural resources of the colony. The colonists believed that "it was by promptly checking the first encroachment upon private rights that public rights would be most effectually guarded." As a reformer who opposed the collusion of big capital and government, Robson saw the issue from a somewhat different perspective. If Stamp were permitted a total monopoly, he could impede settler expansion. Robson claimed that "to allow the forest on the slopes of our outer harbour to remain in its primeval condition is to deny to the farmers and the colonists a ready market for produce and labour." Forests were an obstacle to settlement, but they could also be beneficial if the government permitted them to be "metamorphosed into money by the lumberman's axe." In the process, a great source of wealth could be exploited to form an economic base for the emerging colony. In the opinion of a colonial booster such as Robson, nature was a commodity to be improved and exploited through human labour.[76]

Eventually, the government acceded to the colonists' demands and granted timber leases to Rogers and Miller in November 1868. Following this dispute, the informal disposal of timber resources was gradually curbed. Governor Seymour reiterated to the disappointed Stamp that "the mere verbal permission of the Governor, revocable at pleasure, cannot be held to grant any exclusive right." After Confederation, British Columbia's timber licensing system was established by the Land Act of 1884, and by 1896, legislation had affirmed the principle of Crown ownership of all timber lands. The dispute over the trees helped redefine the legal status of this natural resource, ignoring any prior Aboriginal understandings of its use and ownership.[77]

Although Jonathan Miller and other contractors continued to log the Stanley Park peninsula until as late as 1885, it is impossible to know precisely

Figure 1.7 A man stands next to a cedar tree with a noted circumference of fifty feet. This photograph was taken along the park road in 1889 by Charles S. Bailey. Major Matthews Photograph Collection, St Pk P22 N251, City of Vancouver Archives

how much timber they took or what impact this had on the forest ecology. Historians know that Miller's lease lasted from 1868 to 1871, probably on the same terms as Rogers, who paid an annual rent of $40. In an 1899 *Victoria Daily-Colonist* interview, Miller confirmed that he had worked out of a camp at Brockton Point during the 1860s and 1870s, and he claimed to have "took off millions of feet of lumber." This was probably an exaggeration given the limitations of nineteenth-century logging technologies. It is more likely that he cut selectively, focusing on Douglas fir and using human energy supplemented by teams of oxen. The largest trees were probably spared because they were too big for oxen to haul or mill machinery to accommodate. Although the peninsula was logged until the 1880s, this was not the clearcutting that is so common today. According to forest historian Richard Rajala, the steam donkey and technological innovations in yarding, which increased harvesting capacity and more rapidly depleted forest resources, were not introduced until after the 1880s. Nevertheless, industrial logging in the 1860s and 1870s probably altered the forest ecology of the peninsula and placed greater pressure on its timber. Stamp's preliminary construction work at his Brockton Point site denuded it of trees, and selective logging left numerous large stumps in its wake, some of which remain in place.[78]

Despite the inroads of logging, most of the peninsula remained forested into the 1880s. An 1889 photo series taken by Charles S. Bailey, a prominent turn-of-the-century city photographer, shows the nature of its woodlands (Figure 1.7). His photos particularly focused on the spectacular large trees, often noting the circumference and posing a man at the base for scale. It was the forest – once a prized commodity for the lumber barons of Burrard Inlet – that became the primary object of interest for late-nineteenth-century park advocates.[79]

Cows, Pigs, Chickens, and Horses

During the 1860s, Europeans began to settle alongside Aboriginal people on the Stanley Park peninsula, bringing new ideas and land practices. Colonization led to tremendous cultural and economic changes for Aboriginal people, but it also resulted in significant ecological modifications that historians have not fully appreciated. Although Barman examines European settlement, she does not note its ecological impact. Similarly, Margaret Ormsby's innocuous observations about flowers at Fort Victoria relegate immensely important aspects of the biological exchange between the Old and New Worlds to the realm of symbolism, stating: "There were many

outward signs of inner adjustments, but none more symbolic than the
flower garden inside the log pickets, where the native lady's slipper and
the moccasin flower had been replaced by mignonette, stock, hollyhock
and wall flower, all sweetly reminiscent of 'home.'"[80] Although it is an
evocative metaphor for Aboriginal dispossession, the flower garden at Fort
Victoria was more than mere symbol. It was a small component of a broad
and deliberate effort to biologically transform the Northwest Coast into
Western Europe. European colonization of the coast occurred centuries
after other New World colonies were established in Central and South
America as well as the eastern parts of North America. To borrow Alfred
Crosby's term, these lands became "Neo-Europes," where European migrants
established themselves through the mass transfer of biota from Europe to
reproduce familiar flora and fauna. Alien plants and animals – partners in
this biological expansion – accompanied settlers, but unlike the microbes
that infected the people of the New World, they were deliberately imported.
This is how Stanley Park came to be inhabited by cows, pigs, chickens,
and horses.[81]

Imported plants and livestock provided essential food sources and labour
that facilitated resettlement and the displacement of Aboriginal peoples
from their lands, and thus they were key to transforming the landscape of
the Northwest Coast. The introduction of domesticated animals was especially significant since Aboriginal people had virtually no experience
with them. As Virginia DeJohn Anderson argues, domesticated animals
in early America were not only alien to Aboriginal people, their status
differed entirely from that of their wild counterparts. Unlike wild animals,
cows were private property.[82]

Coast Salish nations, however, were accustomed to their own indigenous dogs, the only domestic animal on the coast prior to European contact.
George Vancouver noted their presence and speculated that their fur was
used to manufacture fabrics. August Jack Khatsalano claimed that the
Squamish kept "lots [of] dogs, Indian dogs, not whitemans dogs," at Whoi
Whoi before European colonization. Because many European colonists
saw the domestication of animals as characteristic of civilized society, they
sought alternative explanations for the presence of dogs among people
whom they considered savage. Believing "that the Japanese visited the coast
of North Western America long prior to any other people," John Keast
Lord, naturalist for the British North American Boundary Commission,
concluded that the "Indian Dog" must have come from Japan, for "the
dog is not indigenous." Of course, Lord was incorrect. Archaeological
evidence has since proven that a distinct species of dog emerged in North

America as early as eleven thousand years ago. Like many colonists before him, Lord dismissed it as "nothing more than a tame coyote or prairie wolf." Such disparagement of "Indian Dogs," Anderson suggests, may have arisen "simply because of their connection with Indian people."[83] In fact, the practice of keeping indigenous dogs may have helped accustom Aboriginal people to European livestock.

During the 1860s and 1870s, a handful of European and Asian migrants settled on the Stanley Park peninsula, establishing houses, yards, and gardens, some of which persisted until as late as 1958. Jean Barman's detailed research provides some of the best information on these early settlers, but her work overlooks the ecological significance of their imported biota. A few people clustered at Brockton Point in the 1860s as Vancouver, initially known as the Granville townsite, emerged and the lumbering industry took root. Three Portuguese sailors, who had come to British Columbia during the Fraser River and Cariboo gold rushes, settled on the peninsula and worked as fishers and local businessmen. Joe Silvey, Gregorio or "Joe" Fernandez, and Peter Smith all married Squamish women from Whoi Whoi and built houses at Brockton Point, where they were later joined by Joe Mannion, John Baker, and Tomkins Brew. As settlement continued at the nearby Granville and Hastings townsites, a small Chinese village was established at Anderson's Point. Thus, by the mid-1870s, the peninsula was inhabited by Europeans, Asians, and Aboriginals.[84]

Although the colonists at Brockton and Anderson Points did not engage in large-scale farming, they cultivated home gardens and raised livestock. Evidence from the 1920s reveals fenced properties with gardens and chicken pens, most probably used for household food production. Alfred Gonsalves, who lived at Brockton Point, claimed that his family "raised a few vegetables, and got a piece of ground and made a garden" there. He described their gardens as small plots between clearings in the woods, where "you can plant all kinds of stuff in between stumps." Another observer, Edward Trimble, claimed that the residents "had gardens in there, there was some potatoes and cabbage and such like growing." The Chinese settlers raised bulls and hogs that grazed freely. Although fishing and longshoremen work remained the primary economic activity of most of these individuals, they introduced new plant and animal species through modest forms of agriculture and animal husbandry. This was not only a significant ecological change: it also represented new uses of the resources of the peninsula as living space. The food production practices of the European and Asian newcomers took advantage of its natural resources in a new way.[85]

Aboriginal food production economies were most disrupted by the colonial seizure of coastal and freshwater fisheries. Douglas Harris argues that these fisheries, "the principal source of subsistence and wealth for Native peoples in British Columbia, were neither unregulated nor un-owned." Prior to colonization, kinship rights restricted access to certain fishing sites and regulated the catch. When the Crown colony was created in 1858, the fishery fell under English common law, which permitted all British subjects free access to it. Fish became an open-access resource and stocks were soon depleted. As was the case with timber, colonial law fundamentally changed human relations with this resource. Believing that the fish were inexhaustible, early Fraser River canneries over-harvested them, gradually edging out the Aboriginal fishery. By 1888, Aboriginal people were hemmed in by the law and restricted to the new concept of a limited food fishery. This compelled many Coast Salish nations to adopt new food production strategies.[86]

When Spratt's Oilery opened in 1882, the industrialization of the fisheries had a direct impact on Whoi Whoi (Figure 1.8). Hoping to capitalize on the abundance of herring in Coal Harbour, Victoria businessman Joseph Spratt established the oilery there, using dynamite to kill the fish and selling the oil for a variety of purposes. August Jack claimed that before the oilery opened, "there were millions of herring in Coal Harbor," but two years into the enterprise, the fish disappeared. Duncan McDonald, an early BC colonist, claimed that "after extracting the oil they took the refuse and dumped it outside the Narrows and they say that drove the herrings away." Others believed that the company's use of dynamite scared off the fish. Regardless, Spratt's Oilery drove off one of the primary marine resources used at Whoi Whoi.[87]

August Jack described the pre-colonization food production economy of Whoi Whoi as follows:

> Lots meat, bear, deer, beaver; cut meat up in strips and dry – no part wasted, not even the guts. Clean out the guts, fill him up with something good, make sausage, just like whitemans. Only head wasted; throw head way. Then salmon – plenty salmon, sturgeon, flounder, trout, lots all sorts fish; some sun dry, some smoke dry. Indians know which best wood for smoke dry. Lots crab and clam on beach.[88]

He also explained how Aboriginal women procured berries, vegetables, and roots. Eventually, however, these practices were disrupted because, as Khatsalano pointed out, "whitemans food change everything. Everywhere

Figure 1.8 Spratt's Oilery, 1884. Major Matthews Photograph Collection, Bu N50, City of Vancouver Archives

whitemans goes he change food." Like other Aboriginal people on the Northwest Coast, the inhabitants of Whoi Whoi adopted some of the alien foods. August Jack claimed that they had a "little garden; just clear space before whiteman come. I never see, but I think they have it (ground) ready like; then when the whitemans come Indians just put in potatoes, turnips."[89]

The potato and turnip patches at Whoi Whoi may have altered food plant production, but the adoption of livestock signalled a substantial change in the relationship with animals. August Jack recalled that his father purchased cattle from New Westminster, where he "bought one cow; then the cow had a little one; it was a bull; then they got lots. We had 12 cows running around, and 8 pigs. They were running loose around Stanley Park when they got road put up."[90] They also kept horses for travel and the occasional race at New Westminster. The livestock was not killed for personal consumption, however; Khatsalano insisted that they ate neither beef nor pork. Instead, the milk and meat were sold to Europeans. He remembered how his family used the land and resources to raise cattle, integrating into the new colonial economy:

> The cows, at night, were put in the stable; in the day they ran loose in the park; or along the beach; they got wild grass mostly – along the beach – but there was some English grass, not much, some, enough to carry us over the winter, and if there was not enough, Father bought hay from Black's and Maxie's. Mother milked the six cows in the morning – the other six were dry – and put the milk in big high milk cans – about five gallons – and took it to Hastings Mill in the canoe.[91]

August Jack's family took advantage of the changing economy of the inlet by selling provisions to the local logging camps. In addition to supplying milk to Hastings Mill, Supple Jack "used to shoot the steers, then butcher them, and send them to the logging camps." In 1876, the Indian Reserve Commission census recorded two horses, seven cows, and 151 fowl at Whoi Whoi. Clearly, by the 1870s, its Aboriginal inhabitants had adapted to the ecological changes of colonization by incorporating domestic animals and new food plants into their economy.[92]

The Indian Reserve Commission

The 1876-78 Indian Reserve Commission and the BC government ultimately dispossessed the Coast Salish inhabitants of the peninsula by outlawing its use as an Aboriginal living space and denying the creation of a reserve. When British Columbia joined Confederation in 1871, the provincial and federal authorities had yet to settle the question of First Nations land rights. Although a few treaties arranged by Governor James Douglas in the 1850s and 1860s covered parts of Vancouver Island, Aboriginal title in most of the province had not been extinguished through treaties. By 1871, British Columbia had rejected the tenets of the 1763 Royal Proclamation, which had guided federal Indian policy in the rest of Canada. Ottawa had generally followed a strategy of extinguishing Aboriginal title through treaty negotiations, allocating large reserves, and paying annuities. In contrast, British Columbia avoided treaties, opting to create small reserves and hoping to assimilate the indigenous population into its emerging industrial labour force. Provincial and federal authorities fought over the question of Aboriginal land rights for five years before appointing a three-man Indian Reserve Commission in 1876, which

Figure 1.9 Gilbert Malcolm Sproat, 1870. A-01770, British Columbia Archives

was led by Captain Edward Stamp's former associate at Alberni, Gilbert Malcolm Sproat (Figure 1.9). Ottawa and Victoria were represented by two former Hudson's Bay Company fur traders, Alexander Caulfield Anderson and Archibald McKinley, respectively. In late 1876, these three men set out from New Westminster to tour the Aboriginal nations of the province and assess their reserve needs.[93]

From its inception, the commission was plagued by conflict between the federal and provincial governments. BC premier George Walkem and Lieutenant Governor Joseph Trutch, both prominent settlers of the colonial era, were intent on upholding the province's parsimonious Indian land policy. Walkem preferred that Aboriginal people should mingle with whites and culturally assimilate rather than live separately on large reserves. According to R. Cole Harris, sizeable reserves and the promotion of agriculture conflicted with Walkem's vision – that Aboriginal people "should enter the workforce where, as labour was scarce and in demand, they would find employment in almost all branches of industrial and domestic life." In essence, Walkem and Trutch hoped to turn the BC Aboriginal population into a much-needed source of cheap labour. Nowhere was this more evident than at Burrard Inlet.[94]

All three commissioners were prominent colonists who were very much influenced by current ideas and preconceptions regarding Aboriginal people. Both Anderson and Sproat published work on the colonial prospects of the province and its indigenous population. Anderson's *Dominion at the West* (1872) assured readers that "the Indians are producers as well as consumers, they form an important element in the consideration of the commercial relations of the Province." It is clear that Anderson relegated Native people to the role of wage labourers because, as he explained, "they excel in many simple manufactures, and are not a little advanced in divers mechanical arts."[95] Sproat's body of work is somewhat more complicated, but it shares some colonial perspectives on Aboriginal people and natural resources. In his first book on his experiences at Alberni during the 1860s, Sproat articulated his views on colonization and indigenous dispossession:

> My own notion is that the particular circumstances which make the deliberate intrusion of a superior people into another country lawful or expedient are connected to some extent with the use which the dispossessed or conquered people have made of the soil, and with their general behavior as a nation. For instance we might justify our occupation of Vancouver Island by the fact of all the land lying in waste without prospect of improvement.[96]

Like many early colonists, Sproat saw traditional European agriculture as the root of private property and proprietary rights to land. Even Governor James Douglas regarded the hunting and gathering practices of Aboriginal people as proof that they were simply a "wandering denizen of the forest." Nonetheless, Sproat believed that "any extreme act, such as a general confiscation of cultivated land ... would be quite unjustifiable."[97]

In his 1873 guide for prospective colonists, Sproat's brief assessment of the Aboriginal population was strikingly aligned with the views of Commissioner Anderson. Sproat believed that Aboriginal people were "useful as common labourers, and not without capabilities as artisans; some take to farming and have cattle, others carry on mining with 'rockers' on the Thompson and Fraser Rivers." His final estimation, dating from just three years before he met with the inhabitants of Whoi Whoi, was that "altogether the Indians contribute very largely to the trade of the province."[98]

On 6 November 1876, Sproat, Anderson, and McKinley left New Westminster, travelling north by steamer to settle land claims among the Musqueam, the Squamish, and the Tsleil Waututh of the Fraser River and Burrard Inlet. Sproat knew nothing more about the Coast Salish than what George Vancouver had recorded in his journal. He knew that Vancouver had encountered only about fifty Aboriginal men in 1792, who had probably come in canoes from Whoi Whoi. Sproat's second assumption was based largely on the accounts of early colonial authorities, who believed that the Squamish were recent arrivals in the area. As he put it, this contention was justified because the "general public opinion in the neighbourhood now appears to be that the claims of the Skwawmish to land at Burrard's Inlet are not founded upon ancient occupancy or use. I do not think they have old associations with the place." Sproat mistakenly speculated that the Squamish had entered the Burrard Inlet area only during the mid-1860s "to make money out of the sawmill owners established in business at that place." According to him, they were migratory wage labourers in the developing lumber industry.[99]

The commissioners arrived at Burrard Inlet on 11 November 1876 and camped at the Capilano Creek Indian reserve on the north shore of First Narrows. Over the course of a week, they met with several Squamish leaders from around the inlet to ascertain their land needs.[100] In his diary, McKinley recorded what he told the assembled Aboriginal people at one of these meetings:

> The Provincial Government have always treated the Indians with liberality and kindness and that it was their purpose to do so still but that they would by no means let them have more land than they could turn to good account &c &c that they would have all they wanted when they shewed that they could make good use of it and that I thought they have too much good sence [sic] than to expect more.[101]

All three commissioners concurred that sizeable reserves were inappropriate in the area. Sproat reported that "there is no available suitable land at Burrard's Inlet for a large Indian Reserve. Even had it been possible to find a large area the white settlers did not appear to desire that the Indians should be concentrated, and the Indians were disturbed in their minds even at the idea of such a proposal."[102] The records reveal that the commissioners tended to place the land rights of white settlers above those of local Aboriginal people. Sproat insisted that the Aboriginal individuals with whom he spoke had no wish to be removed from their homes and placed on a large reserve. They wanted to assure their freedom to work for the sawmill owners on both sides of the inlet. In general, McKinley found that the Squamish "are industrious and are considered very useful laborers." Sproat echoed this sentiment and remarked that having an Aboriginal population scattered around the inlet would help everyone, because "the mill owners too and the shipping frequenting the Mills are benefited in a corresponding degree by having a local source of labour constantly available."[103]

On 16 November, Sproat, McKinley, and Anderson crossed the inlet for an arranged meeting with the people of Whoi Whoi. Once again, Sproat stood on the grounds where his former associate, Captain Stamp, had attempted to establish a sawmill in the heart of a large Aboriginal village. Whereas Stamp had used the guns of his ship to intimidate the Aboriginal people at Alberni into abandoning their land, Sproat would use the power of the provincial and federal governments to dispossess the Native inhabitants of the Stanley Park peninsula.

According to the official census conducted by George Blenkinsop as part of the Indian Reserve Commission, fifty Aboriginal people lived at Whoi Whoi in 1876. At the time, this was the second-largest concentration of Aboriginal people at Burrard Inlet. As Barman has shown, McKinley erroneously believed that Whoi Whoi was established *after* Stamp's attempt to construct his mill in 1865. This led the commissioners to conclude that its inhabitants were "squatters." Sproat relayed this assessment to Ottawa and Victoria, arguing that "the Indians have no old associations with the spot. Some persons think they were quite aware in settling upon it, that it was a special Government Reserve which neither white men nor Indians could be permitted to possess, but perhaps the charitable view that they acted ignorantly may be the truer view."[104] McKinley claimed that he met with Supple Jack and "told him he was wrong in squatting on the Govt Reserve knowing it to be such when he did so." Originally, the commissioners sought to establish a small Indian reserve on the peninsula, hoping to protect about six to eight acres where the people had lived "for several years and had made some improvements." However, when they made this recommendation to F.G. Vernon, the chief commissioner of lands and works, he denied the request. Other than citing the status of the area as a government reserve, Victoria gave no reason for rejecting the commissioners' recommendation. It is most likely that the Province hoped to sell the land for a considerable sum once the expected transcontinental railway was completed, as promised under British Columbia's terms of entry into Confederation. In fact, it attempted to do just that eight years later. In the meantime, the commissioners assured the Aboriginal inhabitants that they would probably remain undisturbed for the foreseeable future and would be given plenty of time to find residences on the new local Indian reserves. Supple Jack and the families at Whoi Whoi were devastated by the news; as Sproat recorded, "they were very downhearted on hearing our decision."[105]

Having made small enlargements to the few Indian reserves in the area, and having officially dispossessed the people of the Stanley Park peninsula, the commissioners departed from Burrard Inlet. In law, the colonial authority of the federal and provincial governments was exercised swiftly, but in actuality, Whoi Whoi remained populated into the 1880s. Its residents were not physically removed until the government reserve was transformed into a park. Nevertheless, the Indian Reserve Commission completed a process of colonial transformation that had begun many years earlier.

Before the establishment of Stanley Park, this was a heterogeneous space exploited for its resources in a variety of ways. A spectrum of ideas and attitudes about nature had changed this environment. By 1886, industrial logging and urbanization had removed many of the trees from the Burrard uplands, leaving the Stanley Park peninsula as a lone forested island. City builders in the newly incorporated Vancouver sought to transform it once again. Their new approach attempted to overwrite past uses of nature and bring that spectrum of ideas into focus behind the single concept of a public park.

2
Making the Park Public

As European settlement intensified, Vancouver's land east of Coal Harbour became increasingly urbanized, whereas land to the west was designated as Stanley Park. Although city council set it aside as a natural retreat from the city, it was intended to serve the needs of the emerging urban environment as it came to occupy a significant place in the lives of Vancouverites.

Just as colonization transformed the peninsula, so too did its designation as a public park. Park creation, or "emparkment" as some have called it, was not simply a matter of preserving land from urbanization; it was a different kind of urbanization in which nature was exploited for the cultural and physical benefit of city-dwellers, becoming a recreational resource for non-consumptive use.[1] The invention of Stanley Park did not separate humans from nature but instead altered an already deeply interwoven relationship. The next two chapters explore two concurrent stages of Stanley Park's development and how emparkment transformed the peninsula.[2]

This chapter looks at the creation of the park in law as public space from 1887 until the early 1930s and how ordinary people used it, sometimes in contradiction to the wishes of authorities. As Ari Kelman argues, law was a fundamental organizing principle for the production of public space in urban areas. He contends that "to understand the history of urban public spaces one must first grapple with how protean definitions of the public have been across time, and the impact that constant shifts in the meaning of that phrase – the public – have had on the production of landscapes in the city." The federal government's designation of the peninsula as a park for Vancouver shifted the definition of "public" at the end of the nineteenth century. Colonial authorities had constructed the peninsula as public property since its designation as a government reserve in 1859, but the idea of a park produced an entirely different kind of public space.[3]

The definition of "public" changed in two key ways that altered how humans interacted with nature in Stanley Park. The first involved the establishment of a new governing authority. The creation of Stanley Park involved overcoming the complexities of federalism and public property under Canadian and British law and establishing a new legal regime on the peninsula to homogenize its use. The second stage of redefining "public" required the imposition of a new environmental ethic. Writing in connection with the American conservation movement, Karl Jacoby refers to this ethic as a new "moral ecology." As a result of its imposition, Stanley Park's human inhabitants could no longer exploit its resources for food, shelter, or any other form of private consumption. Nor could industrial interests do so for commercial profit.[4] Consumptive uses of Stanley Park's resources, including hunting, gathering, fishing, and wood harvesting, became illegal once the park was created. Rather than embodying heterogeneous uses of nature, the invention of the park enforced a single idea of non-consumptive recreation under state ownership and authority.[5]

Nonetheless, ordinary Vancouverites challenged this authority. They illegally harvested timber and plants, collected sand and rocks, and even hunted in the park. The depths of its forest and the abundance of its natural resources permitted them to do so while simultaneously placing material limits on the authority of the Park Board. The families who lived in the park constitute the most obvious example of a challenge to the Park Board vision of public space. Although Jean Barman contends that the families were forcibly evicted because "the space had to be made to appear natural," this chapter shows that the evictions had more to do with private property rights and Aboriginal land claims.[6]

Petition for a Public Park

Stanley Park was founded on speculation and ambition. The efforts to create it coincided with the emergence of Vancouver itself. It was both speculative and ambitious for a small lumber town such as Vancouver, which had fewer than five thousand people in 1886, to establish a public park consisting of nearly a thousand acres. And though there is no clear explanation for its genesis, there are a few likely possibilities, the reasons for which lie in the context of the emergence of the Terminal City.

Prior to 1885, Vancouver was a frontier village housing a lumber society.[7] European settlement of the area was initiated by a gold rush on the Fraser River in 1858. Thousands of miners ventured to this distant edge of the British Empire in search of mineral wealth. As the mining boom of the 1850s and 1860s subsided, settlement on Burrard Inlet concentrated near the two sawmills at Hastings and Moodyville. Conditions in these small lumber communities were to change dramatically with the promise of rail.

British Columbia entered Confederation as the sixth province of Canada in 1871 on the guarantee that Ottawa would build a transcontinental railway connection to the Pacific coast. This guarantee of a link with the rest of Canada stimulated what would become one of the province's largest commercial activities – real estate speculation. In the 1870s, opportunists from Victoria and New Westminster began pre-empting lots on Burrard Inlet.[8] Most were government insiders who hoped that their privileged information regarding the railway construction would inflate land values. In 1885, when the CPR announced that Coal Harbour and English Bay would be the terminus for the promised railway, the trickle of speculation became a torrent. To the chagrin of those who expected Port Moody to be the terminus, land speculators took to the Granville townsite with a flurry of acquisitive energy. According to Robert A.J. McDonald, in a "new western town, where expectations of high financial returns from city building provided the 'indirect and intangible' element that stimulated rapid urbanization, much of the growth-generating activity centred on the sale and servicing of land."[9] Anticipating the completion of the terminus, Vancouver incorporated on 6 April 1886 with an economy fuelled by wood and speculative real estate.

The CPR was the biggest benefactor of the land boom. Its vice-president, William Van Horne, negotiated with Victoria for ownership of 5,800 acres in central Vancouver and nearly all of the West End, making the CPR the largest landholder in the city. Norbert MacDonald argues that the CPR profoundly shaped the development of Vancouver: not only did it instigate the city's real estate bonanza, but it also laid out the street pattern, shifting the commercial and financial centre west toward its own property near Granville Street.[10]

Lauchlan A. Hamilton, a CPR surveyor and land commissioner who played a critical role in the development of Vancouver, was also a principal player in the creation of Stanley Park. Hamilton's contribution exemplifies the significance of the CPR in the early history of the city. He surveyed the first streets in 1885, working in the bush and marking the location of the roads. He was an alderman on the first city council, elected in 1886,

Figure 2.1 Arthur Wellington
Ross and Malcolm MacLean.
Ross was the first person to
suggest the creation of Stanley
Park. His brother-in-law MacLean
was the first mayor of Vancouver.
PA 025819, Library and Archives
Canada, and 677-734, City of
Vancouver Archives

and is even credited with creating the Vancouver coat of arms. In 1886, Hamilton tabled a motion to convert the large government reserve at the western tip of the Burrard peninsula into a public park.[11]

On 12 May 1886, at its second meeting, city council read a letter from Arthur Wellington Ross requesting that it petition Ottawa to "grant [the] Reserve on First Narrows for a City Park."[12] Ross, a federal MP from Manitoba and a close affiliate of the CPR, was deeply involved in the Vancouver land boom during the 1880s. He had previously participated in a similar phenomenon in Winnipeg from 1881 to 1882.[13] A local real estate broker, he also happened to be the brother-in-law of Vancouver's first mayor, Malcolm MacLean (Figure 2.1).[14] Two months before Ross contacted city council, he had written to Minister of Militia and Defence Adolphe Caron regarding the government reserve at First Narrows:

In my opinion it can be made one of the finest parks in the world and in connection with the proposed establishment of national parks along the line of the Canadian Pacific Railway would be quite an attraction to tourists travelling over our national railway and the above proposed arrangement would not in any way interfere with the right of your department to these lands.[15]

Ross's recommendation to city council was his second attempt to convert the peninsula into a park. Alderman Lauchlan A. Hamilton moved that a petition be drafted "praying that the whole of that part of the Coal Harbour peninsula known as the Government Reserve or such part as in the wisdom of the Government they might see fit to grant be conveyed to the City of Vancouver for a Public Park."[16]

This initiative was intimately tied to the speculative real estate market in Vancouver, serving as it did the interests of the major property owners, especially the CPR. Initially, William Van Horne's intent had been to extend the railway terminus to English Bay, bypassing Coal Harbour by cutting through the government reserve (Map 4).[17] Both Van Horne and his associate Henry Beatty felt that English Bay was a more suitable port than Coal Harbour due to the difficulty of navigating the turbulent waters at First Narrows. Beatty believed that "vessels should at all times be able to come right into English Bay without defection while the difficulty of navigation of the first narrows is a serious drawback to Coal Harbour." Assuming that the peninsula had been reserved for military purposes, and hoping that the CPR might purchase part of it, Van Horne instructed Hamilton to conduct a survey to "enable the Department of Militia to determine how much of the ground should be retained by the Government for defensive purposes, and how much they can spare to us." As it turned out, Ottawa was unwilling to part with any portion of the reserve, a decision that forced the CPR to find another means of profiting from this choice piece of real estate.[18]

Since Ottawa was unwilling to part with the reserve and allow it to be sold into private hands, the CPR encouraged its conversion into a public park. The presence of a large park immediately adjacent to its West End property would tremendously benefit the CPR. Ironically, businessmen such as Edward Stamp and Sewell Moody had once valued the trees of the peninsula because they could be logged for commercial gain, but by 1886, the trees could turn a greater profit if they remained in place.[19]

In the nineteenth century, North American city parks tended to appreciate the value of nearby property, a fact that helped instigate the establishment

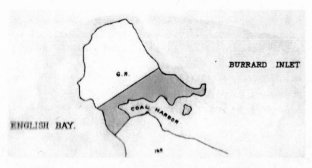

Map 4 The shaded area in this 1885 map by Lauchlan A. Hamilton shows the land that the CPR hoped to obtain to extend its railway terminus to English Bay. J.S. Matthews, "The Naming, Opening, and Dedication of Stanley Park," *Vancouver Historical Journal* 2 (1959): 11

of several parks in the United States and Canada. According to Terence Young, this was one of the four virtues of the American parks movement, along with increased tourist potential. Roy Rosenzweig and Elizabeth Blackmar argue that New York City's Central Park was originally conceived by elite New Yorkers who were interested in inflating uptown property prices for land speculation and that a myth was formed to disguise this dubious genesis. Early park development in Winnipeg had boosted real estate values in neighbourhoods abutting Assiniboine Park. CPR officials were well aware of the link between parks and real estate, and the company's prominent role in the 1885 creation of Rocky Mountains Park reveals that it recognized the great economic potential of park tourism. Stanley Park fit this model well.[20]

In this respect, Stanley Park's origins resemble those of other North American parks. According to W.C. McKee, Arthur Ross's hope was that it would increase the attractiveness of the CPR's West End. And indeed, the West End emerged as Vancouver's first elite neighbourhood for the wealthy and influential, particularly CPR administrators, a status that was partially due to the presence of the park.[21]

However, economic aspirations form only part of the story, as is illustrated in the artwork of Lauchlan Hamilton, which reveals the complex relationship between utilitarian and aesthetic motivations for park creation during this period. Hamilton was the first European to produce landscape art featuring the Stanley Park peninsula (Figure 2.2). His view of it was multifocal: As a CPR employee and a West End property owner, he would profit greatly from the creation of a landmark city park on his

Figure 2.2 Watercolour painting by Lauchlan A. Hamilton of English Bay, looking toward the Stanley Park peninsula in 1885. Major Matthews Photograph Collection, St Pk 77, City of Vancouver Archives

doorstep – this much was obvious. But as a surveyor and an engineer, Hamilton was privileged with another perspective. His 1885 street survey was a premonition of Vancouver, born from his training and translated onto paper. During the day, he walked through the forest, sketching a plan for the city that would one day replace it. He drafted future streets and roads, naming them for – in his estimation – great men of history (including himself and numerous other CPR employees). These lines criss-crossed the tangle of Douglas fir, red cedar, spruce, and hemlock that would soon disappear. This urban vision was counterposed by his work of the afternoons and evenings, when he painted watercolours of the forest. As he quietly depicted the landscape, Hamilton knew that the transcontinental railway would soon make a city and that the city would unmake the forest. To record it, he carefully painted the trees of the government reserve against the spectacular backdrop of the North Shore mountains. When Arthur Ross concocted his scheme to create a park, Hamilton leapt at the opportunity to preserve his painted landscape in reality.

At the insistence of Hamilton and Ross, Mayor Malcolm MacLean forwarded a petition to the governor general of Canada, requesting "that the said reserve should be handed over to the [City of Vancouver] ... to be held by them as a public park."[22] After consulting with the minister of militia and defence, the Privy Council approved the mayor's request on 8 June 1887 and granted permission to use the reserve as a park. The City's tenure of Stanley Park would rest on this arrangement for the next twenty-one years.[23]

In Vancouver, the small elite group that promoted the creation of Stanley Park did not face the problem of returning private land to the public domain, which plagued its US counterparts, because the colonial government had already separated the peninsula from the private land market in 1859. Its challenge was navigating the legal complexities associated with public space in the Canadian and British context. Stanley Park opened in September 1888 and was dedicated in October 1889 by its namesake, Frederick Arthur Stanley, the sixteenth earl of Derby and governor general of Canada, "to the use and enjoyment of peoples of all colours, creeds, and customs, for all time." Lord Stanley's statement, now inscribed on his statue at an entrance to the park, captured one aspect of the meaning of public space – it explained *who* could use the park, but it did not define *how* it could be used or who would govern its use. The 1887 agreement with Ottawa permitted Vancouver to use the peninsula as a park, but it maintained that control could always be returned to the Department of Militia and Defence for military purposes. The minister of militia and defence specifically requested that "the Dominion Government retain the right to resume the property when required at any time." Despite this, the Order-in-Council that created Stanley Park was a vague document that did not provide a clear picture of who held legal title.[24]

The Battle for Deadman's Island

The complicated status of Stanley Park's ownership did not pose a significant problem for city council and the Park Board until Ottawa leased Deadman's Island to a private individual for industrial development in 1899. The board, and many Vancouverites, saw this small tidal island as part of the park. A favourite spot for picnickers, it was even painted by the prominent Canadian landscape artist Thomas Mower Martin in 1899 (Figure 2.3). In 1890, the Park Board constructed a bridge to connect it to the mainland.[25] After Minister of Militia and Defence Frederick Borden signed a lease with industrialist Theodore Ludgate in February 1899, which

Figure 2.3 An 1899 image of Deadman's Island by Thomas Mower Martin.
PDP04429, British Columbia Archives

permitted clearcutting the island and constructing a sawmill, a prolonged
dispute broke out between city council, Victoria, and the Dominion government that would eventually resolve the matter of legal authority over
Stanley Park.

As day broke on 24 April 1899, Theodore Ludgate descended on
Deadman's Island, accompanied by a crew intent on clearing the land and
constructing a sawmill. They approached the beachhead in a small flotilla
of boats, only to be met by Mayor James F. Garden, City Solicitor Alfred
St. George Hamersley, and twenty-five police constables poised to block
any attempt at logging. This "early morning invasion," as the *Vancouver
Province* called it, initiated the long conflict between Ludgate and Vancouver authorities, known locally as "The Battle for Deadman's Island."
At the end of the dispute, the highest court of the British Empire would
determine the legal status and ownership of Stanley Park.[26]

A handful of boats floated offshore, carrying reporters and other curious
spectators. The mayor and Ludgate spoke briefly before Ludgate returned
to his crew. According to reports, Ludgate reached for an axe, walked to
a nearby tree, and plunged the blade into the trunk, whereupon the mayor
immediately ordered his arrest. As the arresting constable moved into action, the crew quickly took up their tools and began to clear some of the
bush and trees. The full force of constables then rushed to apprehend the

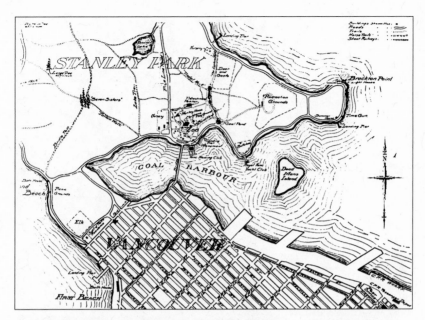

Map 5 Deadman's Island lies in the middle of Coal Harbour, between Stanley Park and urban Vancouver. City officials and Vancouverites had long considered it a part of the park. Stanley Park, 1911, Maps Collection, Map 368, City of Vancouver Archives

entire crew, a standoff that ended without a shot being fired, as the police unceremoniously ushered the "invaders" off the island.

This dramatic confrontation had less to do with an insignificant island in Coal Harbour than with the adjacent residential neighbourhood and urban park. Deadman's Island straddles the border between the park and the city and was a focal point in the legal creation of Stanley Park (Map 5). Even though the park had officially opened to the public in 1888, the legal authority to govern it remained unclear for more than twenty years. The 1899 dispute over Deadman's Island revealed a fundamental lack of consensus regarding how public space should be governed and used.

The businessmen who had created Stanley Park also led the struggle to preserve Deadman's Island, operating through a complex political, economic, and social network to achieve their goal. The 1899 conflict demonstrated that they could manipulate the shape of the urban environment through various political connections at the local, regional, and national levels, but it also exposed the limits of their power. This group sought to enhance the authority of the Park Board in order to guarantee local control of Stanley Park. It had long sought a proper lease so as to regulate the use

Figure 2.4 Theodore
Ludgate leased Deadman's
Island from Ottawa in
1899, hoping to construct
a sawmill there. Major
Matthews Photograph
Collection, P. Port. 532 n.
1179b, City of Vancouver
Archives, and PA 025996,
Library and Archives
Canada

of the park and its protection but had failed to acquire one. The lease of
Deadman's Island to Theodore Ludgate raised the spectre of industrial
encroachment, leading advocates to seek better legal footing in connection
with Stanley Park.

Theodore Ludgate was a shrewd entrepreneur who had previously managed a sawmill in Traverse City, Michigan (Figure 2.4). Born in Peterborough,
Ontario, he first worked as a Crown timber agent. As early as 1898, Ludgate
set his eyes on Vancouver as a potential site for a new sawmill, and he
visited the city on a number of occasions to find a suitable location. Backed
by a group of investors from the Chicago area, Ludgate chose Deadman's
Island.[27]

Knowing that the island was commonly perceived as part of a military
reserve administered by the Department of Militia and Defence, Ludgate

skilfully employed his political connections – including Joseph Martin and George Maxwell, two prominent BC Liberals – to obtain access to it. Joseph Martin was the BC attorney general in Charles Semlin's government and head of his own law firm; Ludgate hired him to lobby Frederick Borden on his behalf. In making his case to Minister Borden, Martin argued "that it could not in any way injure [Stanley Park] to part with this small portion; [Deadman's Island] is really of no value to the reserve, and it would be a great boon to the city of Vancouver to get an immense mill ... in their midst." Ludgate assured Borden that he would bring in over $250,000 of investment and create as many as a thousand jobs for the city. George Maxwell, a former Presbyterian minister and MP for Burrard, lent further support to Ludgate's proposition and argued that it would "be of great advantage to the city."[28]

Ludgate's offer to build a sawmill was an attractive development opportunity for Vancouver. In 1899, the provincial logging industry was growing rapidly; increased immigration to the prairies after 1896 had amplified the demand for BC lumber, and the local market was also escalating at a tremendous rate as Vancouver expanded. The city was still emerging from its first significant economic downturn since the real estate boom of the 1880s, and workers were desperate for employment. Ludgate's attempt to establish a new mill could not have come at a more economically opportune time.[29]

Taking heed of this pressure, Borden consulted with two commanding officers in the Department of Militia and Defence to judge the value of Deadman's Island for military purposes. Major-General Edward T.H. Hutton disagreed with Martin's claim that constructing a sawmill on the island would not interfere with its military use.[30] However, Borden did get approval from Lieutenant Colonel D.A. Macdonald, who saw no problem with granting the lease as long as the department could resume control of the land at any time. Prompted by this assessment, Borden approved the lease on 14 February 1899. For the fee of $500 a year, Ottawa authorized Theodore Ludgate to clearcut the island and construct his mill.[31]

Divided on the Deadman's Island controversy, Vancouverites disagreed regarding how public space should be developed at this stage in the city's growth. During the first days after the lease was signed, it seemed that they would rally to prevent the construction of the mill, but their vocal opposition masked deeper divisions between the West End elite and the working-class residents of the Eastside. During the first week of the controversy, a petition was sent to Ottawa protesting the lease, and a delegation went from Vancouver to meet with the minister of militia and defence as well as Prime Minister Wilfrid Laurier. A close examination of the protest reveals that it was led by a small group of businessmen from the West End.

The protest delegation was composed of Board of Trade members who rallied the support of city council and other organizations to resist Ludgate's industrial ambitions. On 21 February 1899, William Godfrey, chair of the Board of Trade, held a special meeting in hopes that the board would protest the lease. The board duly passed the following resolution:

> The opinion of the meeting was thoroughly averse to the leasing of Dead-man's Island by the Federal Government as a site for a saw-mill or for any other purpose. The island is within the limits of Stanley Park and the citizens have always regarded it as part of the Park in accordance with the Order-in-Council passed by the Federal Government some time in 1887 that the locating of such a saw-mill on Deadman's Island would be fraught with exceeding danger to the Park in case of fire and that the City having made improvements on the island the Board feels that in the knowledge of these facts the claims of the City Council to the island will be recognized by the Government.[32]

Although the resolution seemed to suggest that the board was united in rejecting the project, the opinions expressed at the meeting were far more diverse. Prominent supporters of the lease, including George W. DeBeck, George Maxwell, and Charles Woodward, spoke out against the resolution, asserting that a sawmill would provide jobs for Vancouver workers who had suffered through the recent economic depression. Allegations were also made that opposition to the mill came primarily from West End residents who feared that it would obstruct their view of the park. When J.C. McLagan spoke against the mill, stating, "I believe in planting industries in the best places," an unknown voice at the back of the meeting sarcastically shouted, "In the east end for instance!" This exchange exemplified the common belief that West End business leaders worked to concentrate industry in the Eastside while maintaining the West End as a prestigious residential neighbourhood. Angus Everett Robertson makes this case in his work on the historical geography of Vancouver, demonstrating how businessmen used their economic clout to shape the growth of the city.[33]

Initially, the Vancouver Trades and Labour Council (VTLC) opposed the lease and sent its chairman, Harry Cowan, as a labour representative in the protest delegation. However, it then held a second vote, led by J.H.

Watson, reversed the original decision, and recalled Cowan. Mark Leier argues that the Deadman's Island debate drove a wedge between the leadership of the VTLC and its members.[34] According to Leier, "The different trades could be expected to have different positions on issues, such as parks, depending on how each would profit or lose: boilermakers, stonecutters, and iron moulders supported the logging of the island, for it would create employment among their members, while those unlikely to prosper, such as printers, fought for the preservation of park space."[35] This second vote may actually have been a reflection of the mounting support for Ludgate, led by George Maxwell, among Eastside workers. The withdrawal of organized labour further revealed that the protest against constructing a mill on Deadman's Island was orchestrated primarily by West End elites and that the city's working class favoured using public space for the creation of jobs rather than parks.

Whereas West End residents saw Stanley Park as an essential part of their neighbourhood, their Eastside counterparts did not necessarily share this view. Where some saw a magnificent park, others saw valuable unused waterfront property. Industry dominated the waterfront of Vancouver's Eastside. Hastings Mill, the Vancouver City Foundry, and the BC Sugar Refinery commanded the shoreline to the north, and the railyards of the CPR and other industries crowded the edges of False Creek to the south. Those who favoured constructing a mill on Deadman's Island saw the city waterfront as an industrial place. George Maxwell believed that "in all big cities the water-fronts are used in this way and if we are to be a manufacturing City we must make room for these industries." Charles Woodward recognized the imbalanced distribution of industry in Vancouver and suggested that "if the island was off Hastings or somewhere lower down the Inlet, there would be no kick about it." William Brown, alderman for Ward 3, rejected the aesthetic arguments for the preservation of the island because he "did not believe that a man ever got a square meal off scenery," and furthermore, he believed that "the City would never prosper unless it made good use of every foot of land it possessed." This utilitarian perspective rejected the idea of the public park.[36]

Ultimately, the conflict was rooted in the issue of who had authority over urban public space – that is, which level of government was entitled to determine how it should be used. Charles Hibbert Tupper, a social elite and resident MP from the West End, could "admit that a large portion of the labour element in Vancouver are in favour of [the lease], and, from an economical point of view, it may be a good thing for the city, but there are serious questions remaining as to why and how this property was handed over." These serious questions, which would eventually reach the highest courts of the province and the British Empire, were grounded in decades of confusion over the ownership of Stanley Park.[37]

Redefining public authority to govern the peninsula and securing legal title over the land were essential to the creation of Stanley Park. When Theodore Ludgate arrived on Deadman's Island in April 1899, James Garden employed the powers of the city police to stop him from clearcutting its forest, but this was merely a temporary solution. Garden and his supporters believed that the island came under the purview of the Dominion government's Order-in-Council, which gave the park to the city in 1887. Ludgate cited the authority of his lease; it too came from the Dominion government, though from the Department of Militia and Defence.[38] Less than a month later, Victoria entered the fray when Ludgate returned to the island on 8 May 1899 and commenced construction. The Province's chief commissioner of lands and works, Francis Carter-Cotton, declared that Stanley Park and Deadman's Island lay within the domain of British Columbia, and therefore Ludgate held no legal title.[39] This placed the BC attorney general (and political rival of Carter-Cotton) Joseph Martin in a significant conflict of interest. Martin had been hired to represent Theodore Ludgate in his bid to lease the island, but now his own government stood opposed to such a lease. As a result, some demanded that he resign from cabinet. In a bid for calm, Martin travelled to Vancouver and convinced Ludgate to cease work until a resolution could be reached. Initially, Ludgate acquiesced, but his patience soon reached its limits.[40]

On 15 May, Ludgate's crew returned to the island and began clearing it, working for more than an hour before the provincial police arrived. Believing that he held legal title, Ludgate confronted the officers and refused to vacate. The police left but returned two hours later with the mayor, who threatened to arrest Ludgate if he did not halt his crew and leave immediately. The recalcitrant industrialist stood firm, refusing to go unless taken by force, whereupon three constables wrestled him to the ground and dragged him away. The mayor read the riot act and ordered the remaining men to vacate within thirty minutes. They did so, but the damage had already been done: during their brief hours of work, the crew had managed to topple half the trees on the island. According to one report, "the immense trees cut down on all sides have completely changed the appearance of the island for familiar land marks have disappeared." With Ludgate now in police custody, Victoria turned to the courts to resolve the question of who held legal title to Deadman's Island and Stanley Park.[41]

Earlier attempts to purchase or lease Deadman's Island had illustrated the general sense of confusion over the ownership of the park. Many believed that it was a British colonial military reserve created in 1859 and turned over to the Dominion of Canada in 1884, whereas others thought that it belonged to the BC government.[42] The issue became controversial in March 1886, when an industrialist named Alexander Russell applied to the BC chief commissioner of lands and works to purchase Deadman's Island. This caught the attention of the federal deputy minister of the interior, who was concerned regarding the confusion over who owned the reserve. Joseph Trutch, the Dominion government agent for British Columbia, was instructed to speak with BC premier William Smithe to clarify the issue but failed to persuade Smithe of Ottawa's view. The BC government maintained that at the time of Confederation in 1871, all reserve lands remained under its authority. The dispute became all the more worrisome for the minister of militia when he discovered that Victoria intended to sell lots on the peninsula. The matter was finally dropped when Premier Smithe decided not to sell any portion of it. This skirmish between Ottawa and Victoria was merely a prelude to the larger court battle that would ensue over Deadman's Island and the Ludgate lease.[43]

In February 1899, when Frederick Borden granted the Ludgate lease, the provincial government assisted the City of Vancouver's campaign to assert its authority over the island. Initially, Borden argued that his department retained control of it because it had not been included in the 1887 Order-in-Council that created Stanley Park. He contended that the order had applied only to the "military reserve," not to Deadman's Island, which he argued was a "naval reserve" and thus distinct from the rest of the park. Rejecting Borden's claim, Francis Carter-Cotton decided to take possession of the island in the name of the Province, a move that would prevent Ludgate's project from proceeding.[44]

In exasperation, Deputy Minister of Militia and Defence L.F. Pinault wrote to Carter-Cotton, stating that he was "at a loss to understand how you can now claim to be the proprietor and take possession of the same, on behalf of your government without any legal proceedings."[45] Carter-Cotton and the provincial government were prepared to go to court to defend the contention that the island had always belonged to British Columbia, a position that he claimed "has been held by my predecessors in this department for many years." Thus, the matter was turned over to the Supreme Court of British Columbia.[46]

From December 1900 to February 1901, Supreme Court justice Archer Martin presided over the case to determine the ownership of Deadman's

Island and Stanley Park.[47] Victoria's lawyers argued that the site had never been designated as a military reserve by either Governor James Douglas or Colonel Moody in 1859 and therefore became provincial property in 1871 under sections 109 and 117 of the British North America Act.[48] The attorney general of Canada, co-defendant in the case, argued that the land had indeed been designated as a military reserve and was turned over to Ottawa by the British Colonial Office in 1884 along with all other military reserves in the province. Both sides presented historical evidence, and former lance-corporal George Turner of the Royal Engineers testified regarding the survey of Burrard Inlet that he had conducted for Colonel Moody in 1863. As Jean Barman has demonstrated, though Turner had marked the area as a "military reserve" in his field notes, there was no documented evidence that Moody had officially declared it a military reserve in 1859.[49]

In his decision, Justice Martin stated that only the governor of the colony had had the power to declare a land reserve in 1859.[50] He concluded that Ottawa had failed to present adequate evidence to show that Stanley Park was designated a military reserve in that year; the original Land Proclamation of 14 February 1859 was too vague in its use of the term "reserve." "The conclusion might almost be reached," he speculated, "that Colonel Moody probably brought about the temporary reserve of this land as a prospective coal area." Ultimately, Martin ruled in favour of the Province and granted the land to provincial authorities, thus upholding the injunction against Ludgate.[51]

Ottawa brought the case to the BC Court of Appeal before Justices Montague Drake, Paulus Irving, and Chief Justice Gordon Hunter in 1904. Its lawyers presented a new map and argued that it marked Stanley Park and Deadman's Island as part of a military reserve. The map showed naval reserves coloured in blue, Indian reserves coloured in brown, and military reserves coloured in red. Victoria's lawyers refuted this new evidence, suggesting that it was unclear whether "red" referred to a military reserve or to land that was merely temporarily unavailable for pre-emption. Significantly, the map was undated and unsigned, which meant that it could have been produced at any time and was not necessarily official.[52]

In spite of these counter-arguments, Ottawa won its appeal in a two-to-one decision in the summer of 1904. Justice Drake declared that its evidence proved that "Stanley Park, including the island in question, was and is a military reserve."[53] Thus, it came under federal jurisdiction. Justice Irving concurred with Drake, stating that the map was evidence that the land was a military reserve. Upon final appeal to the Judicial Committee of the Privy Council in 1906, Ottawa and Ludgate were again victorious. Despite a fundamental lack of documentary evidence to show that Moody had created a military reserve at Coal Harbour, the Privy Council decided that since George Turner's survey marked the land as a military reserve and the Colonial Office's schedule of reserves transferred to the Dominion in 1884 included one at Coal Harbour, Stanley Park was therefore a military reserve. Unfortunately for the City of Vancouver, this meant that the final court of appeal upheld Ludgate's lease and automatically lifted the injunction.[54]

Although the 1906 Privy Council decision meant that the City of Vancouver failed to secure possession of Deadman's Island, it did lead to one substantial gain – the federal government finally granted Vancouver an official lease of Stanley Park, which gave it legal authority to govern the site.[55] The negotiations for this lease had begun early in 1904, before the first Ludgate trial was complete, when the Park Board entered into discussions with Victoria for a ninety-nine-year lease of the park.[56] These discussions, and proposed amendments to the provincial Public Parks Act, were premature since the Privy Council had not yet determined the ownership of the park. By April, the City had started to negotiate with Ottawa. Park advocates hoped that a lease would "insure the title to this Park for practically all time to come." It would secure proper legal title for the City so that a local governing authority could regulate use of the park.[57]

In June 1905, as negotiations neared an end and a draft lease had been completed, the federal and city authorities became locked in a disagreement over terms. Ottawa wished to impose a new Park Board on the City to manage Stanley Park, and the lease stipulated that the board would consist of six members, three appointed by the City and three by the Dominion. The *Vancouver Province* stated that it could not "see any reason for the Dominion authorities reserving the privilege of making appointments," an opinion shared by the Park Board and city council. The City held its ground until 1908, when Ottawa capitulated, agreeing that control of the Park Board would continue to rest with the Vancouver electorate. Twenty years after David Oppenheimer opened Stanley Park to the public, the City of Vancouver signed its first official lease.[58]

The dispute with Ludgate did not end in 1906, and a second Privy Council decision was required to uphold his title, but the tide began to turn against him in 1911. That year, the Liberal government lost the federal election, and Robert Borden's Conservatives appointed a new minister of militia and defence, Sam Hughes. Less supportive of Ludgate than his predecessor, Hughes decided to challenge the lease yet again. Although

Figure 2.5 These two images reveal the transformation of Deadman's Island from the 1890s to 1931. Major Matthews Photograph Collection, M-3-16.1, St Pk N27, City of Vancouver Archives

the Privy Council had twice upheld the lease, it had never considered the issue of renewability. Both the Exchequer Court of Canada and the Supreme Court of Canada eventually ruled that the lease was not renewable.[59] With the lease due to expire in 1924, plans for industrial development on the small island were quickly abandoned. In the end, Ludgate and his business partner, Evert Kinman, cleared the trees but never built a mill. Historical photographs reveal the transformation of the site, once admired for its tight cluster of towering conifers (Figure 2.5).

Immediately following the Dominion's Supreme Court victory over Ludgate, the Park Board requested that a lease for Deadman's Island be drafted along lines similar to the Stanley Park lease of 1908.[60] From 1918 to 1929, the Department of Militia and Defence retained title to the island while the Park Board and the Vancouver Harbour Commission discussed which of them should govern it. Finally, in his annual report for 1929, the superintendent of parks noted that

> negotiations have been proceeding for some years past with the Federal Government with a view to securing Deadman's Island for park purposes for all time on terms similar to those contained in the Lease of Stanley Park to the City. These negotiations have confidently expected that the cherished hopes of the Park Boards, past and present, will be realized in the announcement of the Federal Government that Deadman's Island has at last been declared a public park.[61]

Early in January 1930, Ottawa notified the Park Board that Deadman's Island was now leased to the City of Vancouver for use as a public park.

Making and Breaking the Rules

The Vancouver Incorporation Act of 1886 had not included provisions for the creation or regulation of city parks. Instead, the Public Parks Act governed all public parks in British Columbia and empowered the Crown to appoint trustees to administer "any public park or pleasure ground for the recreation and enjoyment of the public." This act applied to the Municipalities Act and permitted a municipal council to manage a park with the permission of the provincial government. However, in 1887, when Ottawa granted permission for Vancouver City Council to operate Stanley Park, there was no BC statute to regulate this authority.[62]

Initially, city council managed the park through the Board of Works and appointed its first caretaker, John Hurst. His job was to "constantly walk around the Park and prevent the brush and timber from burning and [see] that no one be allowed to cut any timber on the Park without permission from the Board of Works." Essentially, this was the only rule that governed the park prior to its official opening in September 1888.[63]

The day before the park opened, city council passed a by-law creating a committee to manage all public parks in the city. Consisting of three aldermen and three "private citizens" whom city council would appoint

Figure 2.6 Henry Avison
in 1893. During his term
as ranger, Avison lived in a
cottage in the park. Major
Matthews Photograph
Collection, VLP 149, City
of Vancouver Archives

annually, the committee was intended to "manage and report upon all
matters relating to the improvement, ornamentation and preservation of
all Public Parks belonging to the City of Vancouver and to carry out all
such works connected therewith as the Council may authorize." The by-
law did not specify how the committee should manage the parks and did
not grant it the power to create regulations defining their use.[64]

Not until April 1889 did the provincial government amend the Vancouver Incorporation Act to provide for the establishment of an official
Board of Park Commissioners.[65] This amendment enabled the Park Board
to regulate the use of public parks in Vancouver. A year later, city council
acted on the amendment and passed a by-law creating a new elected Board
of Park Commissioners with the power to generate by-laws.[66]

In 1889, the Park Board hired a twenty-eight-year-old Irish immigrant
named Henry Avison as park ranger (Figure 2.6). After arriving in Vancouver
during 1887, he had worked as a construction foreman, grading Pender
and Georgia Streets. As ranger, Avison was responsible for protecting
the park from fires, maintaining its road, and preventing the cutting of
cordwood; in an area consisting of nearly a thousand acres, he was also

the sole on-site official for the enforcement of all park regulations. The City later provided Avison with a uniform, helmet, and badge to be worn on Sundays and holidays, the busiest days in the park.[67]

The regulations that Henry Avison enforced during the next seven years were largely composed of informal motions passed at board meetings, and they generally called for the protection of waterways, trees, animals, and other property. During those first years, no codified park by-laws existed. With thousands of people visiting the park every day, the board was anxious to establish strict rules to govern its use. To this end, it sought assistance from other North American jurisdictions, soliciting copies of the regulations from Calgary, Winnipeg, Toronto, and New York City. In 1896, it passed its first comprehensive by-law for "the regulation, protection, and government of the parks of the city."[68]

When Henry Avison left Vancouver in search of Klondike gold, the board hired George Eldon, an English immigrant who had come to Vancouver in 1886, as his replacement. During his tenure, Eldon struggled to enforce the by-laws, and in 1902, the board arranged for a policeman to patrol the park. In 1904, Eldon's title was changed to "superintendent of parks," expanding his authority to cover all city parks. Eventually, the board increased the police detail and introduced mounted officers to monitor the trails and roads (Figure 2.7).[69]

The by-laws reflected the board's understanding of the purposes of a public park and its own stewardship role. As Mayor Oppenheimer stated while opening the park in 1888, it would be used as a great retreat from the city, a forested oasis for the citizens of Vancouver. The board's regulations attempted to establish this division between park and city – a vision that was highly influenced by middle-class notions of non-consumptive use. Because Vancouver borrowed many of its regulations from elsewhere in North America, its rules for Stanley Park shared a common set of ideas with the American park movement. The park may have been public property, but as Rosenzweig and Blackmar suggest, "public property was not to be mistaken for common property." Furthermore, "the park represented a new concept of public property held in trust for the community's cultural rather than its economic benefit." Frederick Law Olmsted, as the first superintendent of Central Park, sought to instruct New Yorkers on how to use the park as public property rather than an unregulated commons. Olmsted excluded those aspects of the city that were alleged to lead to nervous exhaustion and saw the park as an antidote to the fast-paced and competitive individualism of urban life. His regulation of the park reserved its natural resources for the purposes of leisure and recreation.[70]

Figure 2.7 Mounted police officers were first hired to patrol the park in 1904.
Major Matthews Photograph Collection, SGN 75, City of Vancouver Archives

Vancouver's park regulations eliminated traditional consumptive uses of nature. As explained in the previous chapter, Aboriginal people had always consumed the resources of the peninsula and continued to do so after it became a government reserve. Non-Aboriginal settlers followed suit, using the plant and animal life for food, fuel, and shelter. When the reserve was reinvented as a park, the Park Board outlawed these practices. Karl Jacoby argues that members of the American conservation movement similarly erected a series of rules to guide the use of national parks, radically redefining legitimate uses of nature. He suggests that "for many rural communities, the most notable feature of conservation was the transformation of previously acceptable practices into illegal acts: hunting or fishing redefined as poaching, foraging as trespassing, the setting of fires as arson, and the cutting of trees as timber theft." In national parks such as Yellowstone, these rules conflicted with the practices of rural and Aboriginal communities, whose "moral ecologies" differed from those of progressive conservationists.[71]

This phenomenon also occurred in large urban parks. Olmsted's first regulations for Central Park outlawed the consumption of wildlife and plants, which were once considered common property. In many North American cities, working-class people used unoccupied lots as common space for fuel and foraging well into the twentieth century, particularly in younger towns in the west. Vancouver was no exception to this trend, and many of its residents treated Stanley Park as a vast urban commons.[72]

The Vancouver Park Board strictly protected all plant and animal life in the park from damage or removal; it proscribed unregulated burning and dumping of "any dead carcase, filth, dirt, stone, or any offensive matter or substance"; and it prohibited the free grazing of cattle, a common practice during the colonial period. Despite its efforts to impose control, its rules encountered resistance.[73]

George Cary, an early Vancouver resident, recalled that people commonly hauled wood from the park to make split shingles and that they hunted grouse in its forest. Another settler recounted hunting wild ducks, noting that he "used to shoot them down in Coal Harbour." Even in 1904, the Park Board was alarmed to discover that Vancouverites were "robbing ... the swan and geese nests in the park." In 1908, a man named E. Miller Small requested permission to cut four slabs of wood from stumps or fallen timber there. Later that same year, Superintendent George Eldon reported that someone was covertly removing sand from Second Beach at night.[74]

Perhaps the most audacious case of delinquent use occurred in 1910, when an unknown trapper was found living in the park. He evaded capture for weeks until park employees discovered a raccoon and a dog caught in two of his traps. Eventually, by following the trap lines, the superintendent stumbled upon "two rude shacks or shelters, completely hidden away in the densest section of the wildwood," where the mysterious trapper "had been able to carry on his calling." Even today, an anonymous, shifting population finds comfort, shelter, and freedom from police surveillance in the park's forest. Such individuals were commonly discovered throughout the twentieth century, sometimes under tragic circumstances, as in October 1911, when park employees found the dead body of a man from Vancouver's "floating population," according to a newspaper report.[75]

It is difficult to determine how many people transgressed the rules in Stanley Park, but a 1922 letter from Thomas H. Ingram reveals the extent to which plants were taken. Ingram claimed that

for about seven years we lived in Englesea Lodge and it was a common sight every Sunday, and most other days, to see car after car come out of the Park

loaded with ferns etc, and literally hundreds of pedestrians carrying hand-
fuls. I have repeatedly tried to do what I could to stop it but am generally
told that it is none of my business. Women are by far the worst offenders.
I notice few men trouble to pick anything unless requested so to do by
women with them.[76]

Unlike the flower- and fern-picking public, Ingram saw the park as a
pleasure ground for leisure. He signed off as "Yours for a Public Park for
the Public," a view that conflicted with the moral ecologies of those who
exploited the park's natural resources for their own consumptive use.

Vancouverites also challenged the rules that governed the recreational
use of the park. On 11 April 1914, Mr. M.C. Schwaber wrote to the Park
Board, describing a recent unpleasant incident:

Visiting Stanley Park yesterday and walking along the main path leisurely
I passed a group of men and boys who were playing baseball. Not thinking
of any danger in a public Park where one goes for relaxation, I was struck
by a ball which came flying towards me so unlooked for and with such force
that if I had not been protected by a fairly heavy coat, which happened to
be closely buttoned, I might have been seriously injured possibly ruptured
for life the ball struck a very sensitive spot and I suffered the most excruciat-
ing pain for many hours. I shall be very thankful if this accident will leave
me with nothing worse than pain.[77]

Mr. Schwaber's unfortunate accident demonstrates a major problem that
plagued the Park Board during its early years: the conflict between passive
and active recreation. Stanley Park was created at the juncture between
the early romantic period, in which parks were intended for passive leisure,
and a later rationalistic phase, which emphasized active recreation. The
transition to the second phase was never completed at Stanley Park, where
the board attempted to separate passive and active recreation areas.[78] At
times, however, the romantic and rationalistic aspects came into conflict.
Park visitors still experience similar clashes as cyclists and evening strollers
battle for supremacy on the seawall. As Robert A.J. McDonald has shown,
Vancouver's elite class of the early twentieth century saw the park's vast
forests as intended for passive leisure, whereas working-class people desired
a more usable space filled with playing fields and sports stadiums.[79] The
sheer size of Stanley Park's forest played a role in the persistence of this
divergence. Terence Young argues that, because national and state parks
exceeded the scale of many urban parks, the romantic vision became

particularly associated with them. In the case of Vancouver, the size of Stanley Park enabled many people, particularly the West End elite, to see it as a wilderness for passive enjoyment. Schwaber's 1914 encounter with the ball-players illustrated the conflict between passive and active uses of nature in Stanley Park.

Early by-laws set restrictions on active leisure, prohibiting any person from playing "football or any other game within a public park or square, except in such portion thereof as may be set apart for that purpose by the Board."[80] Most sporting activities occurred at Brockton Oval, the site of Edward Stamp's ill-fated attempt to construct his sawmill in 1865. In June 1888, the city leased the oval to the Brockton Point Athletic Association, a select amateur organization, according to Barbara Schrodt, "with the influence necessary to maintain private and exclusive control of a public facility."[81] The oval was the sole sports facility in the city until the construction of the athletic grounds on Cambie Street. The Brockton Point Athletic Association set strict limits on who could use the oval, and it adhered to a middle-class notion of sporting behaviour. Between 1888 and 1912, the board regulated sports in the park through this organization.

By 1915, new sports facilities had been added to the park, including tennis courts, a lawn bowling green, and a playground, each of which required new regulations.[82] The facilities and the rules revealed a loosening of the restrictions to satisfy the demands of playground lobbyists and sporting organizations in the early twentieth century. In 1934, by-laws expanded the active leisure regulations to include separate areas for playgrounds and sports activities. Most of these new uses of the park, and their accompanying infrastructure, were restricted to areas that were largely devoid of trees or had previously been cleared, as in the case of Brockton Oval. The tennis courts, lawn bowling green, and playground were all constructed near Second Beach on the low-lying, thinly forested isthmus between the park and the West End.[83]

Early by-laws were also designed to promote quiet and passive use of the park by curbing loud and rowdy behaviour. No one was permitted to "behave improperly or be disorderly, or use boisterous, insulting or indecent language, or obstruct any other person therein."[84] The wording of this by-law reflects the board's attempts to promote passive leisure and to use the park according to middle-class notions of conduct. Again, many of the views expressed in the by-laws were common in other North American urban parks in the late nineteenth and early twentieth centuries. Over time, however, Stanley Park's increasing popularity – with hordes of weekend visitors – forced the board to alter its policies and permit more active uses. By breaking the rules, ordinary people reshaped the acceptable uses of the site. However, one group still posed a major challenge to the production of public space in Vancouver: the forgotten families of Brockton Point and Lumbermen's Arch.

Park It Somewhere Else: The Stanley Park Eviction Trials

By the 1920s, the families who remained in Stanley Park were mostly descendants of the Aboriginal inhabitants of Whoi Whoi and early European colonists. City and park officials commonly referred to them as "squatters," a term that falsely conjures images of illegitimate, temporary, and dilapidated housing. As Jean Barman and others have shown, the families lived in modest permanent houses surrounded by fences that delineated one property from the next. They owned automobiles, worked in the city, and raised children. Unlike those who labelled them "squatters," they saw the park as living space, not a site reserved for leisure.

The eviction of the families was not, as Barman contends, grounded solely in the effort to construct the appearance of an uninhabited wilderness. Instead, the records of the 1920s eviction trials show that the families were removed because they challenged the very notion of a public park by possessing private homes within it. Furthermore, the Coast Salish lineage of some of the residents threatened to set a legal precedent for Aboriginal land claims in British Columbia. The Park Board's policy of leaving the families undisturbed from 1913 to 1923 was not, as Barman puts it, "a game of cat and mouse" – it was a calculated way of managing the question of Aboriginal title and property rights. In 1923, after years of procrastination, the federal government, on behalf of city council and the Park Board, took the remaining families to court. A constellation of state power, brought into focus following the Deadman's Island dispute, facilitated the ensuing legal conflict. The trials were the final stage in dispossessing the original inhabitants of the peninsula, thus concluding the process of colonial regime change and the legal creation of Stanley Park.[85]

The creation of most North American parks involved the eviction of their inhabitants. As mentioned above, Jacoby notes that leaders of the American conservation movement labelled park inhabitants as squatters and demeaned their uses of nature as uncivilized. If nature were to be reserved, people had to be removed. According to Theodore Catton, removing the inhabitants enabled the creation of vignettes of primitive America, an imagined time and place when nature was untouched except by the Aboriginal people who lived in harmony with it and who left little

Figure 2.8 Some early tourist postcards featured images of the "squatter" dwellings at Brockton Point and Deadman's Island. Unknown artist, *Deadman's Island, Stanley Park and Snow Capped Mountains, Vancouver, BC*, postmarked 10 September 1908. Author's collection

or no impact on the land. The dispossession of park inhabitants also occurred in North American cities. Central Park was home to more than three thousand people in the 1850s. Similarly, a houseboat village stalled the establishment of a recreation area on Burlington Bay in Hamilton, Ontario, from 1920 to 1940. Recent work by Ted Binnema and Melanie Niemi, however, has challenged some of the arguments about parks and dispossession by demonstrating that the construction of uninhabited wilderness was not necessarily the primary objective of park promoters during the eviction cases.[86]

The Stanley Park families were not evicted because the Park Board wanted to create an uninhabited wilderness – several of its employees already lived there, including the superintendent, the operator of the waterworks house, and the Brockton Point lighthouse keeper. Although some newspaper editorials and board commissioners publicly bemoaned the presence of the families, their dwellings were not always considered incongruent with the landscape. In fact, some early tourist postcards featured images of the Brockton Point and Deadman's Island houses (Figure 2.8). The board evicted the residents because they challenged the integrity and definition of public space in Stanley Park. For decades, city council and

Figure 2.9 Settlement at Brockton Point. J. Wood Laing, "Old Squatters' Shacks, Stanley Park," 1910s[?]. Photograph Collection, 677-228, City of Vancouver Archives

the board had perceived the families as a serious threat to their authority. The construction of the park road in 1888 had forced the Aboriginal inhabitants of Whoi Whoi to move to the nearby Musqueam and Squamish reserves, except for a woman known as Aunt Sally, who remained at Lumbermen's Arch.[87] Three main clusters of settlers lived in the park – a Chinese community at Anderson Point, a boathouse community on Deadman's Island, and a mixed heritage Aboriginal-European community at Brockton Point (Figure 2.9).[88] The Park Board first attempted to evict these groups in October 1888 but found that the City lacked the legal authority to do so because it had no lease for the peninsula. City Clerk Thomas McGuigan's opinion was that "it will be difficult for this corporation to deal with persons trespassing on said reserve or to keep it in proper order until they can show their right to same, and I doubt if the Order in Council would suffice." Mayor James Garden made a second attempt in August 1898 but failed to garner the necessary legal authority to remove what he described as "a number of small dwellings of a very undesirable character existing on the foreshore and other parts of the said park harbouring squatters, undesirable characters, such being detrimental to the interests of the public."[89]

Nonetheless, by enlisting the aid of the City Health Department, the Park Board found a way to evict the Chinese settlement at Anderson Point. In May 1889, it requested that "the Council be asked to instruct the Health Inspector to take steps towards removing nuisances along the Park Road especially the Chinese."[90] The city health inspector gave Ranger Henry Avison the authority to eject the Chinese and burn their homes. According to Sarah Harris, Avison's daughter,

> the Park Board ordered the Chinamen to leave the park; they were trespassers; but the Chinamen would not go, so the Park Board told my father to set fire to the buildings. I saw them burn; there were five of us children, and you know what children are like when there is a fire. So father set fire to the shacks; what happened to the Chinese I do not know, but the pigs were set loose and the bull untied, and they got lost in the forest of Stanley Park, and they could not track them down until the snow fell. Then my Dad tracked them down, and they shot them in the bushes, and the bull's head was cut off, and my father had it stuffed and set up in our hallway in our house, the "Park Cottage."[91]

This callous and sudden eviction was representative of the racial antipathy directed at Asian people in Vancouver during this period.[92]

The boathouse community lived on Deadman's Island throughout the dispute between Theodore Ludgate and the City, which ran from the 1890s to the 1930s. At one of the Ludgate trials, William Hammersley testified that he had lived on Deadman's Island since January 1887 and was the first of the boathouse inhabitants. Ottawa evicted Hammersley and twenty or thirty other people from the island in 1924. Peter Marsulia, another island resident, contested his eviction, but the court ruled that he did not hold legal title to his land. Despite these evictions, working-class people continued to build houses along the shores of Deadman's Island into the 1930s.[93]

The families at Brockton Point had lived in the park for three generations or more, most of them dating back to the gold rush era of the late 1850s and early 1860s. Many had ties to the original Coast Salish inhabitants. Alfred Gonsalves, who lived on the south shore of the point, had inherited his property from his father, Joseph Gonsalves, who was said to have purchased it from a Portuguese sailor named Joe Silvey in 1875. Silvey himself had received it from Squamish chief Kiapilano after marrying his daughter, Khaltinaht. Agnes Cummings, Maggie West, and Tim Cummings, who lived on the point's north shore, had inherited their property from their father, James Cummings, a Scottish sailor who arrived in the province during the 1870s and settled on the peninsula with his wife, a Bella Coola woman named Lucy, or Spukh-pu-ka-num. The couple purchased their plot from a young Irish millworker named Joe Mannion, who had obtained it from an Aboriginal healer named Klah Chaw, also known as Doctor Johnson. Klah Chaw's claim to the site was said to have preceded any European settlement on the coast of what later became British Columbia.[94]

The Park Board allowed the Brockton Point residents, as well as Aunt Sally (said to be the only "full-blooded" Aboriginal person still living in the park), to remain undisturbed for thirty-five years because of their Aboriginal claims to the land. It had no wish to agitate the families for fear of triggering a legal conflict that would raise the "Indian Land Question" in the courts and possibly enable the families to establish private property claims in the park. Coast Salish people in the Lower Mainland were active in the movement to settle the unresolved question of Aboriginal land title in the early twentieth century.[95] Chief Joe Capilano from the Squamish reserve in North Vancouver was a principal leader in the Indian Rights Association and once led a delegation to London to petition Edward VII to have the issue of Aboriginal land rights brought before the Privy Council. The City, along with the provincial government, sought to avoid this at all costs.[96]

When the McKenna-McBride Royal Reserve Commission was established in 1913 to settle outstanding Aboriginal issues, the Park Board hoped that it would resolve the matter. To this end, the board secretary wrote to the commission on 29 May 1913, proposing "to bring before your Commission the question of Indian Squatters in Stanley Park," to which the commissioners replied that they "find that the subject therein referred to does not come within the scope of the Commission." Lacking the commission's support, the board decided to allow the inhabitants to live out the remainder of their lives in the park, but it never acknowledged their title to the land. This policy was tested in 1918, however, when Tim Cummings requested that water service be provided to his house at Brockton Point. The secretary of the water committee wrote to Superintendent W.S. Rawlings, notifying him that "the Council thought the best way of getting over the difficulty, without antagonizing the Indians, from whom we have very great concessions on the North Shore, would be to install this public service tap, without any reference to the Indian at all." City council and the Park Board deliberately avoided acknowledging

Cummings's title while not antagonizing the Squamish people of the North Shore reserve.[97]

In 1919, Chief Joe Mathias of the North Shore Squamish Indian reserve hired a solicitor to inquire into the legal status of the "groups of Indians and half-breeds" living in the park. In its response, the Department of Indian Affairs jettisoned its responsibility, denying Indian status for all but one of the families in Stanley Park. As Chief Inspector of Indian Agencies W.E. Ditchburn put it in his assessment of the question, "while there are at least eight families living on the park property, there is only one of pure Indian blood [Aunt Sally], the balance being either half-breeds or whites, therefore the Department has no particular interest in the other seven families." Once the department denied Indian status to the families at Brockton Point on the grounds that they were not "authentic Indians," Vancouver City Council was in a position to pursue legal action against them.[98]

The legal battle began in 1921 when a Brockton Point resident attempted to lease a portion of his land to an outside party. This action threatened the City's title to Stanley Park and its status as public space. Acting Superintendent of Parks Allen S. Wootton notified Corporation Counsel George McCrossan of the situation and requested an opinion on the legal position of the Park Board. City Solicitor E.F. Jones wrote back to Wootton stating that he

> would like to know the exact time this man has been squatting on the part of the park which he now occupies. Unless he has occupied these premises for sixty years, he cannot obtain a prescriptive title, as the park is the property of the Crown in the right of the Dominion of Canada, and it requires sixty years to obtain prescriptive title. If he has not occupied these premises for the time above mentioned, I would advise that the board take immediate steps to ensure a formal entry, so as to defeat adverse possession.[99]

Jones's letter outlined the legal concept that would play a central role in the subsequent eviction trials – that of adverse possession, or "squatters' rights," which could be claimed on any federal property if one could demonstrate sixty or more years of continued occupancy. George McCrossan made five recommendations to the City:

- The Park Board should avoid being put in the position of plaintiff, leaving the burden of proof of adverse possession with the families.
- Ottawa should be asked to lead the prosecution.

- The Health Department should condemn the homes as it did with the Chinese settlers.
- The board should restrict the families' access to the park road.
- If the residents managed to prove adverse possession, the City would have no choice but to pay them for their land in order to regain possession for the public.

With these points in mind, the Park Board went to court.[100]

All eight families were involved in the litigation, which proceeded through several stages of the criminal justice system before a final verdict was given on the question of adverse possession. Because the case had commenced on 23 April 1923, the defendants were required to prove that their homes had been established before that same day in 1863. After hearing evidence from the defendants' lawyers and Crown prosecutors, Justice Murphy of the BC Supreme Court determined that the families did not settle in the park before 23 April 1863, except for Aunt Sally (who had died just days before the trial began) and her daughter, Mariah Kulkalem, who had Aboriginal claims that pre-dated European settlement.[101] Most of the families appealed to the BC Court of Appeal, where Justices MacDonald, Martin, and McPhillips ruled in a two-to-one decision (Chief Justice MacDonald dissenting) that they had in fact demonstrated the minimum number of years to claim adverse possession. But this victory was fleeting, as the Crown made a final appeal to the Supreme Court of Canada, which overturned the appellate court's decision in 1925 and reinstated the lower court decision of Justice Murphy. The court declared that the Brockton Point residents were illegal squatters, a decision that enabled their removal in 1931 (though Agnes and Tim Cummings were allowed to stay until Agnes's death in 1956 and Tim's in 1958). Implicit in the Supreme Court decision was that no part of Stanley Park would become private property.[102]

As Jean Barman has shown, the decision to evict the Brockton Point inhabitants hinged on the documentary evidence produced by the Crown, which was based on George Turner's 1863 survey of Burrard Inlet and what was referred to as the Turner map. The map allegedly proved that the settler families had not lived on the peninsula in 1863 and thus could not qualify for adverse possession. According to the Crown, Colonel Moody had instructed Turner to include all dwellings and settlements in his survey of Burrard Inlet. Except for one marked house that was determined to belong to Aunt Sally, he had made no record of houses, fences, or any other indication of settlement on the Stanley Park peninsula.[103]

For their part, the defendants presented four witnesses; three were elderly Aboriginal men, and the fourth, Edward Trimble, was not Aboriginal. All four claimed to have seen the dwellings before 23 April 1863, and the three Aboriginal men testified that they had personally known the settlers at Brockton Point. However, Justice Murphy expressed doubts regarding their credibility:

> With regard to the Indian evidence, I must say it was unsatisfactory. I do not think the Indians intended at all to deceive the Court. Naturally they were very old people and could only fix dates by the Cariboo gold rush. They contradicted themselves – two of them at any rate, very materially, because they said those buildings were made of lumber and lumber from the mills here. They did not say they were from mills here, but it would be the only place where lumber could be obtained. It is possible that lumber might have been whipsawn, but I think no one would be justified in coming to the conclusion that one would whipsaw lumber to build houses in Stanley Park where cedar, which could be easily split, was available. As against that I have the map, and it seems to me that is evidence which, even if the onus were on the Crown, would conclude this case, on the point of 60 years' possession.[104]

In privileging the Turner map, Murphy discounted the testimony of the Aboriginal men, which was not uncommon in the early twentieth century. According to legal historian Constance Backhouse, because non-Christian Aboriginal people did not swear an oath on the Bible, many Euro-Canadians considered them less credible than white Christian witnesses. The elderly Aboriginal men might have given some contradictory evidence, but the Turner map was no less flawed.[105]

The defendants argued that the location of the marked dwelling on the map, which was said to belong to Aunt Sally, was nowhere near the actual location of her house. They also alleged that Turner had conducted his survey in February 1863, which meant that it did not disprove the existence of settlement two months later, on the critical date of 23 April 1863. Nonetheless, the Turner map prevailed until the BC Court of Appeal overturned Murphy's decision. According to Justice Martin, Murphy was too prejudiced against Aboriginal people, and he himself knew "of no good reason in general for placing the testimony of our native Indians at all on a lower plane than that of others."[106]

In exchange for a small annual rent, the City left the Brockton Point families undisturbed until 1931, when all but Agnes and Tim Cummings were evicted. Their claim pre-dated that of the other residents; their father was said to have purchased his Brockton Point plot from Joseph Mannion's wife, Takood, who was the daughter of Klah Chaw, the Aboriginal healer who first lived there. In reference to the claim, Justice Martin of the BC Court of Appeal said that "it is difficult to imagine a stronger position in law than that of the holder of a possessory title antedating the birth of the colony itself."[107] The claim verged very closely on the controversial matter of First Nations land rights. Justice McPhillips explicitly raised this issue by questioning the very validity of the Crown's ownership of the site:

> There being no express extinguishments of the Indian title in British Columbia the question whether there was earlier possession in the Crown than that of the defendant and those under whom he is entitled to claim possession, is brought up somewhat graphically and it might reasonably be said that there could be no prior possession in the Crown to the possession shewn by the defendant.[108]

Thus, it was in the interest of all three levels of government to avoid bringing this matter before the courts by permitting Agnes and her visually impaired brother, Tim, to remain in place for the next thirty-three years for a nominal rent.

Renisa Mawani argues that the creation of Stanley Park involved "a simultaneous evocation and erasure of Native peoples." After evicting the Brockton Point families, the board reduced the park's Aboriginal presence to a simulacra of "Indian-ness" through the erection of totem poles and the proposed construction of a model Indian village by the Art, Historical, and Scientific Association of Vancouver (see Chapter 1). In 1933, it rejected Joe Mathias's proposal to lead demonstrations of Squamish culture and material practices for tourists at the totem pole display, which reinforces Mawani's argument that only imaginary versions of Aboriginal people had a place in the park. Aboriginal people could exist there only as symbols of an imagined past, where they harmoniously co-existed with nature, not as actual human beings living in the park.[109]

Ultimately, the Park Board evicted the Brockton Point families to defend the definition and integrity of public park space in Vancouver's urban environment. When the federal government awarded Aunt Sally's daughter, Mariah Kulkalem, her property after failing to evict her, the board was anxious to see it returned to the public domain. Kulkalem agreed to sell it for $16,500, and the board assumed that Ottawa would purchase it, but the federal government refused to do so. In the end, board chairman

W.C. Shelly bought it himself for $15,500. The board lauded Shelly "for his public spirited and generous action in securing the 'Aunt Sally' property, Stanley Park, in order to prevent the exploitation of this property by private interests which threatened."[110]

Shelly's apprehension regarding the Brockton Point residents rested on his contention that the park should remain public space. In a letter to F.J. Burd of the *Vancouver Daily Province,* Shelly responded to an earlier editorial, which had suggested that the settlers should be allowed to remain in their homes. His letter revealed his principal reason for evicting them:

> If the present squatters were permitted to obtain title to the property by effluxion of time due to carelessness and passivity of the City or Crown, the large area in which several squatters are now in occupation would become private property for apartment house or hotel sites and even dock or wharves. It would be nothing short of desecration to permit Stanley Park to be invaded in that way because of a certainty the use of the Driveways for such commercial purposes would be claimed and could not be refused.[111]

He added that, in light of this threat, it was "essential to preserve the park as a public domain, that the actions in question be proceeded with, and that the title of the Crown and the City be protected." Shelly's argument succinctly defined the production of public space in Stanley Park: the board must maintain legal title over that space in order to define how it could be used. The eviction of the "squatters" was the final stage in the process of making the park public.

3

Improving Nature

On 27 September 1888, the opening of Vancouver's landmark urban park signalled great promise for the young Pacific metropolis. Under a cloudless sky, the waters of Burrard Inlet sparkled in the sunlight as spectators gathered at Prospect Point to mark the official opening of Stanley Park. Provincial and civic dignitaries marched in procession from Powell Street to the park and took their places on a platform before the crowd. Mayor David Oppenheimer gave a speech to formally open the park and to deliver authority for its management to the newly appointed park committee. This is one of the best-known moments in the history of Vancouver, famously chronicled by the city's first archivist, James Skitt Matthews. However, historians have failed to note the significance of Oppenheimer's remarks on that day. Vancouverites take for granted the natural beauty of Stanley Park, the so-called jewel of the city, but when Oppenheimer spoke of it in 1888, he saw *future* potential, not inherent beauty. He recognized its many "natural advantages" but considered them deficient without the aid of human intervention. He believed that, in a process of careful improvement, "art will unite with nature in making this the finest park on the continent." Only the union of human artifice and natural scenery would "ultimately realize our present hopes of being able in a short time to say we have the most beautiful park in the world." In short, Oppenheimer and other early park advocates saw a natural landscape in need of a helping hand.[1]

This perspective might seem extraordinary to the contemporary tourists and admirers who value Stanley Park as an untouched area, unaware of the enormous, but largely concealed, human effort that has gone into managing its production. As Richard Walker states in the case of Golden Gate Park, this kind of interventionism "runs counter to present-day environmental sentiment, which favors less human impact and more respect for native vegetation." The improvement of nature through human modification, however, was not inconsistent with its preservation or with North American understandings of the value of parks in the late nineteenth and early twentieth centuries. An examination of Stanley Park's early management shows that advocates and Park Board officials actively sought to "improve" nature by controlling non-human forces that threatened to alter the visual or aesthetic appearance of the "virgin" forest. Their primary concern was the construction and preservation of scenic beauty and the enhancement of wild, unrestrained nature. Those alterations in turn transformed both the landscape and the ecology of the peninsula.[2]

Environmental history enables us to better understand the shifting meanings of nature and wilderness, complicated terms that are as much a reflection of social and cultural constructs as they are material realities. The modern concept of wilderness in the United States, as Paul Sutter reveals, has its origins in interwar debates about the impact of highway construction on national parks. Sutter finds that wilderness "was a product of intellectual engagement with specific circumstances," which ultimately reinvented its meaning. The work of Sutter and other historians shows that wilderness, like parks, is an idea subject to change by historical circumstances. As William Cronon puts it, this is part of "the trouble with wilderness," for "wilderness hides its unnaturalness behind a mask that is all the more beguiling because it seems so natural," a mask that suggests an inextricable, yet somehow inscrutable, interconnection between humans, nature, and the idea of wilderness. Of course, humans are a part of the natural world; their actions shape, and are shaped by, complementary and sometimes countervailing non-human forces. "The idea that there is a continuous interaction between man and his environment – man changing it and being influenced by it – also has its mythological antecedents," according to Clarence Glacken, "but its full development belongs basically, I think, to rational thought, because such a conception requires a sense of history." Similarly, the meaning of wilderness is shaped by the interaction between people and the environment. The people who created Stanley Park shared the common modernist belief that engineering and scientific intervention could produce an aesthetically satisfactory landscape, one that was grounded in a romantic and static vision of nature.[3]

Humans played a greater role in shaping the landscape and ecology of the Stanley Park peninsula after its 1887 designation as a park than at any other time. After 1887, human relations with nature changed on the peninsula, though they continued to shape what can be characterized as a hybrid environment, one in which the relationships between species are influenced as much by human actions as by those of non-human actors.

In the early decades of the twentieth century, Park Board improvements were consistent with a broader North American trend in landscape design known as naturalistic constructivism, which sought to disguise anthropogenic interventions to make park spaces appear more natural. Anne Whiston Spirn identifies the origins of naturalistic constructivism in the work of Frederick Law Olmsted, whom she claims "was so skilful at concealing the artifice that both the projects he had so brilliantly constructed and the profession he had worked so hard to establish became largely invisible." Richard West Sellars describes a comparable approach taken by the US National Park Service, which modified parks to promote favoured plant and animal species in order to produce pleasing scenes and a verdant landscape for tourists. He contends that "maintaining such a setting amounted to facade management – preserving the scenic facade of nature, the principal basis for public enjoyment." Similarly, Linda Flint McClelland finds that traditions of landscape architecture, dating as far back as the work of pioneering designer Andrew Jackson Downing, influenced the design of American national parks into the 1930s. A principal concept was that landscape design should *appear* natural or naturalistic. Landscape architects used trees and other plants to disguise evidence of human intrusion.[4]

Although the Vancouver Park Board adopted the basic tenets of naturalistic constructivism, or facade management, they were modified by the ecological characteristics of a Northwest Coast coniferous forest. Unlike other North American urban parks, such as Central Park, Druid Hill, Golden Gate Park, and Mount Royal Park, Stanley Park was not designed by a single landscape architect. From its inception, it was valued for its dense forest, the centrepiece of its landscape, and thus was never subject to much rapid, wholesale reconstruction, as was the case, for instance, with the western sand dunes of Golden Gate Park. Instead, the board sought to improve its appearance through long-term alterations that gradually transformed the landscape, particularly via its forestry policies. Rather than relying on the advice of landscape architects, the board employed engineers and forestry scientists to enhance nature in the park. Although they were not trained in the techniques of naturalistic constructivism, these experts changed the landscape and ecology while simultaneously concealing their efforts, producing the illusion that the park was untouched.[5]

Nevertheless, the park's design was not solely the product of human actions; other forces played a central role in shaping it. Erosion, fire, insects, animals, drainage, and other natural features impeded improvement projects such as road construction and forest preservation. Indeed, the projects were often a struggle *against* the autonomy of nature.[6]

Access

Once Stanley Park was created, city council's first challenge was to provide access to it. Ocean tides often rendered it inaccessible by foot, and the few people who were brave enough to make the journey did so by boat. In fact, since the 1860s, very few non-Aboriginal people had been to the peninsula, except for its residents and the crews who had cut timber there. Though it was praised for its splendour – the lofty cedars, hemlocks, and firs amidst a tangle of underbrush – its natural conditions needed alteration if better access were to be provided.

In October 1887, Vancouver ratepayers approved a by-law that enabled city council to raise $20,000 through debentures to build a public road around the peninsula. The by-law stated that it was in the "interest and welfare of the City of Vancouver that improvements should be made and a public road or drive should be constructed" in order "to give the citizens access to the Park."[7]

The Board of Works, the first public body responsible for the park, managed the construction of the road. Engineers divided the project into six sections, built from November 1887 until September 1888, just before the opening of the park. The road's serpentine route roughly followed the first path surveyed around the edges of the peninsula by CPR land commissioner Lauchlan Hamilton in 1885. Contractors erected a bridge across Coal Harbour to link city streets with the new road. Once complete, the project, which required the labour of more than fifty men and numerous animals, had laid roughly thirty-seven thousand feet of road at a cost of $19,982.84. The reconfiguration of the peninsula's perimeter, the removal of thousands of cubic feet of earth, and the destruction of hundreds of trees constituted a major transformation of the landscape and ecology. Crews covered the road with a light gravel made of crushed shells, which according to an engineer's report, "present[ed] a remarkably white appearance, [and] added greatly to the attractiveness of the park." Workers procured the covering from nearby middens composed mainly of clam and mussel shells, and human remains, which they uncovered during construction (described in Chapter 1). Anthropologist Charles Hill-Tout recounted the disturbance of these middens in a letter to Vancouver's city archivist in 1932 and confirmed that the material "was used largely for priming the roadbed around the park."[8]

The curvilinear route of the road was inspired by the Greensward Plan, which was created by Calvert Vaux and Frederick Law Olmsted for the design of Central Park. Influenced in its turn by the early British landscape tradition, the Greensward Plan established many North American standards for park design in the late nineteenth and early twentieth centuries. Drawing on his experience as an apprentice to Andrew Jackson Downing, Vaux intended the circuitous roads of Central Park to contrast with the rigid grid design of New York City's streets. If Central Park were to be a rural retreat for city-dwellers, as Vaux and Olmsted envisioned, its roads should break from the pattern of the city to provide pleasant country drives. Vaux and Olmsted tried to follow the natural contours of the park's topography to incorporate a naturalistic feel into the roads. They also constructed buildings, bridges, and furniture in a "rustic" style, using stripped-bark logs and rough stonework of simple design. As landscape architects disseminated these ideas, they applied them to national parks where roads revealed scenic vistas of sublime landscapes, particularly in Yosemite and Yellowstone.[9]

Vancouver's first park committee aspired to create a network of roads, paths, and bridges that mimicked this form of landscape design.[10] In 1888, however, the final report on the park road pointed out that "much requires to be done in making drives and serpentine walks, underbrushing in close proximity to the road, planting evergreens, grass-seed, and making rustic arbors and seats." Dissatisfied with this state of affairs, the park commissioners noted that "a large amount of debris [was] left along the sides of the road injuring to a great extent the beauty of the drive and which should certainly be removed." Their principal concern was that the debris should be burned so that the edges of the road would display no signs of the improvement project. Underbrushing (clearing undergrowth) and replanting would give the road the appearance of blending into nature as though it had always existed. With careful use of these techniques, the human impact on the landscape could go virtually undetected (Figure 3.1).[11]

In spite of these efforts at naturalism, nature itself impeded the completion of the road. Contractors faced potential cost overruns due to poor weather, as winter rains delayed the project and frosts washed out newly built sections as crews worked their way around the park. The uncooperative weather postponed construction of the final section for several months. Finally, in May 1888, city council sought a further $5,600 to complete the

Figure 3.1 Stanley Park's first road curved around trees and followed topographical contours to provide a naturalistic appearance. Charles S. Bailey, "Rustic Bridge on Stanley Park Road, Vancouver, B.C.," 1889[?]. Major Matthews Photograph Collection, St Pk P24.1 N241, City of Vancouver Archives

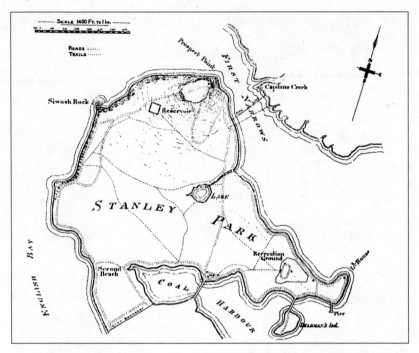

Map 6 Stanley Park's road network in 1898. Just south of Siwash Rock, the Park Board was forced to re-route the road away from the cliffs, parts of which were unstable. Tourist Guide Map of Vancouver City and Park, 1898, Maps Collection, Map 35, City of Vancouver Archives

work, with the result that, by June, W.D. Creighton and William Downie boasted the honour of being the first to travel around the entire park in a wheeled vehicle.[12]

Early observers noticed several structural weaknesses in the road. Mrs. P.S. Saville, an early Vancouver pioneer, recalled her first visit to the park on Dominion Day 1888, when the road was still incomplete. She "walked along the park road, or driveway," noting that "it was all mud." Saville's recollection was an early indication that the heavy rains so common in Vancouver would be a problem for City engineers. One of the first park commissioners, A.G. Ferguson, not only donated personal funds for road improvements but also lent some of his expertise as a civil engineer to help grade the road in an effort to improve drainage. Although mud and frost made the road largely unusable during the winter, it suited the needs of visitors, most of whom walked along its winding course during the summer (Map 6).[13]

In a 1901 article on Stanley Park, the *Vancouver Province* proclaimed that its road was "known all over America as an ideal cycling and driving course, not entirely on account of the beautiful and ever-changing vistas of forest, mountain and sea, but also owing to the excellent surface dressing of the roadway which, after being carefully graded and drained, is covered several inches deep with a top dressing of ground clamshells." Although the clamshell gravel provided a pleasant and natural-looking appearance, the soft surfacing was unsuited to the local hydrology (Figure 3.2). The *Province*'s enthusiastic booster article failed to note the gradual degradation of the road as both human and non-human forces wore down its surface.[14]

The road required constant attention. In 1889, the Park Board was forced to adjust its route near Prospect Point, where the cliffs were too steep and unstable, building 1,700 yards of new road to avoid the cliffs and provide better grade and drainage. Engineers adjusted the grade throughout 1889 and resurfaced parts of the road with rock instead of the famous, but inadequate, clamshells. Conditions were so poor in the autumns of 1890 and 1891 that the board was forced to close all roads.[15] Although the road had been resurfaced with a composite of wood, rock, and crushed clamshells by 1893, it remained a persistent problem for park officials as hydrology and afternoon picnickers conspired to erode it. Its purpose was to bring people closer to nature but not the forces of climate and erosion that so plagued park officials. As Mike Davis argues, nature in the city is "constantly straining against its chains: probing for weak points, cracks, faults, even a speck of rust." Overhanging branches, cliffs, frost, floods, and mud created a series of obstacles for engineers, who struggled to keep the roads and trails open. But their troubles were only compounded by the increasing human use of the park.[16]

In 1905, as visitors multiplied and the automobile became increasingly common, the road had come under greater pressure. As David Louter finds in the national parks of Washington, road design and the use of the car became defining features for park visits during the early twentieth century. He contends that the integration of automobiles into parks was a process that "required thinking of roads not as the antithesis of primeval nature but as constructions that enabled people to know primeval nature better." But Louter's analysis of experiencing nature through a "windshield wilderness" overlooks the extent to which road construction was mediated by the natural environment itself. As in Canadian and American national parks, automobile use in Stanley Park increased during the early twentieth century, and motorists demanded more open access to its roadways.

Figure 3.2 This 1895 photo shows the gleaming white surface of Stanley Park's shell-gravelled road, hailed by boosters for its aesthetic qualities and decried by engineers for its poor drainage and weakness. Walter Edwin Frost, "Compliments of the Season," 1895. Photograph Collection, 447-1, City of Vancouver Archives

Organizations such as the Vancouver Automobile Club pressured the Park Board to lift restrictions on automobile use and even launched a test case to challenge the park by-laws in 1905. The board wished to limit the use of cars because tires damaged the road, whose soft and loose surface was extremely vulnerable to the weight and speed of motor vehicles. Census records not only showed that automobile use was on the rise but that the park's popularity was growing as well. Between 26 July and 1 August 1905, 14,664 people visited the park, a figure that had increased to 32,840 by 1909.[17]

These trends, combined with the forces of erosion, compelled the board to rebuild the road. In 1906, after settling the legal challenge from the Vancouver Automobile Club, it launched a widening and resurfacing program. Chairman Charles Tisdall announced that the road would be broadened to accommodate two-way traffic and to provide more space for pedestrians and cyclists. The board hoped that this project would prevent traffic accidents, but its high cost delayed completion for years, with the result that the narrow width of the road and the annual winter rains and frost continued to create hazardous driving conditions. In February 1907, Tisdall banned all traffic in the park because a recent thaw had so saturated the soil with moisture that it could not sustain the weight of an automobile. The problem recurred during the following year, with one report stating, "the reason for this is that park roads are very soft, and between frost and rain have become cut up." The Park Board admitted that the road surface was no longer equal to motorist demands and required complete reconstruction.[18]

In 1910, the Park Board first used macadam surfacing – a technically superior form of gravelling developed by Scottish engineer John Loudon McAdam in the early nineteenth century – to improve the road. The process involved using heavy rollers to compress three layers of variously sized rock into an interlocked, stable, waterproof surface. Macadamizing also laid the rock on a convex slope to provide better drainage and raised the roadbed high enough that culverts could be placed under it to carry the water away. To save on the cost of materials, the board hired its own rock crusher to process rock from the shores of Second and Third Beaches.[19]

Disappointingly, however, the macadam road could not withstand the pressures of intense traffic and quickly proved inadequate. The tires of speeding automobiles tore up the roads, sending rock and dust into the air. In the summer of 1911, the Park Board considered oiling the road to reduce the dust and later turned to the City of Burnaby for advice on oiling methods used in the neighbouring suburban municipality. In 1913, the board contracted the Cotton Company to experiment with spraying oil on the road to keep down dust and hold the surface together. Park engineer Allen S. Wootton recommended "at once getting a considerable quantity of asphalt mixed, ready for repairing such places as may be necessary, as it is almost impossible to keep down newly laid water bound McAdam [sic] when subject to heavy auto traffic." Eventually, the annual oiling of the macadamized road proved too costly, and the board was forced to resurface it with asphalt.[20]

Why did the Park Board select such an inferior road-surfacing technology? Although macadam had increasingly proven unsuitable for automobile traffic in American cities, Vancouver had only just started to experiment with bituminous hard surface roads in the 1910s. Macadam was cheap, and it was commonly used in North American parks because it provided a more rustic look than asphalt. In addition, there was some concern that asphalt and other bituminous surfaces would adversely affect roadside vegetation. Macadamization seemed to improve drainage and erosion problems, but the roads in Stanley Park demanded sturdier pavements.

Not everyone in Vancouver saw the various road construction projects as an improvement on nature, however. Most could agree that some form of transportation system was necessary if access were to be provided to Stanley Park, but expansion of the original road system met resistance in certain quarters. Some Vancouverites opposed it because it was expensive, often consuming a large portion of the Park Board's annual budget. For instance, the 1909 construction cost for the road was the most expensive item in the annual estimate. In 1912, grading, widening, and macadamizing the road from Prospect Point to Beach Avenue was estimated to cost $30,000, over half the total cost of capital expenditures for park improvements.[21]

Another group became concerned that widening and improving the road threatened the forest. In 1910, a small group of enthusiasts, consisting mainly of the West End residents who opposed the Deadman's Island lease, met to protest the cutting of trees in the park. Once again, they held their meetings in the offices of the Board of Trade. F.C. Wade, an educated middle-class lawyer who held strong romantic sentiments regarding nature in the park, led the meeting and organized a society for the protection of what he, and others, called "Stanley Forest." Criticizing the Park Board's removal of sixty-eight trees during the road-widening project, the group passed a resolution recommending that the board should "appoint an expert forester to prepare a plan for the guidance of the present and future unskilled and untrained park commissioners." Perceiving the roadwork as the destruction of nature rather than an improvement, Wade's group sought to "preserve the forest solitudes and silences and other beauty spots in Vancouver from further present and future desecration."[22]

This protest group also resisted proposals to improve access to the park, which called for the construction of an electric streetcar line through the forest. Like the present-day Stanley Park causeway connector, its two proposed routes bisected the peninsula (Map 7). Citizen groups in several North American cities resisted the efforts of private corporations to expand streetcar service into major urban parks. In San Francisco, advocates

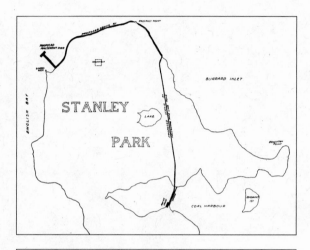

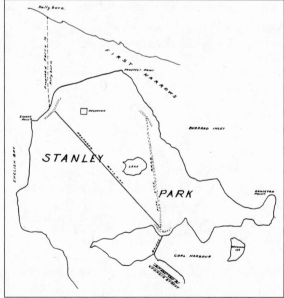

Map 7 Two proposed routes for electric streetcar service in Stanley Park (1906).
Stanley Park proposed railway, December 1906–June 1913, Board of Parks and Recreation fonds, Correspondence, 48-C-5, file 1, City of Vancouver Archives

Figure 3.3 During the early years of Stanley Park, thousands of people crossed this bridge to spend their weekends at the Coal Harbour entrance to the park, putting increased pressure on the bridge and the surrounding area. C. Bradbury, "Crowds Leaving Stanley Park over Coal Harbour Bridge," 1905[?]. Major Matthews Photograph Collection, St Pk P157 N217, City of Vancouver Archives

avoided a similar controversy by running the streetcar line outside park boundaries on an adjacent street. Conversely, in St. Paul, Minnesota, Superintendent Frederick Nussbaumer believed that parks should be accessible via cheap public transportation, and he supported the streetcar service in Como Park. In 1906 and 1910, Wade and his companions fought two separate plebiscites on the question of streetcar service in Stanley Park, defeating both proposals.[23] Wade abhorred what he saw as the encroachment of human artificiality in the park and believed that "we owe it as a duty and a trust to those who will come after us to keep this magnificent stretch of coast and forest in its pristine condition and sylvan beauty, rather than destroy its solitudes and beautiful shoreline and prospects by the intrusion of the tram with its noise, artificiality and disconcerting din."[24] In the debates over road construction and streetcar service, Wade's class-based

bias against affordable mass transportation was accompanied by a change
in thinking about the role that humans played in the park. Elite Vancouverites had become increasingly uncomfortable with obvious evidence
of artifice. If art and nature were to unite in Stanley Park, it would have
to appear more natural than artificial.

Losing Lost Lagoon

Because access to the interior of Stanley Park was limited to a few rough
trails, the entrance at Coal Harbour was the most popular area for visitors.
Park Board census information from 1900 to 1920 reveals that most visitors
crowded the shores of the park near the bridge that crossed the harbour.
On weekends, thousands of people streamed across the bridge to enjoy
the benefits of nature that were said to exist in the park (Figure 3.3). As
the public face of the park visible from the city, Coal Harbour was a prime
candidate for beautification and improvement.

   Coal Harbour challenged public expectations of the ideal landscape. Its
tidal range was wide, which meant that low tides drained most of its western
basin (Lost Lagoon), and high tides pushed seawater as far as Second
Beach, salinating the soils and creating marshy conditions (Map 8). The

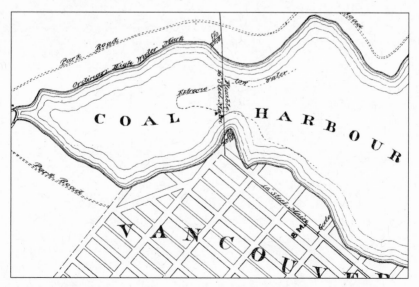

Map 8 This engineer's drawing, of the extreme low water mark in Coal Harbour
during the 1890s, shows that most of the western basin was empty at low tide.
Vancouver Waterworks Company fonds, 509-B-6 file 1, City of Vancouver Archives

Figure 3.4 Second Beach in 1896, prior to improvements. Major Matthews
Photograph Collection, St Pk P296 N182, City of Vancouver Archives

result – an enormous muddy basin and a low-lying, mostly treeless marsh
– was decidedly unappealing. Pauline Johnson immortalized the tidal
phenomenon in her 1911 book *Legends of Vancouver*, describing how she
chose the name of Lost Lagoon: "This was just to please my own fancy,
for, as that perfect summer month drifted on, the ever-restless tides left
the harbour devoid of water at my favourite canoeing hour, and my pet
idling place was lost for many days – hence my fancy to call it the Lost
Lagoon."[25]

The saline soils of the marsh left the vegetation patchy and vulnerable
to high winds; its few trees were often ravaged by winter storms (Figure
3.4). Initially, the Park Board sought to improve the site by draining the

marshlands near Second Beach and raising the topographical grade of the isthmus in order to construct picnic grounds. It intended to establish a bathing area at Second Beach to complement the popular beach at English Bay. In 1900, the plan called for the removal of driftwood and boulders, the construction of bathhouses, and the creation of a picnic area. As the superintendent reported in 1914, "The lower section of the Picnic ground here [Second Beach] has been swampy and practically useless for public use in the past, and it was decided to fill this in with sand, the total quantity required being some 17,000 cubic yards." The board hired the Pacific Dredge Company to pump sand onto the low-lying area near Second Beach in 1914, a measure that dumped fill on the picnic grounds and the beach, raising the isthmus that joined the park to downtown Vancouver.[26]

These improvements were only one component of a larger scheme to manage the "ever-restless" tides of Coal Harbour. In 1909, the Park Board and city council launched a project to improve the park entrance after the wooden pilings of the Coal Harbour bridge started to decay. The board closed the bridge to vehicle traffic during repairs and appointed a bridge committee to develop alternative solutions to crossing the muddy flats of the harbour. Accordingly, park commissioner W.R. Owen suggested that Lost Lagoon be filled in and converted into athletic grounds. Owen may have derived this idea from a 1902 proposal to fill in the basin for an exhibition ground. Like the Second Beach project, which converted marshlands into a picnic and bathing area, Owen's plan sought to reclaim Lost Lagoon for active recreational purposes. Most board members rejected his proposal, opting instead to keep the water in the basin by constructing an artificial land-bridge, or causeway, across the harbour. The bridge committee also suggested the construction of a causeway, so that Lost Lagoon "could be always kept flooded and the mud flats done away with" (Figure 3.5).[27]

In November 1910, the board invited aspiring landscape architects to design the causeway and the improvements to the park entrance. Elliott Rowe, manager of the Vancouver Tourist Association, recommended G.K. MacLean, the landscape architect who designed the grounds for the provincial asylum in Coquitlam. Civil and hydraulic engineer Arthur Monteith and architect J.J. Blackmore also applied for the competition, but all were rejected.[28]

After hearing from six more architects, the Park Board decided to defer its decision until late in 1911. But when it learned that famed British landscape architect Thomas H. Mawson was touring Canada and giving lectures on town planning at the behest of Governor General Earl Grey, it sent a

Figure 3.5 Prior to the 1915 construction of the causeway, a chief complaint about Coal Harbour was that low tide exposed its unattractive mudflats for extended periods of time. These two photographs, taken in 1914, show the shifting tides of Lost Lagoon. Photograph Collection, 789-123 and 789-130, City of Vancouver Archives

telegram to Mawson, requesting his services for the Coal Harbour project. Mawson visited Vancouver in March 1912 to consult with the board.[29]

Due to public controversy over the project, the board asked Mawson to prepare three possible plans for Coal Harbour. As Robert A.J. McDonald argues, debate regarding the enterprise tended to follow class lines, with three competing groups: "a middle-class Park Board, anti-development elite, and labour." Each of the three improvement schemes reflected the class perceptions of one particular group. Elite and labour representatives advised the Park Board in connection with two of them. As Mawson recounted, "the alternative schemes were a concession to two opposing ideas, both vigorously promoted." The third proposal was Mawson's own design and clearly his favourite.[30]

The first scheme, known as the "landscape plan" and favoured by the city's elite class, was to develop the entrance along naturalistic principles by retaining the tree-fringed outline of Coal Harbour and constructing a causeway in roughly the same place as the old bridge. The second proposal "seeks to fill up and convert the entire area of Coal Harbour into a series of playing fields, with intersecting boulevards and driveways." Labour organizations favoured this version because the city lacked adequate active recreational space. Although Mawson approved of expanding the recreational facilities, he believed that "the sacrifice of the water area seems too big a price to pay for it." The third proposal featured a grand architectural composition. The causeway would form the eastern curve of a wide boulevard that would circle a large round ornamental pool. At the centre of the pool, an eighty-foot stone column would be topped with a bronze statue of either James Cook or George Vancouver. The boulevard would be adorned with three massive civic buildings housing a stadium, a natural history museum, and a restaurant (Figure 3.6).[31]

Despite the vigorous opposition of elite critics such as F.C. Wade, the Park Board unanimously selected Mawson's third design. According to McDonald, most board members were middle-class reformers who were drawn to its grandiose promises, which had the potential to spectacularly alter the landscape. However, Mawson's vision was never fully realized, and the construction of the causeway, just a few years later, appeared to follow the principles of the "landscape plan" instead. McDonald attributes this largely to the economic depression that struck Vancouver in 1913 and the outbreak of the First World War in 1914, but he overlooks significant ideological and architectural factors that contributed to the demise of Mawson's favoured proposal.

The third design reflected Mawson's own architectural and intellectual influences as a leading advocate for town planning and the City Beautiful movement. The movement focused on beautifying urban environments as well as providing comprehensive town planning to enhance city life and is generally associated with neoclassical formalist architecture, with grand monumental buildings and civic centres. Thomas Mawson's commitment to the ideological and architectural foundations of the City Beautiful movement conflicted with elite cultural sensibilities and perceptions of nature in Stanley Park. He envisioned the relationship between park and city in terms that differed entirely from those of his opponents, who held romantic sentiments regarding nature (as expressed during the road construction and streetcar controversies). Breaking from the traditions of Downing, Vaux, and Olmsted, Mawson rejected the idea that the urban park should be treated as a rural retreat, separate from the rest of the city. He saw parks as a component of beautifying urban landscapes, and therefore they needed

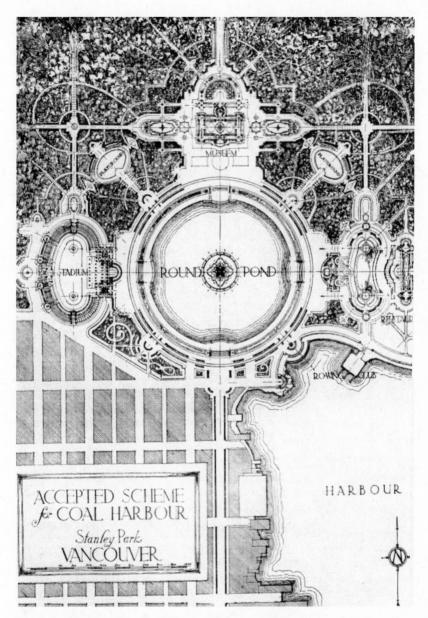

Figure 3.6 The accepted scheme for Coal Harbour promised to transform the entrance to Stanley Park into a grand civic centre resembling those of European capitals. Maps Collection, Map 728, City of Vancouver Archives

to be integrated into the built environment. One of his main criticisms of Vancouver in 1912 was that "at present Stanley Park may be said to be 'apart from' rather than 'a part of' Vancouver City." In his 1911 book on civic art, he was equally critical of English parks, noting that "we fail to plan our parks and gardens in relation to their surroundings. A tract of land is secured and enclosed by a tortuous boundary line, the land perhaps occupying the position through which a main artery should have been driven." Here was the root of Mawson's third proposal, which would place a civic centre – the cultural heart of the city – on the doorstep of the wilderness.[32]

Mawson's architectural style was based on the idea that the natural and the cultural should be dramatically merged. He was entirely opposed to the naturalistic style of landscape design common in North American parks, which sought to conceal the art of the landscape architect. When it came to urban parks, Mawson believed that "we can rely less and less upon nature as we approach densely-populated areas with their smoke or chemical-laden atmosphere, and, in proportion as we lose the help of nature, so must we seek the aid of art and invention." He placed particular emphasis on bold architecture but recognized the importance of natural features in large urban parks like Stanley Park, where "we would naturally endeavour to keep the place as rustic and simple as possible; but this cannot be done by trying to make details which are palpably artificial look as though they had grown, when they ought to look as though they had been well and lastingly done by the village craftsman." Park design, according to Mawson, was the product of art, and therefore the human role in nature should be evident. Mawson had met with Pauline Johnson shortly before her death. Although he was enthralled with her poetic ability, he was largely unaware that his plans for Coal Harbour would forever destroy the tidal phenomenon that created Johnson's legendary lagoon.[33]

F.C. Wade's opposition to Mawson's third plan was emblematic of a North American view of parks, rooted as it was in romantic landscape design where human modifications were masked with naturalistic building materials and techniques. Mawson's proposal made the human impact on nature more apparent than Wade and others could tolerate. Mawson's preference for neoclassical architecture and formal design, European styles that were largely alien to North American parks, was also significant.[34] Mawson urged the Park Board to consider his plan "along the lines of the Paris model, not in detail but in the broader application of principles, regarding your Civic Centre as the Arc de Triomphe, Georgia Street as the Champs-Élysées, the Coal Harbour as the Place de la Concorde and

Figure 3.7 F. Fellowes's plan for the Coal Harbour causeway demonstrated a consensus on the tidal flats of Lost Lagoon. Abandoning Mawson's grand scheme, Fellowes prepared a simple causeway to separate the lagoon from the rest of the harbour. "City Engineer's Plan for Coal Harbor Causeway," *Vancouver Sun,* 14 July 1914, 1

Tuileries Gardens, and the Museum of the Natural History of British Columbia as the Louvre."[35] This European analogy was never achieved in Vancouver, and Thomas Mawson's plan for Coal Harbour, like most of his designs for urban landscapes in Canada, remains a brilliant, if idealistic, architectural fantasy.

For a time, the federal government became involved in the issue. Some alleged that the elite opponents of the Mawson plan asked Minister of Militia and Defence Sam Hughes to prohibit the clearing of any trees in Stanley Park around Coal Harbour, knowing that this would render the plan unworkable. According to the lease signed in 1908, tree removal had to be approved by the minister. In defence of the Mawson plan, the Park Board submitted a list of improvements made from 1887 to 1912, showing how few trees had been cut. The board was adamant that it was acting in the best interest of preserving the park by executing Mawson's scheme. Not until Mawson personally met with Hughes to discuss the matter did the minister drop his objections.[36]

By the time the Department of Militia and Defence consented to the Mawson plan, the 1913 economic depression had reduced it to an impossible dream. Thus, the City gave the project to its chief engineer, Frederick L. Fellowes, who ultimately designed the Coal Harbour improvements and the causeway (Figure 3.7). Despite the controversy over the issue, the various competing interests did achieve a broad consensus – everyone agreed that the muddy tidal flats were a problem and that the shoreline needed renovation. So, between 1915 and 1917, a causeway was constructed to close off Lost Lagoon from the ocean waters of Burrard Inlet. A disappointed Mawson bemoaned the selection of Fellowes: "Unfortunately, the City Council instructed their engineer to carry out the scheme, and as this gentleman was unsympathetic towards our proposals, and at the same time trained to a different conception of construction, the result, so far as realized, does not come up to our expectations or attain the high level aimed at in our designs."[37]

The consensus on the causeway demonstrated that the elite perception of nature, held by Wade and others, did not preclude the idea that it could be improved. When Wade pleaded, "For God's sake hands off Stanley Park," he did not necessarily mean all hands. Humans could play a part in the construction of nature; as he put it, the tidal waters could be "cleansed" through the addition of a causeway. To explain it another way, Wade was perfectly comfortable with improvements to rationalize the aquatic and terrestrial environments of the park. His emotions were stirred only when improvements, such as paved roads, streetcar lines, athletic fields, and monumental buildings, made the human impact obvious and potentially opened the park to greater use by working-class Vancouverites. Wade also saw an important role for humans in the enhancement of the park's forests.[38]

Keeping the Virgin Forest Chaste

During the debate over widening the park road in 1910, F.C. Wade and the self-proclaimed "Lovers of Stanley Forest" sought to improve nature in the park through the use of expert knowledge. Wade chastised the Park Board for mismanaging the forest and accused it of lacking sufficient expertise in forest management. He asserted that "as Stanley Forest is the city's most valuable asset we are of opinion that the park commissioners should in future act on the advice of expert foresters of the greatest eminence." Like other conservationists of his day, Wade placed tremendous value in the power of scientific forestry, and he and his supporters *endorsed* the expansion of human intervention in the park through the application of modern forest management strategies.[39]

The Park Board first sought to improve the forest by eliminating disturbance brought by fire. In the summer of 1888, just before its official opening, Stanley Park burned. Dry weather conditions combined with careless roadwork and the accumulation of debris from road construction spread several small fires until dozens of blazes lit up the forest and filled the air with smoke. The pall of smoke worried anxious observers, who were concerned that "the fire has been burning ... for several days, and in the present state of things there is no one whose duty it is specially to see to the protection of this portion of the city's domain." They feared that, without active intervention, the fires would irreparably destroy the beauty of the park. The fires worsened during late summer, prompting pessimism among critics who felt that "probably by the time steps are taken to protect this magnificent heritage of the city there will be nothing left but a lot of blackened stumps." This kind of public commentary portrayed the park as a valued municipal landmark that required special intervention against fire in order to avoid the production of an unsightly scorched landscape. Park authorities proved incapable of stopping the flames. Serendipitously, a spell of late summer rain extinguished both the fires and the public angst. As a result of the fires and public pressure, city council temporarily hired a caretaker to patrol the road to guard against future blazes.[40]

Little is known about the role of fire in Northwest Coast forests. In this region of primarily coniferous trees, some ecologists believe that "large wildfires typically correspond to episodes of drought rather than simple patterns of fuel history." That is, climatic conditions spark fires rather than more predictable patterns associated with the buildup of debris on the forest floor. Studies reveal that southwestern British Columbia's great variability in fire frequency during the Holocene can be linked to climate through large-scale atmospheric circulation patterns. During the contemporary phase, known as the Fraser Valley Fire Period, Aboriginal people used fire prior to colonization to alter the ecology of local environments and to encourage the growth of target succession plant species. Vancouver's Camosun Bog, examined by Sally Hermansen and Graeme Wynn, is one example of a site that Aboriginal people burned to encourage the growth of food plants such as blueberries. Robert Boyd finds that, for Aboriginal people, fire was "by far the most important tool of environmental manipulation throughout the Native Pacific Northwest." Nancy J. Turner contends that BC First Nations used landscape firing neither casually nor sporadically but deliberately and for a variety of purposes. Thus, for centuries before Stanley Park was created, natural and human-induced fire played a role in fashioning the landscape.[41]

The nineteenth-century Coast Salish, European, and Asian inhabitants of the park peninsula probably changed its fire regime by introducing a greater likelihood of anthropogenic fire. The construction of housing, small-scale agriculture, and the need for home heating all created new sources of ignition. Furthermore, industrial logging may also have increased debris and slash, producing new anthropogenic fuel for forest fires.

Similarly, the creation of the park further altered its fire regime. Infrastructure construction increased the risk and incidence of fire, and fed a preservationist impulse to protect the trees by implementing fire control.[42] Stephen Pyne describes fire control as a threefold strategy: prevention of ignition, modification of the environment, and suppression of small blazes. The Park Board followed all three.[43] Its regulations sought to prevent ignition by outlawing the use of fire: "No person shall light any fire in any public park or place in the custody, care and management of the Park Board, except in such portions thereof and at such times as may be authorized."[44]

To diminish the impact of accidental fire, the board modified the environment by removing debris and slash to reduce the stockpile of fuel. The third and most complicated strategy, the suppression of small fires, was the responsibility of the caretaker, whose job was to patrol the park and alert the fire services of any small blazes before they became unmanageable. The board later tasked the park superintendent with this chore; about twice a week, he checked for fires and for fallen timber or branches on the road. Firefighters had a limited ability to cope with conflagrations deep in the forest, far from the roadways and a convenient water supply. Richard Rajala notes that federal forestry officials who sought to suppress fires on forest reserves consisting of thousands of acres had a similar problem. Axes, hoes, and shovels were the main tools for manual fire suppression until the 1920s, when technological developments in portable pumps and chemical extinguishers improved fire control in Stanley Park.[45]

Eventually, expansion of the water supply solved the problem of fighting flames deep within the forest. In 1910, the Park Board commenced the construction of a system of watermains and fire hydrants to distribute water from the city reservoir at Prospect Point to various locations throughout the park. From 1910 to 1914, in consultation with the city waterworks superintendent, the board extended the hydrant system to Second Beach, Ferguson Point, Brockton Point, and Prospect Point. Although the hydrants improved firefighters' access to a water supply, the system proved inadequate during the particularly dry summer of 1920. Superintendent W.S. Rawlings reported dozens of large fires that could not be put out, because they were too far from the hydrant system, which was unable to supply sufficient water or pressure over such a distance. He pleaded for an expansion of the hydrant system and insisted that "every precaution has been taken by day and night patrols to keep guard, but this is only a small measure. The danger of fire increases every year as the park becomes more developed and with it is the corresponding anxiety. We have been extremely fortunate in the past, but this good fortune may not always follow us."[46] The board did not expand the system until 1924, when ratepayers approved a plebiscite for a $65,000 scheme to install fifty-six new hydrants. The board adopted an increasingly elaborate system of fire control to preserve what it saw as a valued natural landscape. When it came to fire, board members pursued a highly interventionist forest policy.[47]

By controlling fire, the board hoped to maintain the image of an undisturbed natural forest. Ironically, clearing paths and roads to make the forest more accessible to firefighters and cutting through the woods to lay and bury pipes probably caused a good deal of ecological disturbance, but these increasingly intrusive interventions stirred far less public alarm than did the spectre of forest fires.

In 1910, an acute insect and fungus outbreak struck the park, posing a new challenge to the board's forest management policies. Noticing considerable areas of dead and defoliated trees, board officials and the public feared that Vancouver's crown jewel appeared to be fading. In response to the public demand for immediate action, the board sought help from the federal Department of Agriculture's entomology division. The division conducted a brief examination and found "that some of the most valuable large trees were dying fast and that certain bark boring beetles and wood destroying fungi appeared to be the principal causes of damage done." Three years later, the Dominion botanist, Hans T. Gussow, led a more comprehensive survey, in which he blamed the continued presence of insects and fungi for the thick underbrush of fallen and dying trees. His report observed that the "ground is densely covered with under growth, [and] dead trees and limbs also cover the ground at every place, so that the whole is an almost impenetrable jungle, shutting out light and air." Gussow also attributed the problem to edge, or remnant, effects. As he explained,

Stanley Park ... is part of an immense area of woodland which has been exterminated as the city grew, and what is left now, though an area of considerable size, is somewhat exposed and unprotected, hence, as is common in the preservation of isolated areas of forest, the trees along the edge begin to die slowly and will continue to do so from insect pests, fungus attacks and physical exposure unless every possible means are taken to encourage favourable conditions for the growth of the trees by destroying all material

carrying infection and preventing the spreading of contagious pests and
diseases by up to date methods of forestry.[48]

Although the causes of the problem remained uncertain, Gussow's conclusions marked a turning point in thinking about the management of
Stanley Park. Gussow's report argued that suppressing fire was not enough
– active management and the expenditure of human energy were required
to produce a stable forest. Without "up to date methods of forestry," un-
controlled non-human forces would eventually destroy the park.

The insect and fungus problem continued throughout 1913, killing "large
numbers of some of the finest specimens in the park," according to one
board estimate. Nearly all the coniferous species were affected, especially
western hemlock and Sitka spruce *(Picea sitchensis)*. Again, the board turned
to the federal government for the best possible advice, and in response,
the Dominion entomologist, Charles Gordon Hewitt, sent his chief of
forest entomology, James Malcolm Swaine, to investigate (Figure 3.8).[49]

More than any landscape architect, James Swaine played a pivotal role
in remaking the forest of Stanley Park. A young scientist with the entomology division, he was a recent Cornell University graduate, specializing
in the emerging field of economic entomology. In January 1914, after

Figure 3.8 Dr. James
Malcolm Swaine, shown
here in 1943, played a
pivotal role in reshaping the
forest of Stanley Park, along
with other scientists from
the federal Department of
Agriculture's entomological
division. Agriculture Canada,
PA-140403, Library and
Archives Canada

conducting numerous surveys of the park to better understand the problem, Swaine and his assistants produced a preliminary report that summarized the forest conditions and placed blame on particular species of trees. An outbreak of hemlock loopers *(Lambdina fiscellaria)* had ravaged large areas of hemlock, an infestation that was particularly noticeable because the loopers had defoliated the trees. Swaine found that "dead hemlocks comprise the majority of the dead trees in Stanley Park" and added that this situation was particularly troubling because "in addition to being extremely unsightly these dead and dying trees form a breeding ground for injurious insects and fungi, which will surely have a harmful affect [sic] upon the remaining hemlocks if allowed to breed undisturbed." The report clearly revealed that aesthetics were a primary concern. Swaine suggested that the infected and dead trees be immediately cut down and the slash burned. The hemlock should then be replaced with Douglas fir. The park's spruce trees were most affected by an unidentified species of gall aphid, probably ragged spruce gall aphids *(Pineus similis)* or Cooley spruce gall aphids *(Adelges cooleyi)*. These insects form conspicuous galls on the ends of spruce twigs, where they live out a portion of their life cycle. They are not usually fatal to the tree, but they do produce a ragged appearance in foliage and can result in a rusted brown colouration of the leaves. Swaine's remedy was to remove and burn all the affected spruce. He found that the western red cedars suffered most from fungus, but this was apparently a common condition on the Northwest Coast. He recommended that their dead tops be cut off to improve the overall scenic appearance of the landscape. His ultimate conclusion was that the Park Board should remove all dying and dead trees "as soon as their usefulness is gone" and replant the cleared areas with Douglas fir, a species he believed to be more durable and better suited for park purposes. He contended that this approach would gradually put the park in "a permanent healthy condition." Swaine's recommendations were intended to produce a more aesthetically pleasing landscape – one that would retain the sense of an unblemished wilderness and leave no room for the variability and unpredictability of a Northwest Coast forest.[50]

In March 1914, J.B. Mitchell, from the provincial forest branch, also conducted a thorough survey of the infestations. He concluded that, except for a portion of trees with dead tops and hollow trunks, the Douglas fir and cedar were the healthiest species. Mitchell estimated that "of the Hemlock 25% is already dead, and about 60% more or less seriously affected by insect attack, while the 15% remaining are apparently healthy as yet." The spruce were in even worse condition: fewer than 8 percent were healthy,

over 50 percent were diseased, and the remainder were dead.[51] Overall, his
bleak assessment painted a stark picture of the problem: "No particular
area can be pointed out as being unaffected, in fact, the damage done has
been wide spread; but on one area of about 15 acres to the north of the
Park, near Prospect Point, practically every hemlock and spruce has been
killed."[52] Mitchell's report provides some indication of the anxiety regarding
the state of the park in the prewar years. The board continued to seek the
advice of experts in order to resist and correct the impact of natural forces.

Swaine and the Dominion entomologists also offered several recommendations for insect control, including the experimental use of pesticide.
According to Swaine's report, hemlock loopers could be most effectively
eradicated by spraying the infested trees with lead arsenate. To stay the
spread of the gall aphids, he endorsed the application of fish oil soap to the
affected trees. Swaine admitted that this procedure would be experimental
because "control measures for similar insect outbreaks have never been
attempted ... on such an extensive scale" or for such large trees. He saw the
insect problem as an opportunity to expand the entomology division's role
in forest entomology research and the dissemination of insecticides. This
work could cement the division's scientific status. In essence, Swaine would
use the park as a laboratory, a sample Northwest Coast coniferous forest,
to test pesticides.[53]

As the Park Board debated Swaine's numerous recommendations, including clearing underbrush, removing dead and dying trees, and applying
experimental insecticide, the public was largely supportive. One cartoonist
depicted the insects as a larger-than-life menace set to destroy the park
(Figure 3.9). The *Vancouver Sun,* which had vociferously opposed the electric
streetcar and road construction projects, firmly supported the work of
Swaine and his colleagues, and urged the Park Board to heed their advice:

> We have no doubt whatever that it is the conscientious desire of the com-
> missioners to do all they can to stop the spread of disease among the trees
> and keep this splendid forest as an unimpaired heritage for future genera-
> tions. But the policy they adopt in endeavouring to accomplish this should
> be dictated by knowledge, should, in fact, be framed on the advice of
> entomologists of assured standing and not at the haphazard suggestion of
> members of the board or of casual visitors to the city.[54]

This editorial reveals a common faith in the efficacy of science to combat
autonomous natural forces that threatened to change the "unimpaired
heritage" of Stanley Park.[55]

Figure 3.9 A 1914 cartoon depicting the first insect outbreak studied by the Department of Agriculture's entomology division. The artist's representation reveals popular perceptions of the insect threat. "Triumphant," *Vancouver Sun*, 24 March 1914, 1

J.B. Mitchell of the provincial forest branch expressed skepticism about Swaine's insecticide proposal, which he did not see as a practical solution in the long term, because "spraying is a slow and costly operation, which, while quite practicable in the case of ornamental and isolated trees, would be unfeasible for a large area such as Stanley Park, where the crowns of the larger trees only begin at a point higher than the strongest pump could throw a spray."[56] Mitchell favoured other methods of insect control, including "the judicious removal of a certain proportion of the underbrush," which he believed would "have all the desired effects, without giving rise to the sudden change in ground cover which might be injurious to the other trees." Furthermore, he endorsed the continuous removal of dead and dying trees. Finally, to improve the aesthetic appearance of the park, Mitchell tentatively lent support to the topping of dead cedar trees.[57]

Mitchell was not alone in his criticism of the insecticide experiment. The Park Board consulted the US Forest Service and the Oregon game warden, both of whom concluded that "spraying would be ineffective and practically impossible." Using the emerging language of ecology, they suggested that "the balance of Nature must be restored by encouragement of the life of the insectivorous birds." They asserted that the small birds that preyed on the problem insects had been driven off by crows. By placing a large number of birdhouses throughout the park, the board could encourage their return. This solution represented yet another hypothesis regarding the cause of the infestations. The debate demonstrated the limits of forestry and entomological sciences in the early twentieth century, when scientists were only beginning to understand the complex biology of Northwest Coast forests.

Swaine's solutions sought to address the problem by eradicating the insects with chemical pesticides and by reducing the amount of debris on the forest floor, which Swaine believed provided breeding grounds for insects. Rather than seeking the underlying cause of the infestation, he sought to construct an insect-resistant forest through fir reforestation. In the absence of scientific consensus on the cause of the outbreak, the Park Board deferred to federal authorities and proceeded with Swaine's recommendations.[58]

In March 1914, the board permitted Swaine's assistant, R.C. Treherne, to conduct a series of experiments with chemical insecticides. Borrowing a sprayer from the provincial fruit inspector that could reach heights of fifty feet, Treherne drenched twenty-three spruce and hemlock trees near Coal Harbour with whale oil soap and kerosene emulsion (which were commonly used at the time). Swaine insisted that "the work that we are having Mr. Treherne do in Stanley Park this spring is purely *experimental*" and that, although he could identify the insect threat and its remedy, "there are many details to be learned about a problem so extensive and unique as that in Stanley Park."[59]

By July, Swaine had re-examined the park and was more convinced of the effectiveness of his insecticides. Urging their regular application, he claimed that the measures against the gall aphids "have satisfied us that this pest can be effectively controlled by spraying with contact sprays." Regarding the hemlock looper, "the caterpillars are readily controlled by spraying." He also identified an emerging threat from the spruce bark-beetle *(Dendroctonus obesus)*, which could be alleviated by "felling and marking the infested trees." Swaine was adamant that the hemlocks should be replaced with Douglas fir. He argued that "Douglas Fir is the one healthy timber tree of this region. If this were done, the Park would be preserved and would be eventually more beautiful than it has been since the big firs were cut years ago." As he reiterated more explicitly a few months later in the *Agricultural Gazette,* "It should be made a settled policy to replace the hemlock, as it gradually dies, by the much more healthy Douglas Fir." Swaine advocated total reforestation as a means of resisting future insect attacks and improving the beauty of Stanley Park. In essence, his scientific recommendations were a form of landscape art.[60]

Of course, the tree removal did not proceed without controversy. In 1915, the park superintendent attempted to follow Swaine's recommendations to remove dead and dying trees and to clear portions of the under-brush. He reported that the insect infestation had spread from Pipeline Road toward Prospect Point on a tract of thirteen acres, where he found few live trees. The board hired contractors to remove the dead trees, but this simply raised alarms at the *Vancouver Sun,* which accused it of "vandalism" and of attempting to "civilize" the park. "Stanley Park is famous the world over as a forest, within the confines of a city," the newspaper stated, a place "where nature has been allowed to go about her business." Some feared that "weeding" the peninsula would transform it into an "artificial park." Although earlier public commentary had supported the work of the Dominion entomologists, the optics of loggers in the park seemed to contradict popular expectations of a "virginal" and "unimpaired" forest. This was a prelude to future controversies regarding human "intrusions" in Stanley Park.[61]

By April 1915, the board had allowed R. Neil Chrystal (another of Swaine's assistants) to construct a small laboratory in the park to conduct further experiments on the forest. From 1916 to 1919, active management continued along the pattern outlined by James Swaine, becoming, according to the superintendent, "one of the most important branches of the work in Stanley Park." Annual board expenditures on the forestry efforts grew from $487 in 1916 to $2,801 in 1919. The board continued to remove dozens of infected trees, replacing them with Douglas fir as Swaine had suggested. The superintendent expressed satisfaction with the policy in 1917, claiming that "a big improvement in the appearance of the park can be noted from the driveway as a result of this work." In 1918, the entire area behind the Second Beach playground, "one of the most unsightly spots in the park," was logged and burned. Contractors removed nearly all the spruce and hemlock trees from the Big Hill area, and loggers cut new trails to reach deeper sites. The board also encouraged the elimination of red alders, a deciduous succession species that tends to occupy disturbed areas in Northwest Coast forests. The superintendent argued that "their removal gives greater opportunity for the growth of conifers which should be encouraged." The board's efforts during this period transformed the park into a more homogeneous forest, where conifers (especially Douglas fir) dominated the landscape.[62]

However, the insect problem persisted, and in 1919, Superintendent W.S. Rawlings reported that, once again, large tracts were infested with hemlock loopers. Convinced that the problem was beyond his control because the board did not have the necessary equipment to launch another insecticide campaign, Rawlings pleaded with the commissioners, claiming that "a suitable pump for spraying is very necessary." Facing yet another insect eruption, the board retained its belief that the nuisance could be controlled and nature improved. Once again, it turned to the scientific experts of the Dominion entomology division.[63]

Swaine returned to Vancouver in the summer of 1919 to conduct another survey of the forest. He praised the board for its strict adherence to his recommended control measures over the past three years, pronouncing that, "if no control work had been done in the meantime, Stanley Park would have been an eyesore today." However, he noted that many of the hemlocks were in poor shape. "The hemlock," he argued, continuing his earlier campaign against this tree species, "is not thrifty under park conditions and it is the least desirable species for this purpose." Once again, he urged the board to "make Douglas fir and cedar the basis of reproduction, so that eventually Stanley Park will be covered chiefly by these two species." He reiterated the aesthetic reasons for removing dead trees, stating that they "detract from the beauty of the park and are eventually a constant menace from falling branches and tops."[64]

Dominion entomologists George Hopping and R.C. Treherne joined park authorities to study the insect problem, and Superintendent Rawlings forged ahead with Swaine's plans to remake the peninsula. Rawlings kept in contact with Swaine and provided updates on the progress of his work:

The whole of the dead spruce and hemlock, numbering several hundred trees, will have, by the end of this week been entirely cut down and burnt up, in the entire area surrounding Beaver Lake, and you will readily understand the vast improvement this has affected in the appearance of this district,

which heretofore has been one of the big blots in the forest area. A very fine
stand of healthy trees now takes the place of what was a veritable cemetery
of dead timber.[65]

Rawlings tapped into the resources of the city's relief department to recruit
labour for the removal project. The work was slow, he admitted, but "only
by systematic plodding in dealing with a specific area, and completing it,
can the ambition of a natural park of healthy trees and growths be realized."
In Rawlings's opinion, expending an enormous amount of energy to produce a "natural park" was not a contradiction in terms; in improving the
visual landscape, he was improving nature. He continued clearing trees,
occasionally used insecticides to control certain insect flare-ups, and
planted more Douglas fir.[66]

In 1929, Hopping reported a new outbreak of hemlock loopers and tip
moth *(Rhyncionia frustrata),* and he advocated a dramatic new approach
to the problem: using an airplane to dust insecticide over the park. With
little public debate or scrutiny, the board approved this measure, hiring a
plane to coat the park with a powerful poison. Superintendent Rawlings
subsequently reported that "extensive spraying operations by aeroplane
were carried out on June 23rd, when eight tons of lead arsenic was used
to dust the entire park, the cost being $6,750."[67]

Public support for aerial dusting was very strong. In fact, one 1930
editorial, urging the board to act quickly, drew the following analogy:
"Nero, fiddling while Rome burned, has been held up through the ages
as a horrible example of callous indifference and fatuitous indolence. But
fiddling while Rome burns is not essentially different from arguing while
the looper eats up Stanley Park."[68] The dusting campaign demonstrated
the persuasive power of expert scientists. Public officials, and the public
at large, were confident that specialized knowledge could eradicate the
undesirable insect "invaders." No one raised concerns over the possible
environmental impact of arsenic-based insecticide, a deadly poison.[69] Park
Board chairman Jonathan Rogers soon declared victory in the insecticide
campaign:

The authorities at Ottawa advised us that unless we [had] sprayed Stanley
Park for Hemlock Looper last Spring, there would [have been] a very serious
loss in that beautiful park ... the Park Commissioners could not do anything
else but have it sprayed even though they had to curtail their expenditure
in other directions. The spray was very successful having been done by
aeroplane and at least a ninety percent kill being recorded.[70]

Aerial insecticide spraying continued in the park as a standard procedure into the 1960s.[71]

In 1931, following its first use of aerial spraying, the Park Board organized a conference of British Columbia's top forestry specialists to review its management strategies. H.R. Christie, James D. McCormack, A.E. Munn, and G.A. Peck met with the park superintendent to review past reports and to conduct a brief survey of the forest. Their report noted that they examined all aspects of forest management, including "insect control measures, diseased and dead tree removals, tree topping, underbrushing and reforestation." Making a number of policy recommendations that echoed earlier reports by James Swaine and the other Dominion entomologists, they endorsed the continuous clearance of dead and dying trees and lent support to the Douglas fir reforestation efforts. "From the scenic standpoint," they argued, no one could question the value of removing "dead and diseased trees, alder, etc. from the fringes of the main driveways and trails." They cited this as a principal purpose of such forestry work – to improve the landscape features for visitors as they viewed nature from the roads and trails. The delegates sanctioned tree topping – the evidence of which remains today – because they believed it "will not only remove one of the outstanding eyesores of the park, but will remove a real menace from falling limbs and perhaps the whole tree." Their report confirmed what had become an implicit assumption by 1931: "modern forestry methods must be applied" in order to ensure the preservation of the park. The board adopted all the policy recommendations of this conference and thus formalized the work of the previous two decades. Its impact can be seen in historical photographs (Figure 3.10). In the late 1890s, the forest was ragged, variable, and untidy, but by the 1940s, it was more dense, orderly, and homogeneous. With such active management, one report stated, "the future of Stanley Park as a beautiful City park forest area will be assured."[72]

Creature Comforts

Improvements also refashioned the animal landscape of Stanley Park, with subsequent ecological changes and feedback effects.[73] The Park Board set out to eliminate certain animal species and enhance the presence of others for the pleasure of visitors. Pests and predators were hunted and killed, whereas preferred species were encouraged and protected. Exotic wild animals were confined where they could best be controlled – the zoo. This careful husbandry was another form of landscape art and facade

Figure 3.10 The appearance of the trees at Stanley Park's entrance, shown in the 1890s and the 1940s, illustrates the extent to which forest management transformed the landscape. Major Matthews Photograph Collection, LGN 1048, and Photograph Collection, 586-340, City of Vancouver Archives

management, intended to produce pleasing images for recreation. One could spend an afternoon in the park, feeding graceful swans and playful squirrels at Lost Lagoon, unaware that the scene was as dependent upon human intervention as it was on nature. The construction of a modern managed wilderness required the manipulation of animal life. However, these modifications opened niches for opportunist species, which found news ways to elude park policy and operate beyond the purview of human control.

By 1888, when Stanley Park opened to the public, habitats on the Burrard uplands had been transformed by urbanization, leaving the park an isolated forest for a significantly reduced animal population. The Great Fire of 1886 – which destroyed much of early Vancouver – and clearcut logging drove large animals such as deer (Cervidae), bears (Ursidae), cougars *(Puma concolor)*, and wolves *(Canis lupus)* to the suburban fringes of South Vancouver, Burnaby, and the North Shore. Early settlers exhibited hostility toward wild animals that transgressed the perceived boundary between wilderness and the city, illustrating Patricia Partnow's argument that the urban view of wildlife is rooted in a territorial separation of humans and wild animals. Settlers showed little tolerance for these "intruders." A pioneer settler named George Cary recalled the presence of deer in the West End as loggers cleared the land during the 1880s. The deer "got so used to the men slashing that they became quite tame; they would come around, you could see them any day; everyone knew about them." On one occasion, a few deer came too close to the city, making the mistake of mixing the wild with the urban. Cary "heard those deer go by on that board walk, tap, tap, tap, as they walked along the boards," before two men shot them. As people carved out a new urban environment, they did so at the expense of the non-human habitat.[74]

At just under a thousand acres, Stanley Park was too small to sustain significant numbers of large wild animals, but it was home to many small species, including raccoons *(Procyon lotor)*, beaver *(Castor canadensis)*, skunks *(Mephitis mephitis)*, red squirrels *(Tamiasciurus hudsonicus)*, Douglas squirrels *(Tamiasciurus douglasii)*, and a variety of birds. At the time of its opening, the largest animals in the park were domestic livestock kept by the families who lived there (as described in Chapter 1). Eventually, the Vancouver Park Board drove out both the livestock and most of their owners. Cows, pigs, and other domestic animals did not conform to its broader objective of transforming the peninsula into a public park for leisure, representing as they did the consumptive uses of nature. By the end of the nineteenth century, with most large wild animals and most livestock removed, the board set out to remake the animal landscape of the park.

Many visitors expected to see free-roaming animals in Stanley Park as part of their nature experience and were disappointed to discover that its forest was not teeming with wildlife. One Vancouver resident wrote to the Park Board, wondering why "the province is full of wild game [but] none in Stanley Park plenty of feed there and hiding places."[75] Early in the twentieth century, to remedy this defect, the board began to import attractive species of gentle demeanour that would entertain visitors and produce the effect of a sanitized and tamed wilderness.[76]

The introduced species of swans and squirrels best illustrate the board's efforts in this direction. The majestic mute swans *(Cygnus olor)* that cruise the waters of Lost Lagoon owe a debt to early officials who strove to maintain their population. In 1900, board chairman Robert Tatlow procured a pair of black swans *(Cygnus atratus)* from the Zoological Gardens in Sydney, Australia, to inhabit seven ornamental ponds constructed along the broad promenade from Coal Harbour to Lumbermen's Arch. Victoria's Public Parks Board also donated mute swans from Beacon Hill Park. To the delight of visitors, the Park Board stocked the ponds with the popular birds, adding to the already abundant wildfowl population of the park.[77]

It was also common for North American authorities to stock urban parks with grey squirrels *(Sciurus carolinensis)*, an eastern species admired for its charcoaled coat and charming appearance (Figure 3.11). Although Stanley Park was already home to the dark-brown Douglas squirrel *(Tamiasciurus douglasii)*, which is native to coastal British Columbia, the decision was made to import the more popular grey squirrels. In 1909, board chairman Charles Tisdall attempted to purchase grey squirrels from the New York City parks commission and the Baltimore Department of Public Parks and Squares but was informed that they could easily be bought through a third-party company that trapped and distributed animals throughout the continent. After consulting with park commissioners in other cities, the board ordered twenty-four grey squirrels from Wenz and Mackensen, a game preserve company in Yardley, Pennsylvania. Temporarily unable to fill the order, the company sent eight fox squirrels *(Sciurus niger)* instead and shipped twelve grey squirrels to Vancouver in 1911. Since then, grey squirrels have co-existed with the native Douglas squirrels.[78]

Such manipulations of the animal composition of Stanley Park produced unforeseen consequences. Introducing free-roaming species such as swans and squirrels simply provided new menu items for certain native predators.

Figure 3.11 A young boy watches a squirrel climb a tree in Stanley Park, 190[?].
Vancouver Museums and Planetarium Association fonds, Add. MSS. 336, item 677-664,
City of Vancouver Archives

The tenacity of opportunist species such as racoons, northwestern crows
(Corvus caurinus), and even great horned owls *(Bubo virginianus)* challenged the board's efforts. When it introduced the grey squirrels, the board
ignored warnings from William Manning, general superintendent for the
Department of Public Parks and Squares in Baltimore, who shared his
experiences at Druid Hill Park: "The raccoons in the less frequented places
of the Park kill the squirrels during the night, and we are unable to kill all
of the raccoons as they come from adjacent woodlands." And the much-
admired swans were equally vulnerable to predator attacks. One newspaper report described a gruesome scene at the birth of a clutch of cygnets:
"Shortly after the young ones were hatched, an immense flock of crows

attacked the nest in an unguarded moment and killed three of the little ones by picking their eyes out before the old birds could hasten to the rescue." Marauding raccoons regularly pillaged the ponds, further reducing the swan population. Park visitors and their accompanying dogs also commonly clashed with swans, a problem that persists to this day. In his 1916 annual report, the superintendent disturbingly noted that "our water fowl suffered very severely from the depredations of the great horned owl, which driven from the North in search of food, invaded Stanley Park and worked havoc around the Duck ponds."[79]

In response, the board sought new methods to control the native predators, focusing largely on crows between 1900 and 1950. Its reaction to the crows vividly illustrates Anne Whiston Spirn's observation that "in the city, humans subsist in an uneasy cohabitation with other animals," especially those they cannot control. Many observers demonized the crows, describing them in sharply unfavourable terms. M.W. Woods, a Vancouver resident and self-proclaimed "student of nature," offered one such perspective on the crow "problem" in 1908. Woods believed that "there is possibly no bird more rapacious and distructive [sic] than the common black crow," and he blamed the species for the lack of small songbirds in the park. M.G. Johnson, another observer, called the crow "the worst of all winged vermin." Yet another commentator complained that the park was full of "nothing but nest robbing crows." In 1910, hoping to protect its investment in the swans and to please dissatisfied visitors, the board approved a motion to allow members of the Vancouver Gun Club to shoot crows in Stanley Park on Saturday mornings – a policy that was renewed every year until 1961. The gun club had regularly lobbied the board for permission to hunt in the park but failed to win approval until its leadership pointed out that crows, a particularly troublesome nuisance, warranted this modest form of hunting as a means of predator control.[80]

The Stanley Park crow hunt did not proceed without dissent. Some Vancouverites questioned the class interests and scientific wisdom that lay behind the Vancouver Gun Club's hunting privileges. Ronald C. Campbell Johnson wrote to the *Vancouver Daily News-Advertiser* to complain about the legality of the crow hunt, stating, "these commissioners cannot condone such offences and grant class privileges to any particular men." He cited the yacht and rowing clubs as further evidence of unfairly granted class privileges in the people's park. Campbell Johnson was also opposed to what he considered "bad taste and wanton cruelty to destroy our crows," an opinion that was not unique. The *Vancouver Sun* echoed his sentiments in its editorial pages, referring to the hunt as a "slaughterfest." It doubted the science underpinning the policy, arguing that "there is much reason to believe that the depredations of the crow family have been much exaggerated." Furthermore, it suggested that crows were useful birds, for they "perform an immense service in the destruction of injurious insects of almost every description and in performing duty as scavengers." Some Vancouver residents believed that, far from protecting songbirds, the sound of firearms in the early morning hours was "scaring the timid songsters from the park." Nonetheless, this opposition failed to convince the board.[81]

The Vancouver Gun Club was an instrument of a Park Board predator control policy, but shooting crows on a weekend morning was also a recreational activity for its members. Although hunting opportunities abounded in the rural hinterland of British Columbia, the crow cull provided a rare opportunity for city-dwellers to hunt closer to home. George Colpitts's study of human attitudes toward wildlife in Western Canada prior to 1940 argues that local fish and game societies, including the Vancouver Gun Club, played a significant role in promoting wildlife conservation and animal control efforts in rural areas, but the park crow hunt reveals that these organizations also promoted similar efforts in town. During the first half of the twentieth century, Stanley Park brought hunting, traditionally an activity of the rural wilderness, into the urban environment.[82]

The autonomy of the wild animals in the park took an extraordinary turn during the autumn of 1911, when a cougar from the North Shore took up residence in the depths of its forest. In mid-October, the zookeeper awoke to find that five of his animals had been killed – two deer and three goats. Their remains were strewn about the paddocks, evidence of a brutal attack. By that time, the zoo had a vast collection of animals, a tempting smorgasbord for any cougar. The Park Board hired three game hunters from Cloverdale to find and kill the cat. For two weeks, it eluded them and devoured another deer until a team of hounds tracked it down. The hunters volleyed a number of shots into the animal, finally ending the "terror" of Stanley Park.[83]

The cougar episode further revealed the limits of the human relationship with wildlife. The Park Board was happy to introduce novel animals that could be enjoyed almost like ornaments on the landscape, such as squirrels and swans, but it did not tolerate larger free-roaming species that acted autonomously and threatened human life. Many saw the cougar as a menace because it had transgressed the boundary between wilderness and the urban environment. Newspapers portrayed it as "a very crafty animal," and one headline pondered whether the board was dealing with a "Cougar or the Devil." Like the crows, the cougar was seen as an intruding, murderous

Figure 3.12
Cartoon depicting the Stanley Park cougar hunt. Hugh Savage, "Cougar Is Shot Dead by Cloverdale Hunters," *Vancouver Daily Province*, 27 October 1911, 1

villain, endangering human life and safety. After viewing its body, a reporter said that he "could not help thinking how terrible it would have been if it had crept up behind one of the little ones in the park and given it one stroke with its mighty paw." Cartoons in the *Vancouver Daily Province* portrayed the cat as a cunning threat to human enjoyment of the park (Figure 3.12). Rooted in a long-standing tradition of cougar hunting, this attitude was common across the province.[84]

One Vancouverite expressed sympathy for the creature. A.H. Peters was a lone voice that autumn, calling on others to see the cougar as "a noble beast." He cited human intervention to explain its presence in the park, claiming that it was "lured from the mountain fastnesses by the persistent boosting of the Vancouver Tourist Association ... of Stanley Park's wild and prehistoric tangle," where it found that "deer and goats that had, in its native home, often taken days, nay weeks, of unremitting toil to capture, were here provided free of charge or toil."[85]

Although Peters's remarks were accurate, they were drowned out by the excitement of a big game hunt on the doorstep of the city. Cougar hunting

The slain Cougar & his Hunters.
Shot in Stanley Park Oct 26th '11

Figure 3.13 The Stanley Park cougar, slain and presented at the *Vancouver Daily Province* office, 1911. Major Matthews Photograph Collection, Add. MSS. 54, St Pk P271.2, City of Vancouver Archives

was a popular recreational activity in British Columbia. The provincial government and tourist promoters carefully managed the province's image as a wildlife frontier and a hunter's paradise. The *Vancouver Province* followed the hunt with such fervour that its owners even offered a reward for the cougar's capture. When the hunters finally killed it, they delivered the corpse to the offices of the *Province,* where it was photographed and displayed (Figure 3.13). The Park Board later stuffed and mounted the cougar's body in the Stanley Park Pavilion, where it remained for many years. One reporter claimed that "this cougar hunt has been so remarkable as to be almost without parallel in the annals of Canada." He was amazed by the thrill of "hunting absolutely wild big game within the limits of a big city." The cougar episode captured the imagination of Vancouverites and remained part of park lore for many years. In his 1929 recollections, Robert Allison Hood colourfully recounted the story, informing tourists that "looking savage and cruel just as she was in life, the animal is to be seen stuffed, in a case above the mantelpiece, in the Park Pavilion. Thus were the deer avenged." The display of the cougar's body was intended to symbolically represent human dominion over nature and its creatures, yet ironically the story underlines the limits of human authority.[86]

Finally, the zoo, one of the most popular tourist attractions, was the most controlled animal environment in the park, because, as Nigel Rothfels notes, "at their most basic level zoos are for people and not for animals." However, it was never entirely under human control or entirely divorced from the surrounding environment, affected as it was by climate, geology, and other natural characteristics. John Berger's contention that "the zoo is a demonstration of the relations between man and animals; nothing else" ignores the material presence of the zoo itself as habitat for people and animals. The history of the Stanley Park zoo demonstrates the relations between humans, animals, and the environment of an urban park.[87]

The zoo got its start during the 1890s, when the wife of the first ranger tended to a captive bear and a few small local animals just outside the ranger's cottage at the Coal Harbour entrance. This modest collection eventually grew into a more elaborate assemblage, which was viewed by thousands of visitors every year. BC residents donated animals from across the province to display the wealth of its wildlife. In 1904, for instance, a man named Lee Kee offered a black bear *(Ursus americanus)*. A Mr. Corrigan from Hope offered a marmot *(Marmota caligata)*, and W.G. Murphy from Bute Inlet sent a pair of Canada geese *(Branta canadensis)* in 1907.[88]

To meet the demand of the thousands who flocked to the growing zoo, the Park Board sought more exotic specimens from zoological societies and governments across the world. Eventually, the zoo featured a diverse collection, including bears, elk *(Cervus elaphus)*, kangaroos (Macropodidae), plains bison *(Bison bison bison)*, coyotes *(Canis latrans)*, raccoons, seals (Phocidae), and the very popular monkeys *(*Cercopithecoidea*)*. Intended to entertain and delight, the animals were the most rigidly controlled wildlife in the park, but even in their closed area, they were vulnerable to natural forces beyond human control.

Some species were not suited to the climate of the Northwest Coast; nor did their keepers always manage their conditions with proper care. The early facilities were very rough, constructed ad hoc to accommodate the great variety of animals, and did not always provide adequate protection against harsh winter weather. Although Vancouver's climate is mild by Canadian standards, its temperatures dropped well below tolerable levels for some of the exotic species. One report from 1907 noted that not "only with the monkeys, but with many other inhabitants of the zoo which are natives of more tropical climates than this, has the present period of cold weather been particularly hard." The ranger boarded up enclosures and lit fires to protect the vulnerable animals during snowfalls and cold snaps, and he sheltered the swans in the winter, before their ponds froze over. Despite these efforts, however, animals died every winter.[89]

Park visitors also posed a threat to the zoo animals. In October 1905, after a fire killed an opossum (Didelphidae), twelve rabbits (Leporidae), and several birds, the ranger found that its probable cause was a cigar or cigarette stub dropped by a careless visitor. Sometimes, the animals bit back; more than one mother wrote to the Park Board, seeking compensation after their poorly behaved sons lost fingertips to frustrated monkeys. But the greatest threat to the animals was the condition of their captivity. Year after year, the annual reports recorded their deaths. In one year alone, a falling tree crushed an antelope, someone stole a black swan, a bull elk was killed in a fight with another elk, a bear died from a mysterious disease, a dog killed a pea hen, a cougar cub was found strangled in a fence, and several animals died from "natural causes." Describing these deaths as "natural" was probably a case of unintended irony, given the highly unnatural conditions of the zoo.[90]

The introduction of such a wide variety of exotic animal species was yet another example of how, in its first four decades, Stanley Park was the subject of numerous efforts to improve nature. Far from preserving nature as it was when Europeans arrived at Burrard Inlet, the park continued a long history of interdependence between nature and culture. It was a hybrid environment, one that, despite popular perceptions, was an integral part of the city.

4

The City in the Park

Since many Vancouverites think of Stanley Park as a wilderness space separate from the city, it might seem incongruous that it is bisected by the causeway connector, Highway 99, which is one of the busiest traffic arteries in the Lower Mainland (Figure 4.1). Thousands of motorists speed along it (or crawl during rush hour), moving into the city in the mornings and out to the sylvan North Shore suburbs in the evenings. The bright reds and greens of the traffic lights and the 6,500-foot highway that leads to Lions Gate Bridge contrast with the rustic paths that innervate the park. But those who seek refuge from the clamour of the city are quickly reminded, when they stumble out of the woods and cross the connector via the pedestrian overpass, that the park is part of the city.

The causeway connector is only the most visible evidence of the influence of the city, for remnants of the park's urban past are dotted throughout. Projects such as the Capilano water pipeline, city reservoir, West End outfall sewer, Lions Gate Bridge, and coastal defence installations have all left their mark, meeting the non-recreational needs of the city. Employing the techniques of facade management, the Park Board attempted to mask or minimize the impact by isolating the affected areas and cloaking the intrusions with greenery. It also tried to reclaim alienated areas and to disguise their former uses with playing fields and picnic grounds. Throughout these processes, the Park Board struggled to balance the wilderness qualities of the peninsula with its indissoluble role in the built environment of Vancouver.

Figure 4.1 The causeway connector runs through the middle of Stanley Park, forming part of Highway 99. *Author's collection, 2010*

Two aspects of the park's geological inheritance facilitated its incorporation into urban systems such as water, wastewater, transportation, and defence. First, the peninsula lies at one of two narrows in Burrard Inlet, a fact that drew the attention of investors who were interested in constructing water pipelines, reservoirs, and bridges. Second, Prospect Point is situated at the highest elevation in the original boundaries of Vancouver and provides a clear outlook over the entrance to the harbour. This provided a strategic advantage that attracted military authorities, who sought to establish coastal defence batteries to protect the harbour during wartime.

Pipes, Reservoirs, and Sewers

Before bridges conveyed cars into Vancouver, a pipeline conducted its water supply from the Capilano River, running down the slopes of the North Shore mountains and crossing First Narrows, Stanley Park, and Coal Harbour (Map 9). The construction of the pipeline has much in common with that of Lions Gate Bridge, the principal difference being the fundamental lack of public controversy over the former. No plebiscite preceded its installation. No public campaign blocked the construction of a highway to service it. And no elaborate proposal was needed to persuade hesitant voters of its benefits. With little fanfare and almost no public acrimony, the Vancouver Waterworks Company drove the pipeline through Stanley Park.

Prior to 1889, Vancouverites ingested groundwater from shallow wells and expelled it (and other things) into outdoor privies, a combination that in close proximity produced typhoid and cholera. In Vancouver, according to Margaret W. Andrews, "the frontier practice of unfettered response to calls of nature prevailed without public objection for a decade after municipal incorporation." There was no municipal delivery system for fresh water and no sewer system for waste. Like cities across North America, Vancouver searched for a water source that would alleviate part of this public health problem and found it across the inlet at the Capilano River. In his assessment of the Capilano, Chief Engineer Henry Badeley Smith noted the quality of its water, remarking that "no purer water can be obtained from any source than that from this mountain stream." He considered the Capilano especially pure because it flowed "swiftly over a boulder bed, through deep rocky canyons, and along shores as yet uncontaminated by the impurities which follow in the wake of settlement." Like

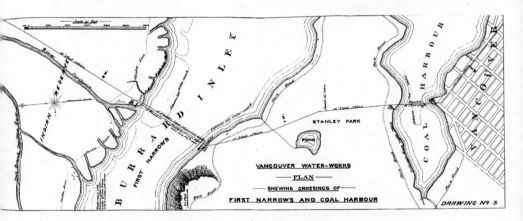

Map 9 The Capilano pipeline connects Vancouver to the Capilano watershed, following a route resembling that of Lions Gate Bridge and its road, which were constructed almost fifty years later. The Vancouver Waterworks Company built Pipeline Road and a utility house to service the line. Engineering Report of Henry Badeley Smith, 1889, Vancouver Waterworks Company fonds, 509-B-6, file 1, City of Vancouver Archives

many other North American cities, Vancouver delegated the task of de-
livering the Capilano's water to a private corporation. George Keefer and
H.O. Smith's Vancouver Waterworks Company dammed the river in 1888
and began the difficult process of piping water down from the North Shore
and under First Narrows.[1]

Many Vancouverites felt that the strong currents of the narrows would
make pipes impossible to lay. City council itself favoured the more distant
Coquitlam River in preference to the Capilano, due in part to the difficulty of crossing First Narrows. Nevertheless, Keefer and his associates
chose the narrows, not because it was a natural point at which to bridge
the inlet, but because it was the cheapest option – taking the shorter route
would diminish their capital costs. The popular misgivings were nearly
realized early in the summer of 1888, when the initial attempt to install
the pipes failed. Chief Engineer Henry Badeley Smith took over operations and led the diving project that eventually buried a twelve-inch
main with flexible joints beneath the inlet by the end of the summer.
Never before had pipes been laid sixty feet deep in water with such strong
tidal currents – a significant engineering achievement that was not lost
on the local newspapers.[2]

Ironically, as Mayor David Oppenheimer presided over the official
opening of Stanley Park, celebrating it as an unsullied retreat from urban
life, the city was encroaching on it. In order to service the pipeline,
Vancouver Waterworks Company employees built a five-thousand-foot
road from Coal Harbour to First Narrows (Pipeline Road). Two days
after the opening ceremonies, crews prepared a trench that would carry
the sixteen-inch main through the park, and they built a low-level trestle
bridge to take the pipeline across Coal Harbour and into the city. The
company erected a building on the south side of the narrows, where a
caretaker maintained the pumps for the project (Figure 4.2). The pipeline
installation was the first significant component of urban infrastructure
in Stanley Park.[3]

The waterworks venture provoked very little public concern, especially
regarding its impact on the park. Critics were primarily concerned with
the feasibility of the project. Referring to the many who doubted the company's ability to lay the pipe beneath First Narrows, the *Vancouver Daily
News-Advertiser* lamented that "there have not been wanting some amongst
us who seemed to desire that the scheme might result in failure, if only for
the reason that their gloomy prognostications might be proved correct."
Not a single voice opposed the construction of the road and the trench,
and no one suggested that it might harm the scenic beauty of the park.[4]

Figure 4.2 The waterworks house stood near First Narrows until the 1950s. The caretaker and his family were permitted to live in the park for several years after the house was no longer needed to manage the pipeline. William M. Stark, "Waterworks House at End of Pipeline Road in Stanley Park, Covered in Snow," 1900[?]. Major Matthews Photograph Collection, St Pk P315 N202, City of Vancouver Archives

After a shipping accident broke the submerged main in November 1889, leaving the city without water for eight days, the waterworks company installed an emergency reservoir at Prospect Point. This involved clearing the forest and excavating an enormous hole, measures that, once again, provoked no opposition. Chief Engineer Smith had identified the site as most suitable for a reservoir due to its high elevation. In 1905, the City replaced the original reservoir, estimated to hold up to 10 million gallons, with an even larger one that was said to be "the greatest excavation ever taken out in British Columbia." The new sixteen-foot hole was lined with concrete and carried roughly 25 million gallons. The removal of thousands of cubic yards of earth certainly constituted an enormous geological change, yet there was no public outcry in response to it (Figure 4.3).[5]

Figure 4.3 The water reservoir at Prospect Point in 1898 before it was replaced by a larger capacity reservoir in 1905. William M. Stark, "The Reservoir," 1898. Major Matthews Photograph Collection. St Pk N37.2, City of Vancouver Archives.

The lack of criticism may be traceable to the fact that, during this period, it was not uncommon for urban parks to be used as buffer spaces to protect the quality of reservoir water. Some early US parks, including Central Park and Prospect Park, were built around existing city reservoirs because they served as popular promenading areas and were an attraction. In this respect, the reservoir in Stanley Park was not entirely out of place.[6] Vancouverites recognized that the pipeline and the reservoir were more necessary to the city than a park. In addition, the pipeline construction began before the park opened, and public sentiment regarding the park was not as strong as it later became. Thus, commentary focused on the importance of a modern water system to promote the growth of the city. "A good water supply," explained the *Vancouver Daily News-Advertiser,* "is the one thing necessary to make Vancouver complete in all matters which tend to make a city a healthy and pleasant place of abode." Cutting roads and digging giant holes in the park were a small price to pay for such vital urban amenities.[7]

The same can be said for the completion of the wastewater system with the installation of the West End outfall sewer, which coincided with the construction of the Coal Harbour causeway between 1915 and 1917. To improve the city's wastewater removal system, the Vancouver Sewerage Board built a large outfall sewer that ran from Second Beach to

Lumbermen's Arch, an endeavour that significantly disturbed the area. Inconveniently, the tunnel for the sewer collapsed twice, beneath the road at Brockton Point and beneath the superintendent's garden. Eventually, workers completed the project, making Stanley Park a conduit for the delivery and disposal of urban water.[8]

It is also possible that there was little public complaint over these infrastructure projects because the Park Board segregated the sewer, pipeline, and reservoir from the naturalistic aesthetic applied throughout the rest of the park, thus minimizing their impact on its scenic beauty. The sewer was hidden underground, along with numerous other culverts and pipes designed to drain both the park and the city. Although the superintendent maintained Pipeline Road like the other roads, it differed from them; it was the only straight thoroughfare in the park, breaking from the curvilinear fashion used elsewhere. It was a utility road, not part of the park's public transportation network. The reservoir was also hived off: accessible only via a short road from the main drive, it was screened from view by a fringe of trees. A 1929 poem by Robert Allison Hood playfully describes this aspect of the landscape:

> Jupiter's bathtub, have you seen it?
> Just a fringe of firs to screen it;
> Naught above but just the sky,
> So he'll never come down when folk are by;
> But when he does he makes a dash
> And leaps right in with an awful splash!
> Thus if it's wet all around the path
> You'll know that Jove's just had his bath.[9]

In 1944, the Greater Vancouver Water Board reported that the main that ran from the waterworks house to the reservoir was leaking and would need to be repaired. However, because the reservoir's concrete lining had deteriorated, the system needed a more major overhaul, with the result that the Little Mountain Reservoir replaced the one at Stanley Park. Deciding to convert the reservoir into a baseball field, the Park Board filled it in and covered it with sod in 1946.[10]

Bridging the Narrows: Dreams

The shallow fjord of Burrard Inlet stretches from Point Atkinson and Point Grey in the west to the muddy flats of Port Moody in the east – a distance

Figure 4.4 An aerial view of First Narrows, prior to the construction of Lions Gate Bridge. Albertype Company, "Air View Showing the West End, Stanley Park, the Narrows, Hollyburn Ridge, and the Lions," c. 1925. PA-031697, Library and Archives Canada

of roughly twenty-five kilometres. The inlet constricts twice: at First Narrows, near Prospect Point, and at Second Narrows, near the boundary between Vancouver and Burnaby. For decades, these narrows fuelled the fantasies of real estate entrepreneurs and investors, who dreamed of mountain suburbs connected to the city by expansive bridges and engineering expertise, particularly at First Narrows (Figure 4.4). As early as 1890, real estate speculator George Grant Mackay predicted in the pages of the *Vancouver News-Advertiser* that a vast First Narrows bridge would one day link Vancouver to the North Shore. His statement was grounded less in prophecy than in a desire to see his 320 acres of Capilano River property transformed into prime real estate. Not unlike dozens of other men in the decades before the construction of Lions Gate Bridge, Mackay called for the bridging of the shores, where nature had so ostentatiously provided the opportunity to promote his own interests. But any scheme to build a bridge at First Narrows (or Lions Gate as it was sometimes called) would undoubtedly affect Stanley Park.[11]

In 1908, the Burrard Bridge Company proposed one of the first of many unrealized and preposterous bridge schemes to the Park Board: it would construct a suspension bridge to convey pedestrians across First Narrows. A sagging footbridge would span 1,280 feet and be suspended from two Tolkienesque towers – one of 222 feet on the north side and a smaller 30-foot version at Prospect Point. The company's solicitors provided the board with blueprints for the audacious undertaking, which detailed the system of elevators that would transport walkers up and down the mammoth north tower. The board rejected the ambitious plan.[12]

The idea of a First Narrows bridge lapsed for a number of years and was not seriously reconsidered until November 1924, when a drawing published in the *Vancouver Daily Province* revived the dream. According to Lilia D'Acres and Donald Luxton, Reeve David Morgan of West Vancouver had convinced the *Province*'s publishers to print a full-page article on the bridge idea, including the sketch – of a suspension bridge modelled on the Clifton Suspension Bridge in Bristol, England (Figure 4.5).[13] In fulsome prose, the article imagined a scene in the future:

> The crowd of tourists climbs aboard the sightseeing car, eager to escape the noise and bustle of the city's streets sweltering in the midsummer heat. The car glides smoothly down Georgia Street – that magnificent thoroughfare, bordered with stately maples and elms. Stanley Park rouses the usual chorus of wonder at its unspoiled natural beauty and primeval stillness; Coal Harbour, with its handsome aquatic clubhouses and fleet of pretty yachts, attracts mild expressions of admiration ... As the car rounds Brockton Point

Figure 4.5 This 1924 drawing stimulated renewed interest in constructing a bridge at First Narrows. "First Narrows Suspension Bridge – Vancouver B.C. 1934?" *Vancouver Daily Province*, 15 November 1924, 21

the northern end of the giant First Narrows Suspension Bridge comes into view, and the occupants of the car crane their necks forward to catch the first glimpse of the mighty structure.[14]

Perhaps the most significant aspect of this narrative was not the bridge itself, but its southern approach. The article described a route around the perimeter of the peninsula by way of Brockton Point. It did *not* foresee a highway bisecting the park.

Of course, North American parks had featured motorist roadways for decades prior to this proposal. David Louter's research on national parks in Washington finds that autotourism in the early twentieth century had become an integrated component of the wilderness experience. According to Louter, roads functioned as "scenic corridors and scenic narratives, making it possible to think of automobiles not just as an acceptable way of seeing national parks but perhaps as the best way." This kind of thinking about the relationship between parks and roads certainly informed the construction and use of Stanley Park's first road. By the 1920s, however, real estate boosters and suburban politicians were promoting autotourism as a means of convincing Vancouver voters to use roadways as a conduit across First Narrows.[15]

In 1926, West Vancouver Municipal Council was aroused by the dream of a First Narrows bridge that would link its isolated mountainside suburb to Vancouver. The Second Narrows Bridge, which had been built in 1925, had recently achieved this for North Vancouver, and West Vancouver wanted a crossing of its own, so the municipal council offered $2 million of tax land to any private contractor that would construct it. This bait attracted two proposals; the first came from James A. Campbell, representing Dwight P. Robinson and Company of Montreal and New York (later incorporated as the First Narrows Bridge Company). Shortly after Campbell commenced discussions with the local municipalities, William C. Ditmars put forth the second scheme on behalf of the Armstrong and Morrison Company of Vancouver in association with Stuart Cameron and Company and Harrington Howard and Ash of Kansas City (later incorporated as the Lions Gate Bridge Company). Local officials formed an inter-municipal bridge committee to consider both plans, scrutinizing the dimensions of each bridge as well as the proposed tolls.[16]

The two schemes ignited a vigorous debate about the merits of a First Narrows crossing. Opponents focused on a number of issues, including the effect on shipping in the harbour, the necessity of constructing another crossing so soon after the one at Second Narrows, and, of course, the impact on Stanley Park. Because any bridge would affect Vancouver's harbour, the federal government, which was responsible for all navigable waterways in the country, would have to approve it. In light of this, the Department of Marine and Fisheries and the Department of Public Works also held a commission in November 1926 to determine how the bridge might affect traffic in Burrard Inlet.

Several groups opposed the bridge on the grounds that it would obstruct the harbour entrance and thus impede commerce. During the 1920s, Vancouver had made several important investments in the harbour, including the construction of Pier D (1920), the Ballantyne Pier (1923), and Pier B-C (1927), and was emerging as a major Pacific port dominated by grain exports from the prairies. Its exports more than quadrupled between 1921 and 1929. The Vancouver Board of Trade, Vancouver Merchants' Exchange, and the Shipping Federation of British Columbia made presentations before the commission to argue that a bridge would ruin the harbour for shipping. They feared that a First Narrows crossing would "advertise to the world the narrowness of the entrance, and place this harbour at once in the category of the river ports and in a secondary position when compared with the rival ports of Seattle and San Francisco." They argued that installing a bridge would be feasible only if the federal government widened the narrows from 1,200 feet to 1,800 feet.[17]

Opponents rightly questioned the wisdom of erecting a private toll bridge so soon after the publicly funded one had been built at Second Narrows. Long the vision of Vancouver mayor Louis D. Taylor, that bridge, a low-level rail and two-lane automobile structure, had linked North Vancouver to the rest of the Lower Mainland. A *Vancouver Daily Province* editorial pointed out that its construction was a necessity because the North Shore lacked any crossings. By contrast, "with the Lions' Gate Bridge, the circumstances are different. We could probably use the bridge to good advantage, but we do not need it very badly." Another astute observer wrote that Lions Gate Bridge would be detrimental to the public interest because it would drain funds from the municipal toll bridge at Second Narrows. Certainly, the Second Narrows Bridge played a crucial role in the debate over a First Narrows crossing in the 1920s.[18]

A principal obstacle to the Lions Gate Bridge project was public sentiment for Stanley Park. Because the park stood between First Narrows and the city, building a bridge would necessitate running a road through the park. The outcry was plentiful and emotive: The *Province* argued that the southern approach to the bridge "should be so arranged that Stanley Park will suffer as little damage from it as possible." Vancouverites wrote numerous letters to the paper, expressing their fear that the road would ruin the park. A.H. Gordon complained that "no vandalism must be permitted in Stanley Park, the wealth of which to the citizens of Vancouver is worth many bridges." An anonymous writer opposed the bridge "for the reason that it would destroy for all time to come part of the beauty and utility of Stanley Park by the cutting of a public thoroughfare through this, one of, if not the world's greatest exclusive natural playground adjacent to any important city." In light of the recent eviction trials for the families living in the park, one observer felt that "if squatters who lived there for fifty or sixty years were undesirable, surely this [the road] would be more so." The road was also seen as a form of privatization; for the "benefit of a few persons, the beautiful Stanley Park, known world wide and one of Vancouver's greatest assets, a park that no other city on the continent can boast of and a wonderful attraction to the thousands that visit it, the sheltered trails of beauty, [would be] converted into a truck highway." These opponents were concerned that the road would divide the forest in two and permit the city to invade the park.[19]

But not everyone agreed with this point. Some saw the highway as a minor intrusion, one that would hardly "vandalize" or "mutilate" the park. And the bridge would enable the city to expand beyond the geographical restrictions of the inlet, as F. Lefeaux pointed out when he decreed, "Wake up citizens of Vancouver! Realize what unique tourist attractions we have at our door, and before condemning the Lions' Gate bridge study the question from all angles, for the construction of this bridge will be a giant stride in the creation of a greater and grander Vancouver." That greater and grander Vancouver was inevitable, according to those who believed that the city was "still expanding. It is the law of nature that all things must grow or stagnate." Claims that the road would ruin the park were rebuked because "the fear of a highway spoiling the beauty of Stanley Park is not logical." Given that thousands of cars toured it every day, advocates for the project could see no difference between the bridge road and the rest of the park's traffic network. In fact, some went so far as to argue that it would open access to new natural areas.[20]

The Park Board did not see the road as just another thoroughfare for visitors – the proposed southern approach to the bridge was entirely different from the one-way perimeter road that looped around the peninsula. The inter-municipal bridge committee invited board members to participate in consultations with the competing contractors to determine the best route through the park to the bridge landing, which would be at Prospect Point. Park engineer Allen S. Wootton provided a report on the two schemes for the roadway. The First Narrows Bridge Company proposed to widen Pipeline Road, which ran from Coal Harbour to the park drive at the inlet and would connect it to the bridge site. The Lions Gate Bridge Company also hoped to use Pipeline Road, along with a new roadway from the northeast end of Beaver Lake, to connect with the bridge. Wootton, who considered both proposals wholly unsatisfactory, cited three reasons for not using Pipeline Road. First, it was intended to service the Capilano water pipeline and the increase in traffic would impede its utility for the waterworks. Second, the "considerable widening of this road, which is fairly straight in line, would give the impression of severing the Park in two," a fear that Wootton shared with Superintendent W.S. Rawlings. Third, allowing a major traffic artery to deliver large numbers of automobiles into the heart of the park was inappropriate.[21]

Wootton's fears that the bridge road would fragment the park resembled concerns expressed by Calvert Vaux and Frederick Law Olmsted during the 1850s with regard to Central Park. Olmsted was vexed that the transverse roads mandated by the City would allow ordinary street traffic to pass through the park, a development that would disrupt the cohesion of his landscape vision. His solution was to sink the roads below grade, which would hide them from the gaze of visitors and present them with uninterrupted vistas. In Olmstedian fashion, Wootton recommended that the "road should be built if possible on a continuous curve so as to avoid the impression of severing the Park in two." When the highway was eventually built, it consisted of a gentle curve that hid Lions Gate Bridge until, at the last possible moment, a final bend suddenly revealed it. Vancouverites can thank Wootton for this.[22]

Ultimately, the Park Board opposed the schemes to bridge First Narrows, concluding that "the character of the Park, regarded as a natural forest, must be adversely affected by anything of so commercial a nature, and the quiet and peacefulness of this woodland retreat would to some considerable extent be lost." Construction of the road "would leave a scar which it would take years to properly efface by a natural forest growth." Unlike the pipeline, the road and the bridge were too great an intrusion. And Vancouver taxpayers concurred.[23]

Under pressure from local newspapers and many Vancouverites, Mayor Louis Taylor, an open supporter of the First Narrows bridge, was compelled to turn the matter over to a public plebiscite. Shortly before the vote, the bridge committee released a pamphlet to convince Vancouverites of the necessity of the crossing. It compared the bridge road with Pipeline Road, stating, "some one has said that such a roadway would desecrate Stanley Park. One would not for a moment say that the present pipe-line road is a desecration." Indeed, the road would benefit the park by opening access and providing a necessary firebreak. In a ludicrous disregard for actual distances, the pamphlet even proclaimed that, after a short ramble from the bridge, a casual hiker could enjoy a stroll on Hollyburn Ridge, located more than thirteen kilometres from the proposed bridge site.[24]

In the 1927 plebiscite, despite the best efforts of the bridge committee and other advocates, Vancouverites rejected the proposed road, and in doing so, they rejected the bridge. The plebiscite had placed Stanley Park at the centre of the issue by asking, "Are you in favour of the construction of a boulevard roadway without cost to the City, through a portion of Stanley Park to afford access to and from the proposed First Narrows Bridge, subject to a satisfactory agreement between the Board of Park Commissioners and the Bridge Company as to location and specification?"[25] In the event, 4,724 Vancouverites responded "No" to the question, whereas 2,099 agreed to it. The initiative was rejected in every district of every ward in the city, a resounding defeat. For the time being, the dream of a First Narrows crossing was dead.

This development can be explained in part by the economic conditions of Vancouver. After a period of recession following the First World War, Vancouver emerged as a significant port city and benefitted from a brief economic boom. The opening of the Panama Canal in 1914 greatly expanded activity in the Port of Vancouver and tremendously improved the local economy. From 1921 to 1931, the combined population of Vancouver, South Vancouver, and Point Grey grew from 175,000 to 246,000. After the downturn of the early 1920s, the provincial economy expanded through most of the decade. This prosperity made it financially feasible for Lower Mainland municipalities to invest in the Second Narrows Bridge. The good times also gave ratepayers the economic luxury of rejecting over $3 million of private investment for a bridge at First Narrows. At this moment in Vancouver's history, the cost of carving a highway through Stanley Park outweighed the benefit of building a bridge at Lions Gate. One must also note the influence of the CPR in the real estate market of Vancouver and South Vancouver, where the company held vast tracts of suburban land. Some individuals associated with the CPR opposed the construction of a First Narrows bridge because it would promote North Shore suburban development over their own real estate interests. Nevertheless, Stanley Park ultimately stood in the way of the bridge plan. The visceral reaction to the

Figure 4.6 Collapse of the Second Narrows Bridge. Stuart Thomson, "Accident, 'Pacific Gatherer' Collision with Second Narrows Bridge, Tug 'Lorne' in Attendance," 1930. Photograph Collection, 99-2152, City of Vancouver Archives

scheme had been rehearsed earlier in connection with the streetcar proposal and Theodore Ludgate's attempt to build a sawmill on Deadman's Island. However, as economic conditions worsened during the 1930s, Vancouverites would be forced to re-evaluate their attachment to the park.[26]

Bridging the Narrows: Realities

Two crashes bolstered the prospects for a bridge at First Narrows: the collapse of the New York Stock Exchange in October 1929 and of the Second Narrows Bridge in September 1930 (Figure 4.6). A clumsy harbour accident brought down the poorly designed bridge, making its replacement a necessity, and the accompanying economic depression improved the situation for the First Narrows Bridge Company. In the 1930s, capitalism failed and British Columbians were not immune. From 1929 to 1933, the provincial economy declined sharply in nearly all sectors including fishing, mining, forestry, farming, and manufacturing. Unemployment in

British Columbia soared during these years, reaching 28 percent in 1931 – the highest in Canada – and forcing the fiscally tight-fisted Conservative government of Premier Simon Fraser Tolmie to open relief work camps throughout the province and abandon its lemming-like faith in the invisible hand of the market. Even the premier could no longer deny that the province was in grave trouble. The absurdist recommendations of the ultraconservative Kidd Commission, which called for massive cutbacks of the already paltry provincial social services, simply angered the burgeoning masses of unemployed, especially in Vancouver.[27]

The city's warm climate and faint promise of public relief and private charity had long lured the unemployed and homeless. According to Patricia Roy, "almost every unemployment problem Vancouver suffered in the 1930s had a precedent during the previous three decades." The so-called mecca of the unemployed also attracted its fair share of unrest as men without work took to the streets on several occasions to demand better relief and employment. When the City had attempted to cut off relief to non-residents in 1915, a march on the relief office quickly turned into a riot down Hastings Street. City officials learned very little from this clash, however; the relief office again slashed transients from the rolls in March 1931, instigating similar protests. Mass unemployment in Vancouver during the 1930s, combined with the parsimony of public relief, translated into commotion in the streets. In the winter of 1929-30, continuous protests and rallies culminated in a late January clash with Vancouver police. In 1931, the City had banned all public meetings, leading to a series of free speech demonstrations and more police violence. These public displays of protest and violence made unemployment the most pressing issue in the Lower Mainland during this period.[28]

"Work and Wages," the political war cry of Duff Pattullo's Liberal Party during the 1933 provincial election campaign, succinctly captured the sentiment of the time. Many believed that the road to economic recovery should be paved with work and wages rather than relief. The slogan also suited the politics of Liberal devotees who feared that the dole was sapping the work ethic in the country's young men. This mentality led to the establishment of the Interior work camps that removed men from the city relief rolls and took potential political radicals off the streets. But not all public works projects were located outside the city. After a two-term interlude by local businessman W.H. Malkin, Mayor Louis Taylor returned to office in 1930 to revive his earlier platform of "a full dinner pail" and "a fair day's wages for a fair day's work," first used in 1915. Taylor believed that large public works projects, which would provide desperately needed jobs, could best improve the provincial economy. He endorsed the construction of the Burrard Street Bridge in 1932 as one such project to provide wages for the city's unemployed.[29]

Stanley Park was also used to relieve the unemployment problem. It was common, especially during the 1930s, for governments to provide jobs through public works projects in parks. This occurred in both Canadian national parks and the national and state parks of the United States. Early in the First World War, the City of Vancouver employed relief gangs in Stanley Park to provide temporary labour for the Park Board, paying the workers twenty-five cents an hour to clear dead and dying trees. These projects tended to be restricted to local married men as a means of supporting Vancouver families, but as joblessness increased, they were expanded to include bachelors.[30] Relief work was a boon for the cash-strapped Park Board, which took advantage of the additional funding and cheap labour to further many long-term projects, especially forestry work and the continuous construction of the seawall. The federal government contributed funding almost annually for relief work on the wall throughout the century. The City employed relief work in the park during other periods of economic depression in the early 1920s and most extensively during the 1930s until 1942. The superintendent reported that 1931 was "a record year of expenditure and development in the history of the Park Board, due largely to heavy improvement works being carried out under Unemployment Relief schemes." Stanley Park bears the imprint of waves of unemployment relief.[31]

When the First Narrows Bridge Company offered a second time to build a crossing at Lions Gate, many saw this as an opportunity to create large-scale employment. In 1930, three years after the 1927 plebiscite, the two competing companies had merged under the name First Narrows Bridge Company, headed by William C. Ditmars and supported by William Stephen Eyre, A.J.T. Taylor, and a consortium of British investors (including members of the famous Guinness family). These foreign financiers – incorporated as British Pacific Properties Limited – also took advantage of Depression conditions and invested in bargain-priced real estate in Greater Vancouver, including the bankrupt Marine Building on Burrard Street and several thousand acres of tax land in West Vancouver. Reeve Joseph B. Leyland of West Vancouver was eager to offer four thousand acres, which had reverted to the municipality during the economic slump, in an attempt to prevent West Vancouver from going bankrupt like neighbouring North Vancouver and Burnaby. The revived bridge proposal was intended to promote suburban development in the new, elite Capilano Estates (commonly known as the British Properties). But before Taylor and his British syndicate could fulfill their aspirations, Vancouverites had to be convinced to permit a First Narrows crossing.[32]

When its charter was renegotiated in 1931, the First Narrows Bridge Company sought Victoria's approval for the project. The following year, the federal government granted tentative approval but required the affected municipalities to follow suit, so the company commenced negotiations with Vancouver City Council and the North Shore municipalities in 1933. Negotiations with West Vancouver and North Vancouver were brief; as in the 1920s, they were almost instantly on board. Vancouver remained the largest local obstacle. Vancouverites had scuttled the project in the 1927 plebiscite, a debacle that the company was determined to prevent.[33]

In April 1933, Vancouver City Council and the Park Board organized a joint committee to negotiate a tentative agreement with the company. Very early in the process, the committee decided that a plebiscite would be held after an agreement was reached. When some of the participating board members and aldermen suggested that the committee should not agree to the principle of the bridge and roadway until after the plebiscite, the company threatened to walk away from the table. The committee quickly retracted its suggestion. The bridge project amounted to roughly $6 million of investment in Vancouver, a sum that the company skilfully used to lure the desperate committee and the public into supporting it.

The First Narrows Bridge Company approached its public campaign with better organization and more aggressive propaganda than in 1926. Its first tactic was to portray the $6 million investment as a gift from benevolent imperial patrons to a city fallen on hard times. In one of several articles sponsored by the company through the Greater Vancouver Development Association (GVDA), a mysterious citizen group probably fabricated by the company itself, the author described the British investors as Vancouver's "fairy godmother." The money was to be seen as a donation to revive Vancouver's economy, and on numerous occasions, bridge promoters stressed that "neither the city nor any of its citizens will be asked to spend one single penny for any part or portion of the entire project." With such generous largesse at hand, another article warned, "any man who turns down the offer of immediate cold cash in these times – or in any times – is a fool to himself and a traitor to his community." The company played a double game, presenting itself as benevolent while constantly threatening to withdraw should voters reject its munificent overture.[34]

Some observers doubted the authenticity of such generosity. George Duncan wrote to the *Vancouver Daily Province,* complaining of the "deluge of propaganda which has been loosed upon us" and noting that "the most attractive local writers have been hired to pen long and glowing addresses in commendation of the generous gifts which are to be bestowed upon us against our own wills." Similarly, C.M. Campbell found that "the Greater Vancouver Development Association doth explain too much and the questionable character of the promotion, as far as Canadians are now concerned, is now obvious." Arguing that the public would be expected to pay tolls for the bridge, he pointed out that the "project is an investment ... and not a gift as we are being led to believe, and the owners will expect real returns on the money invested." But considering the difficult economic times, most people saw the $6 million as a fortuitous opportunity to create jobs.[35]

The bridge promoters and their most ardent supporters believed that the project would ease the epidemic levels of unemployment and launch an economic recovery for the city. One GVDA-sponsored article claimed "the story of the Lions Gate bridge across the First Narrows reads like an advance notice on good times coming." According to this promotional article, the project would employ an "army of bridge workers" for at least two years. Not only would it constitute immediate relief for the jobless, it would also provide "a sizeable amount of money to stimulate the fast-brightening outlook for Vancouver's business growth." This argument was not lost on Mayor Taylor, one of the most vocal supporters of the venture. He believed that "a payroll such as this promises will have not only a direct benefit in the community, but a favourable reaction indirectly." This economic logic was best articulated in another GVDA article written by UBC economics professor J. Friend Day, who asserted that the investment in Lions Gate Bridge would inject "new money" into the local economy. According to this reasoning, private foreign investment stimulates economic growth better than public works because it introduces new money that will provide both direct gains through employment and numerous indirect gains for businesses as workers spend their wages.[36]

Promoters also portrayed the proposal as a tremendous boost for tourism. As Michael Dawson suggests, tourism during the 1930s was changing from its earlier incarnation as a means of encouraging industrial and agricultural investment to an industry in and of itself. Furthermore, tourism during the interwar years was "transformed from an industry intimately connected with railways and hotels to one in which the automobile

assumed central importance." Governments began to invest in tourist bur-
eaus as a means to overcome the economic depression and attract vaca-
tioners' dollars. The bridge company and its supporters argued that the
bridge would provide new tourist opportunities for motorists, who would
be able to reach the recreation areas of the North Shore at Hollyburn
Ridge. Reeve Leyland even predicted that the bridge "may bring nearer a
connecting link between the proposed Garibaldi National Park which will
attract thousands of tourists to this province, resulting in large increases
in business to wholesale and retail merchants." Tourism was yet another
way that Lions Gate Bridge would bring salvation in a time of need.[37]

Once again, the bridge company's greatest challenge was the opposition
to situating a road in Stanley Park. Thus, before the December 1933 plebiscite, it printed the roadway design in the *Vancouver Daily Province,* showing
it for the first time as a gradual curve through the centre of the peninsula
(Figure 4.7). The GVDA attempted to convince Vancouverites that the
thoroughfare would even improve the park; rather than marring its beauty,

> the new roadway through Stanley Park will do for this park what the
> Redwood Highway has done for the scenic beauty of the Northern California
> forest lands. It will bring, within a few minutes by automobile, a series of
> sylvan vistas, of sheltered coppice and leafy glade, at present entirely inaccess-
> ible to all save the more daring who occasionally may venture off the beaten
> foot trails which thread their way through the underbrush.[38]

The GVDA clearly tried to tie the bridge project to the use of roads for
autotourism in national parks and other nature areas. Its article also highlighted the ingenious design of the road, which would render it "invisible
to anybody using the Park except at its landscaped entrance at Georgia
street and at those points where it crosses the woodland trails, and, once
only, where it intersects the existing traffic road." Essentially, the company
had adopted all of Allen S. Wootton's 1926 recommendations, ensuring
that the highway would blend into the forest and provide better access to
nature – an enhancement, not an injury.

Several people wrote to the local newspapers in support of the bridge
proposal and the new road. One writer reiterated an argument that had
been made in the 1920s: "A wide road through the Park would be of in-
estimable value in the case of a fire getting a good start on the west side
with a strong west wind." For his part, William Elgie Bland, a self-proclaimed
admirer of Stanley Park, placed his trust in the Park Board and felt confident that "a valuable addition in the form of a fine drive and walk through

Figure 4.7 A version of this plan was printed in the *Vancouver Daily Province* in April 1933, showing both the road through Stanley Park and the prospective suburban property at Capilano Estates. Major Matthews Photograph Collection, Out P625, City of Vancouver Archives

the very heart of the timbers will be provided." The *Vancouver Sun* proclaimed, "Stanley Park's beauties will be opened to people who never see more than the outer fringe when they drive or walk around the present park road." Supporters of the bridge project justified the construction of the road by portraying it as both useful and benign.[39]

Nonetheless, opposition mounted, refuting claims that the highway would improve the park. One writer in the *Province* wondered "what is wrong with the present road system of the Park, without having to hand over around twenty acres of the Park in order to make a shorter cut through the Park for a private firm?" Although roads were not out of place in the park, this one threatened to remove too much forest cover, and its promoters were criticized for plainly suggesting that the forest should be cleared to make room for it. One critic remarked that they were casually inviting loggers to "slash hell out of our Park, twenty acres of it." George Duncan wrote that "the ugly Pipe Line road was a warning how much harm might be done by rash interference." Others rejected assertions that the road would simply blend into nature, arguing "it is so easy to destroy beauty, but how impossible to replace – and to those who appreciate the beauty of Stanley Park it is hard to understand why it should be marred by a highway through it and why concessions can be granted on something owned by the people." A principal concern was that the road would permit the encroachment of the city within the park.[40] In a moment of deliberate exaggeration, one writer to the *Vancouver Daily Province* sarcastically predicted future improvements after the completion of the bridge project:

> Stop and go signals on the Cathedral Trail, the removal of the B.C. Gas Company's gas tank from where it is to the Seven Sisters' trail, and the leasing of Beaver Lake as an industrial site, removing all the "beauty" of Granville Island [then a major industrial site] to that of Beaver Lake and Granville Island could be the site for the City Hall. Also there is an unexpected domain in Stanley Park suitable for a packing plant or a glue factory.[41]

He even went so far as to suggest that the entire forest be cleared and the park be subdivided for homes, like Capilano Estates. Park advocates were no less vocal than they had been during the 1920s, but as the results of the December plebiscite were to reveal, they were now in the minority.

One critical difference in the 1930s debate was that the Park Board granted approval for the construction of the southern approach through the peninsula. To the regret of many, the board heartily capitulated, with seemingly few apprehensions about the road's potential impact. Given that just two years earlier, it had rejected a proposal from Henry Bell-Irving to use Pipeline Road as a connector to a ferry landing at Prospect Point, its position might seem surprising. But it was under considerable pressure from city council, the Vancouver Trades and Labour Council, and the company to approve a draft agreement before the plebiscite. At a special meeting in August, it sanctioned building a "gradual circuit" road through the park and leasing roughly four acres at Prospect Point for the bridgehead, as laid out in the plans produced by Allen S. Wootton and other City engineers.

Only Commissioner E.G. Baynes voted against the motion; Commissioners Charles Tisdall and Alice Townley were absent from the meeting, though Tisdall later voted in favour of the scheme at a meeting in November. With the consent of the board, opponents to the bridge proposal were at a significant disadvantage in the December plebiscite.[42]

On 14 December 1933, the *Vancouver Sun* announced, "Vancouver awoke today to find itself on the threshold of a new period of commercial and industrial revival." The electors had overwhelmingly approved the construction of Lions Gate Bridge, a complete reversal of the 1927 plebiscite: 17,806 voters favoured the tentative agreement between the City and the First Narrows Bridge Company, which had been signed on 9 November 1933, whereas only 7,615 disapproved. The plebiscite was immediately hailed as a victory for employment. Mayor Taylor took it as evidence that "the public prefers work, not relief," and expressed pleasure "that the citizens have been far-sighted enough to take advantage of their opportunities to climb out of the depression." The *Sun,* which had supported the project throughout the negotiations, roundly criticized the editors of the *Province,* who had refused to endorse it. Some believed that the *Province* was trying to defend the interests of CPR president E.W. Beatty, who had publicly stated his opposition to the scheme. Despite the bickering of the two dailies, electors opted for the bridge, largely as a means to produce jobs. On the same ballot, they also approved the erection of a new city hall as a public works project to address the unemployment problem so visible throughout Vancouver. Although the building would not be constructed for another three years (and under tremendous controversy), the 1933 plebiscite was, as the *Vancouver News-Herald* proclaimed, an "emphatic endorsement to more work and more wages for its citizens."[43]

Federal obstruction delayed the project for two and a half years after the plebiscite. Due to the concerns of Vancouver shipping interests, who, as in the 1920s, feared that the bridge would prevent the widening of First Narrows, R.B. Bennett's Conservative government continued to withhold its approval. By this time, the Vancouver Board of Trade and Merchants' Exchange were calling for the narrows to be dredged and widened to two thousand feet; the proposed bridge would span only fifteen hundred feet. Hoping for more favourable treatment from William Lyon Mackenzie King's Liberals, the company postponed construction until after the 1935 election, when the Conservatives were removed from power. Disappointingly, however, the Liberals proved no more compliant than the Conservatives and delayed the bridge proposal for months until finally approving through an Order-in-Council on 29 April 1936.[44]

Figure 4.8 Approximately 6,500 feet long and 66.feet wide, the bridge road cleared roughly ten acres of forest. Philip Timms, "Clearing of Land for the Lions Gate Bridge Road," 1937. Historical Photographs, Acc. no. 19129, Vancouver Public Library Special Collections

A logging crew commenced construction of the bridge road on 31 March 1937, clearing roughly ten acres through the centre of the park. Photographic evidence reveals the substantial transformation of the landscape (Figure 4.8). The work was contracted to William C. Ditmars's other corporation, Stuart Cameron and Company, and the Park Board sold timber from the clearance for $583.07. It closely managed the project throughout the year, arguing vigorously against plans to change the northern intersection of the road and the park drive from an underpass to a circus and to permit parking on the new highway. Allen S. Wootton also pressured the First Narrows Bridge Company to build a pedestrian overpass on the new thoroughfare, and Commissioners R. Macaulay and Edgar George Baynes consistently criticized the aesthetics of the causeway improvements and the road. Nonetheless, the board could not hide the fact that the city's transportation network had penetrated the park. Lions Gate Bridge opened to pedestrians on 12 November 1938, with a ceremonial crossing by Mayor George C. Miller of Vancouver and Reeve Leyland of West Vancouver.[45]

As if to stave off buyer's remorse, the bridge committee and the company generated a series of promotional pamphlets and newspaper articles to publicize the benefits of the new crossing (Figure 4.9). This literature served as an advertisement for both tourists and construction and real estate investors. Just as the company had claimed during the plebiscite debates, the bridge would offer untold opportunities for tourists to explore the forest playgrounds of the North Shore because, as one pamphlet stated, "the entire region to which the bridge gives immediate access has been described as among the most beautiful in the world." Another souvenir pamphlet claimed that "the new suspension bridge will give quick access through Stanley Park to the beaches, coves, and mountain resorts of the North Shore." Not only was the bridge the means to a better vacation, it was also evidence of Vancouver's construction skills. The longest suspension bridge in the British Empire, it was admired by George VI and Queen Elizabeth, who crossed it during their 1939 tour of Canada. A significant engineering achievement, it was supposed to boost the local construction trade, a fact emphasized by a 1938 souvenir book produced by the company, which was essentially an advertisement for all the contractors who had

Figure 4.9 Lions Gate Bridge officially opened on 12 November 1938, less than two years after construction began. "The Bridge Is Open!" *Vancouver Sun,* 12 November 1938, 1 (magazine section)

been involved in the project, from the steelworks that constructed the towers to the painters. It claimed that the bridge was "a monument to the spirit which will carry on in the face of opposition, calmly and sincerely to successful conclusion, work of great magnitude."[46]

The promotion of Lions Gate Bridge did more than just publicize Vancouver to the world; it manufactured an iconic symbol of the city, one that endures to this day. Indeed, the company propaganda is echoed in a 1996 book by Douglas Coupland, which describes the bridge as "a structure through which all of your dreams and ideas and hopes are funnelled" and as "one last grand gesture of beauty, of charm, and of grace, where civilisation ends ... and eternity begins." In attempting to convince Vancouverites that the bridge represented a new era of prosperity (and was worth the sacrifice of their park), the company portrayed it as a beautiful and natural feature of the landscape, "an embellishment worthy of a province which in itself forms an empire of vast potentialities, immense natural resources, and unsurpassed scenic grandeur." Vancouverites were told that "to Vancouver's people the Lions Gate Bridge is not only a bridge but a symbol of conquest, and earnest of future greatness." This rhetoric – unconsciously repeated throughout the century by casual observers such as Coupland – camouflages what park commissioners and many Vancouverites of the late 1960s and early 1970s would later consider a tragedy and Faustian bargain: the process by which Vancouver, in a moment of weakness, had permitted a private corporation to drive a major highway through Stanley Park. Even more tragic was the fact that the northern approach to the bridge was routed through the Capilano Indian Reserve without the consent of its residents, an issue that was never mentioned during the public debate of the 1930s.[47]

Like the Capilano pipeline, which wove the park into Vancouver's water supply system, Lions Gate Bridge integrated the park into the urban transportation network of the Lower Mainland. Both projects were facilitated by the park's proximity to the narrows, but they were ultimately determined by the economic and social conditions of the city. The bridge proposals of the 1920s and 1930s illustrate how the economic climate influenced voters in two plebiscites on essentially the same question. In 1927, the bridge was deemed unnecessary, but the desperation of 1933 made its disruption of the park a small price to pay for much-needed employment.

Vestiges of War

In 1859, Colonel Richard Clement Moody had recognized the military advantages of the Stanley Park peninsula due to its high elevation over the entrance to Burrard Inlet. Moody foresaw the construction of a fort at the site, where guns could be placed to defend against an American surprise attack on New Westminster. As discussed in Chapter 1, Moody never followed through on this plan, and strategy became a moot point until the First and Second World Wars.

On 6 August 1914, two days after Britain declared war on Germany, Park Board chairman W.R. Owen sent a letter to Colonel J. Duff Stuart, the senior military officer in Vancouver, offering the park for any necessary military purpose. In patriotic terms, Owen explained, "We fully recognize that this Park being a Military Reserve is always at the disposal of the Dominion Government, but my Board feels that at such a time as this, it is appropriate that we should be the first to voluntarily offer to place Stanley Park at our Country's disposal."[48] The Canadian military did not compel the board to take this step; it pre-emptively relinquished control. Owen's letter was probably a response to complaints of poor harbour security following the *Komagata Maru* standoff just months earlier, when a shipload of Sikh migrants was held in the port for several weeks. The subsequent clash with police caused many observers to question the security of Vancouver's harbour and to suggest that defences be installed at its entrance.[49]

Owen's letter also spoke to two key aspects of British Columbia's response to the war: patriotic volunteerism and paranoia-laced fear. Anglo British Columbians greeted the war with an outpouring of support for Britain. British Columbians donated thousands of dollars to the war effort and eagerly volunteered to fight on the Western Front. In total, 55,570 people volunteered and 43,202 went overseas. By the end of hostilities, the province had lost 6,225 men, and 13,607 had returned wounded. The patriotic fervour that filled local recruitment offices also ignited conflict on the homefront. In 1915, anti-German riots broke out at Victoria's Kaiserhof Hotel in response to the sinking of the American passenger liner *Lusitania* and the death of Lieutenant James Dunsmuir, who was among the fatalities. As a result of this kind of violence, Germans and Austrians who lived in British Columbia were interned by Ottawa for the remainder of the war. This xenophobic patriotism was also accompanied by grave concerns for the safety of the province's coastal cities, especially Vancouver.[50]

Many Vancouverites feared a sudden strike by sea more than a fifth column attack by German and Austro-Hungarian spies. According to Peter Moogk, the German naval squadron based at Tsingtao, China, was perceived as the greatest wartime threat to the province's security. Two vessels particularly captured the imagination of British Columbians, the *Leipzig*

Stanley Park   Vancouver   B.C.
August 1914

Figure 4.10 The four-inch guns at Siwash Point stood on guard to protect Vancouver from a potential German naval attack. William Stark, "Stanley Park, Vancouver B.C., August 1914." Photograph Collection, 371-2620, City of Vancouver Archives

and the *Nurnberg,* thought to be in the vicinity of Mexico and California; they could potentially launch a surprise attack on Vancouver. The threat seemed so imminent that Premier Richard McBride covertly purchased two submarines from the United States in the summer of 1914, acting without the consent of Ottawa and making British Columbia the only province to (briefly) have its own navy. The federal government continued to increase its naval presence in the Pacific and received further help from the Japanese heavy cruiser *Izumo* after Japan declared war on Germany. When the Park Board offered Stanley Park to the war effort, the Canadian military acted rapidly to bolster Vancouver's coastal defences.[51]

Military authorities quickly delivered two four-inch-calibre guns from Esquimalt and installed them at the Siwash Point picnic grounds, not far from Siwash Rock, overlooking the entrance to Burrard Inlet. Engineers mounted the guns on two sunken wooden platforms overlaid with steel plates (Figure 4.10). The Park Board cleared several trees to give the gunners a clear line of sight over the water, and part of the park was closed to the public. According to the superintendent, this area extended "from the

old road above Third Beach to the junction of the Main Driveway above
the Big Tree [the present-day Hollow Tree]." Park-goers were prohibited
from using the park from the shore to the main road from Third Beach
to Prospect Point. On 15 August 1914, Stanley Park was armed and ready
for combat. Three days later, explosions from test firings of the guns could
be heard around the inlet. In September 1914, two sixty-pounder field guns
from Ontario were placed at Point Grey to support the park defences.
These installations were intended as a temporary measure until Britain
gained naval supremacy in the Pacific. By June 1915, the guns in Stanley
Park had been rendered inoperational.[52]

During its tenure at Siwash Point, the military proved a poor steward,
and it left the area in significant disrepair. The water supply pipe from the
reservoir, ordinarily intended for fire protection, had been ruined by tap-
ping it for regular use for the gun emplacements. The Park Board requested
that the military make any necessary repairs, and it quickly obliged, though
it kept the site closed to the public for several months. The guns had been
removed, but the steel plate platforms remained, as did the barbed wire
fencing and the underground magazine. Superintendent W.S. Rawlings
politely requested that "if the grounds are not being put to any further use,
I am to ask whether you would be good enough to arrange to have barbed
wire fences, enclosing this area, removed, and the paths leading to Siwash
Rock, opened, in order that the public may have full access to Siwash Rock."
He assured Colonel Stuart that the Park Board had no intention of interfer-
ing with the military use of the space but wanted only to regain access to
Siwash Point if it were no longer needed for the war effort. The site still
required considerable renovation, so the board worked closely with military
authorities to restore the picnic grounds by clearing underbrush, removing
the fencing, and repairing the paths and roads. It provided the materials
and tools, and the military supplied the labour. By the end of April, the
picnic area had been completely restored, except for the platforms, which
remained in place until they were sold in October 1917. The Park Board
returned the Siwash Point landscape to its pre-war condition and erased
all evidence of the military episode.[53]

During the interwar period, drills and military parades were often held
at Brockton Oval, but the park was not called into service again until 1938.
Once more, the looming clouds of war raised concern among Vancouverites,
who lamented the vulnerability of Canada's Pacific coast. In January 1938,
the Department of National Defence notified the Park Board that it would
soon be occupying a site at Ferguson Point, just south of Third Beach,
where it would install two six-inch guns to defend the entrance to Burrard

Inlet. This time, the board had no choice but to accede to the wishes of the military. The department furnished some rough plans for the proposed gun site and consulted with the park commissioners on its construction. Despite the objections of Vancouver's Town Planning Commission, which believed that the guns would harm the beauty of the park, workmen began clearing a new roadway 150 feet east of the original road to divert traffic around the proposed gun emplacements. One report reassured the public that "care is being exercised by Park Board officials to cut down as few trees as possible, in order to preserve the natural beauty at this site." The *Vancouver Sun* explained that Ferguson Point was widely known as a quiet beauty spot and that "the view from the Point is one of the finest in Stanley Park." Unfortunately, this fine view also provided excellent sightlines for the coastal defence guns.[54]

In August 1939, the gun emplacements in Stanley Park were mobilized for war. The two six-inch guns at Ferguson Point were supported by three searchlights at various locations along the park's western shore and an observation post at Prospect Point.[55] These installations formed part of a coastal defence network, with guns placed at Point Grey, Point Atkinson, and First Narrows. The Department of National Defence expanded its occupation of the park in 1940 by closing Third Beach to the public, where it had established barracks for the battery detachment. At first, the Park Board hoped that the beach would be closed only during the winter months, but in 1941, the military required its closure for the remainder of the war. In 1942, the department took control of Deadman's Island for naval training grounds. Naval authorities assured the Park Board that the buildings they planned to erect on the island, now called HMCS *Discovery*, would be "designed to be in conformity with the background of the famous Stanley Park, so that Deadman's Island will become an attraction of interest and a point of beauty." Throughout the war, the board had little choice but to submit to the various demands of the Department of National Defence, from limiting access to parts of the park to permitting the construction of water pumps in Lost Lagoon that would provide fire protection for the West End in the event of an air raid. It did its best to minimize the impact of these measures but had virtually no control over the situation, and the public was largely compliant.[56]

This public acquiescence can be partially traced to widespread fear of a sudden Japanese attack following the events at Pearl Harbor in December 1941. Racism and wartime anxiety fuelled public furor among white British Columbians who pressured their all-too-willing political representatives to push for the total expulsion of Japanese Canadians from the Pacific coast. The dreadful treatment of these Canadians was the most vivid expression of the panic in Canada's Pacific province. Although Vancouverites had vigorously defended the sanctity of their park from several encroachments such as streetcars, sawmills, and roadways, the strategic security of the city always seemed to trump sentimental concerns for nature.

After the war ended, the Park Board repeated its policy of removing or concealing the military's impact. Ferguson Point and Third Beach were quietly reincorporated into the park. At the end of 1944, the coastal batteries were maintained by a skeleton crew and were later removed. Board commissioner Rowe Holland negotiated the re-opening of Third Beach in January 1945, but Major-General G.R. Pearkes insisted that the fencing, barracks, and camouflage remain. The board continued to press the Department of National Defence to remove all the military buildings from the beach area.[57] The superintendent's report for 1945 reveals that, once again, the military had left the park in poor condition: "A tremendous amount of clean up work was necessary, as none of the trails had been touched for four years. The park buildings, turned over to the military were not left in particularly good shape, and had to be re-conditioned. So far the military hutments have been used as temporary quarters for various units in turn but should soon be relinquished."[58] Not until 1948 did military authorities return the entire area to the public and reseed the land with grass for picnic grounds. The Park Board converted a Ferguson Point military building into a teahouse and a Third Beach hutment into a workshop, where Aboriginal carvers could craft totem poles. The remaining military structures were removed, and except for the naval training grounds at HMCS *Discovery*, the board extirpated the military presence from the park. Today, an adventurous visitor can find a few remnants – the concrete base of a searchlight and a lookout post at Siwash Point – but by and large, this part of the park's past has vanished.[59]

As was the case for other aspects of urban infrastructure, the Park Board carefully applied facade management practices to minimize the visual impact of the militarization of Stanley Park. Such measures maintained the illusion that it was not part of the urban environment. This enduring notion of separateness – that the park remained undisturbed by the city – continued to inform popular understandings and lay at the roots of the protectionist environmental politics that shaped Stanley Park in the late twentieth century.

5

Restoring Nature

Where are the Seven Sisters? Once a world-renowned cluster of Douglas firs and western red cedars, they no longer remain in Stanley Park; the Vancouver Park Board removed the last of them in the early 1960s after years of decay. Poet/performer E. Pauline Johnson immortalized them as the Cathedral Trees, but they were more commonly known as the Seven Sisters (Figure 5.1). To Johnson, they were such majestic forest giants that "there is no cathedral whose marble or onyx columns can vie with those straight, clean, brown tree-boles that teem with the sap and blood of life." Though she praised the forces of nature that crafted the fine trees in preference to the human architecture of a cathedral, she found common ground between the two, where one could experience "elevating thoughts, some refinement of our coarser nature." Echoing Johnson's sentiments, Catherine Mae MacLennan's 1935 booklet of poems and stories about Stanley Park referred to the Seven Sisters as "an ancient grove of giant trees." Just a few years before the Park Board removed them, local writer Allen Roy Evans described the Seven Sisters as "a majestic family, impressive not only in appearance, but in the antiquity of their lineage."[1]

These writers invested the trees with such powerful symbolic significance that they became natural monuments, admired by Vancouverites for both their girth and age. However, they were far less enduring than the stones of a European cathedral. Living organisms, they thrived for decades, changed shape, and played host to numerous creatures, but eventually, the Seven Sisters began to die. As they rotted throughout the 1940s, they shed masses of bark, which thundered down with a startling sound

Figure 5.1 The Seven Sisters, or Cathedral Trees, shown here in about 1910, were once a popular feature of Stanley Park but were reduced to stumps after their removal in the 1960s. Rosetti Photographic Studios, "Seven Sisters in Stanley Park," 1910[?]. Major Matthews Photograph Collection, St Pk P230 N263, City of Vancouver Archives

of cracking wood, reducing them to a shadow of their former glory. Due to the public's love for the Seven Sisters, the Park Board tried to preserve what remained of them by fencing off the area and planting ivy to secure the decomposing bark. Even after the trees died, the park superintendent had them topped, leaving only the trunks standing like "giant fence posts towering starkly into the sky." Under extreme public pressure, the board kept them in place until the early 1960s, when they became a danger and were removed before they could be blown over onto an unsuspecting admirer. Nature changed in Stanley Park and the city quietly lost Johnson's famous trees.[2]

The story of the Seven Sisters is more than mere anecdote. It is a micro-cosm of the larger relationship between human perceptions of nature, Park Board policy, and unruly natural processes. The North American parks movement of the nineteenth and twentieth centuries inspired the creation of boundaries to protect nature from the impact of human societies. As discussed in Chapter 3, facade management was used in an effort to preserve and enhance the beauty of Stanley Park. The public perceived the Seven Sisters as an enduring historical landmark, and the Park Board attempted to satisfy this perception by preserving and eventually restoring the dying trees, an approach that it exercised on a grander scale throughout the park. However, despite its best efforts, it could not halt the forces of nature, which brought constant change.

This chapter examines the period between the 1930s and the early 1970s, focusing on the ways in which nature failed to fulfill human expectations and how the Park Board designed policies that attempted to compensate for its lack of cooperation. Powerful natural forces have always moulded the landscape and ecology of Stanley Park, but over the course of these decades, the public's ideal image became increasingly grounded in the idea of an undisturbed wilderness. Furthermore, the Park Board's restoration work was directly influenced by the windstorms that regularly destroyed numerous trees, beginning with a violent storm in 1934. To return the park to its former condition, the board erased the dynamic and chaotic impact of the storms, resisting the autonomous forces of nature and simultaneously concealing its active management of the forest. In doing so, it aspired to satisfy the prevailing myth that Stanley Park was a pre-contact wilderness.

Its efforts were so convincing that the popular perception of the park as historically preserved had been consolidated by the 1960s, and the public had largely forgotten past disturbances by human and non-human agents. When Typhoon Freda struck in 1962, Vancouverites were shocked by both its damage and the board's restoration work. In the 1930s, they had *encouraged* the board to return Stanley Park to its former condition, but in the 1960s, they displayed ambivalence regarding this approach, a development that marked a shift in popular thinking about both the park and the broader meaning of wilderness.

In the wake of Typhoon Freda, the board abandoned the improvement projects it had vigorously pursued in the late 1940s and the 1950s, including an enlargement of the zoo and the installation of an aquarium. During the late 1960s and early 1970s, both the board and the public became increasingly resistant to intrusion in the park. The desperate compromise that had facilitated Lions Gate Bridge and the causeway connector no longer existed, as the board fought urban development projects such as the construction of a third crossing of Burrard Inlet. Though partially influenced by the emerging popularity of ecology and the new environmental movement of the 1970s, this stance was driven by popular memory and perceptions of Stanley Park as a pristine wilderness. As Paul Sutter finds in connection with the modern wilderness idea, this shift in thought "was shaped more by a collective uneasiness with the enormity of change at a given historical moment than it was by the emergence of a new scientific way of looking at nature." After 1962, restoration of Stanley Park relied on a resistance to disturbance and a static vision of nature.[3]

October 1962

Edward Lorenz might have found that the events on the Northwest Coast in October 1962 affirmed his soon-to-be-famous theory of the butterfly effect.[4] Although we may not be able to trace the destructive path of Typhoon Freda to the flap of a butterfly's wings in a Chinese park, its origins were nearly as remote. The 1962 Pacific storm season was particularly volatile in Southeast Asia. After recording twenty-four typhoons, the Joint Typhoon Warning Center noted that "a record year for typhoons has gone into the climatology books," the previous record being twenty-one in 1951.[5] Freda, the nineteenth and most easterly typhoon of 1962, formed off the coast of Japan (Map 10). Between 3 and 10 October, it safely

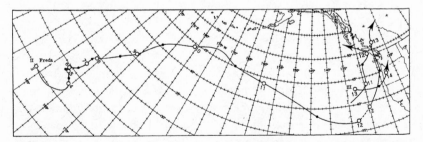

Map 10 The track of Typhoon Freda, 3-13 October 1962. The storm regenerated on 10 October 1962 as an extratropical cyclone and cut up the coast of North America from California to British Columbia, causing millions of dollars of damage and killing several people. "Pacific Coast Storm, October 11-13, 1962," *Mariners' Weather Log* 7, 1 (1963): 16

twisted eastward across the Pacific, making it primarily a nautical threat. However, as it began to dissipate near the International Date Line, it drew warmth and moisture from the mid-Pacific waters. Reinvigorated by the additional moisture, it became an extratropical cyclone, picked up speed, and headed north for California on 12 October.[6] After reaching peak intensity at Brookings, Oregon, it continued up the Washington and British Columbia coasts and struck Vancouver in the late evening and early morning, finally dispersing on 13 October.[7]

In the United States, Typhoon Freda killed thirty-one people and caused damages estimated at between $225 million and $260 million. It overturned boats and airplanes, inflicted minor damage on buildings, and significantly disrupted the power supply and communications. The lumber industry suffered the greatest economic devastation. Freda blew down an estimated 10 billion board feet of timber in Oregon and Washington. The governor of Oregon feared that the salvage effort would precipitate a drop in lumber prices. According to one weather report, Freda "took the greatest toll in death and destruction of any wind storm in the history of the Pacific Northwest." Although it had weakened by the evening of 12 October, when it reached Vancouver, it caused considerable damage there.[8]

A smaller storm had visited Vancouver the day before, with winds strong enough to cause significant power outages in parts of the Lower Mainland. Weather forecasters had failed to gauge its strength, warning only that "a disturbance moving inland this evening should bring a return to the showery weather of the past few days." One man was killed when he stepped on a downed power line. Falling trees trapped cars on the causeway connector leading to Lions Gate Bridge, and Letitia Williams of North Vancouver was luckily left unharmed when a tree crushed the hood of her car. With reports of the storm damage in northern California, forecasters warned of the larger system that would reach Vancouver on the night of 12 October.[9]

At about 11:00 p.m., Typhoon Freda reached Vancouver and battered the city until 3:00 a.m. The weather station at Sea Island reported maximum gusts of up to 126 kilometres per hour, and though the storm had been in decline since passing over Oregon, its hurricane-force winds remained strong enough to rip off the steeple of the Evangelistic Tabernacle on Tenth Avenue. Five people died as a result of Freda: two men succumbed to heart attacks while attempting to repair rooftop television aerials; one man was killed when his car skidded off the road; another was crushed beneath a tree in Richmond; and Renee Archibald was killed

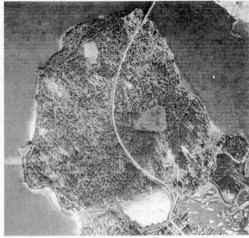

Figure 5.2 Comparing these photographs, of Stanley Park in 1957 and 1963, reveals that Typhoon Freda had cleared and thinned considerable numbers of trees. 1957, BC2350:50, BC 2350:51; 1963, BC5059:231, UBC Geography Air Photo Library

when a two-foot-thick hemlock toppled onto her car as she rode through Stanley Park with her daughter and son-in-law. The All-Canada Insurance Federation estimated that Freda had caused approximately $10 million worth of damage to private property in the Lower Mainland. City council estimated that the cleanup would cost taxpayers about $176,700, most of which would go to reconstruction efforts in Stanley Park.[10]

Typhoon Freda dramatically altered the park's landscape, levelling vast tracts of trees. As a reporter noted, it had become "a sight to shock any Vancouverite as the 1000-acre peninsula lies beneath tons of splintered wood." Others bemoaned the loss of the trees and labelled the event as a "slaughter." Even the national press described "Stanley Park, normally one of the city's most picturesque spots, [as] one of the ugliest in the midst of the storm." Newspaper reports were imprecise regarding the number of trees and the acreage cleared, but aerial photography reveals the extent of the destruction (Figure 5.2). The visceral reaction to the storm was to see it as both a tragedy and an anomaly. Because it had followed a meandering route along an "anomalous easterly flow," it could be perceived as an unprecedented fluke. However, a closer examination reveals that though Typhoon Freda may have been the most powerful storm to hit Vancouver in recorded memory, it was not entirely unusual.[11]

Storm Park

While chronicling the removal of fallen trees and debris to recover the "dignity" of Stanley Park, one astute *Vancouver Province* writer saw Typhoon Freda as a reflection of a similar storm that had occurred on 21 October 1934, nearly thirty years earlier. It had been described in hauntingly familiar terms. Winds gusting up to eighty kilometres per hour had thrown "mainland telephone, telegraph and electrical systems into a confusion of broken wires and fallen poles." The city was battered in almost the same fashion as in 1962: "Roofs were blown off buildings, electric signs were hurled to the streets, hundreds of trees were blown down, streetcar service was interrupted, and scores of small boats were dashed ashore." And not unlike the gales of Freda, those of 1934 laid waste to thousands of trees in Stanley Park. The superintendent estimated that nearly $4,500 (a considerable chunk of the Park Board's 1934 budget) would be needed in the first year alone to clean up and restore just a small portion of the damage.[12]

Like Freda, the 1934 storm passed over Washington and Oregon, leaving a trail of death, destruction, and debris. However, lacking radar and weather observation records, we can never know whether it too was an extratropical cyclone that originated as an errant typhoon in the western Pacific. The renowned meteorological researcher Jerome Namias of the US Weather Bureau produced a study of Typhoon Freda in which he suggested that it was part of a cyclical storm pattern in the Pacific Ocean. Namias focused on the abnormally warm sea-surface temperatures in the eastern Pacific that contributed to the reinvigoration of Freda. He concluded that "the formation growth, decay, and subsequent redevelopment of typhoon Freda along a most peculiar path were probably prescribed well in advance by interactive large-scale patterns of temperature and circulation in the ocean and atmosphere." Along with many others, his work contributed to the study of this phenomenon, known as the El Niño–Southern Oscillation (ENSO).[13]

If the trajectory of Typhoon Freda was related to the warm sea-surface temperatures produced by ENSO, other storms could theoretically occur in conjunction with these larger atmospheric and oceanographic patterns. This forces us to rethink the term "anomalous" in reference to Typhoon Freda. Figure 5.3 shows a timeline of all the storms recorded in the Park Board minutes and annual reports from 1900 to 1960 that significantly damaged the forest of Stanley Park and required clearing and reconstruction. During this sixty-year period, nineteen storms were powerful enough to blow down dozens to thousands of trees. The first of these, recorded on Christmas Day in 1901, did "more felling of trees in the park and on the

Storms in Stanley Park, 1900-1960

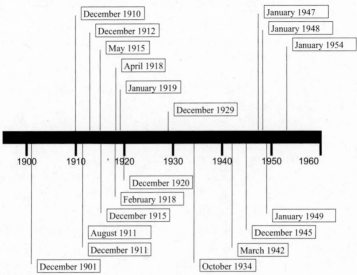

Figure 5.3 Timeline of storms that disturbed the Stanley Park forest from 1900 to 1960. Extrapolated from Annual Reports, 1900-60, Board of Parks and Recreation fonds, PDS 12, City of Vancouver Archives; and Board Minutes, 1900-60, Board of Parks and Recreation fonds, MCR 47, City of Vancouver Archives

park road than men with axes could accomplish in two or three years work." The superintendent estimated that the big storm of 31 December 1912 destroyed up to seventy-five trees around Ferguson Point and Second Beach. Smaller storms, such as the ones in 1915, felled only two dozen trees but created a significant hazard by tossing them across paths and roadways. A report from that year noted that the falling trees were "a very real danger to the public who may happen to be in this neighbourhood, and should an accident occur, the question of responsibility would undoubtedly arise." Clearly, as Figure 5.3 reveals, severe windstorms are not particularly unusual in Stanley Park and should not be considered surprising, especially in light of the most recent examples of 2006 and 2007.[14]

Typhoon Freda may have been the largest storm to disturb the park, but it was not out of the ordinary. In fact, it fit neatly into a pattern of extreme weather that had spanned more than half a century. The widespread shock and dismay in 1962 suggest that this pattern of regular windstorms was absent from public memory. Why, if the park had been hit by nineteen storms prior to Typhoon Freda, did the public find this one so surprising? The answer is rooted in the policies of the Park Board that aimed surreptitiously to erase signs of natural and human disturbance in the park.

Resisting the Autonomy of Nature

The restoration policies of the Park Board, developed after the 1934 storm, represented a concerted effort to resist the random, autonomous forces of nature.[15] When the park was created in the late 1880s, the board had largely conceived of its role as one of stewardship – the preservation of scenic beauty. It sought to improve nature by opening up roadways and paths that provided access to the solitude of the forest. The insect outbreak of 1910 (discussed in Chapter 3) forced it to take a more active approach, so it applied insecticides, instigated more elaborate fire suppression techniques, and removed debris. It readily accepted its new management role, but nature soon proved a non-compliant partner in this endeavour. Regular windstorms created an untidy tangle of fallen trees, rotting stumps, and moss-covered logs; the 1934 storm left such an indelible mark that it compelled the board to consider a new restoration policy.

Today, ecological restoration – renewing and restoring disrupted ecosystems via human intervention – is one of the most controversial responses to the modern environmental crisis. Two of its leading proponents, Frederick Turner and William R. Jordan III, view it as superior to older forms of conservation and preservation. They see a fundamental flaw in preservation efforts that seek to keep the environment pristine by eliminating all human intercessions in nature. Turner and Jordan reject this approach because it defines nature as homeostatic and separate from humans. As Turner asserts, "our job is not to leave nature alone or to coexist peacefully with it; we *are* it, we are its future, its promise, its purpose." Jordan sees hope in ecological restoration, in part because it "asks not how nature may be kept pure and uncontaminated but rather just how it is actually being affected by human activities, and how this influence can be reversed." Together, they view restoration as an instructive means of re-evaluating and realigning our place in the natural world.[16]

Of course, Turner and Jordan have their detractors. Eric Katz and Robert Elliot see ecological restoration as a potential environmental threat. Katz describes it as a "big lie" that could potentially be used to justify unrestrained environmental degradation on the grounds that the planet can always be restored to a healthy condition at some point in the future. Dismissing ecological restoration as "faking nature," Elliot warns that "if natural value can be and will be restored, then the obligation to leave wild nature alone is weakened, perhaps to the point where it has little force, provided, of course, that restoration of natural values is later accomplished." Katz and Elliot both accept a rigid dichotomy between nature and culture. Thus, an artificially restored environment can never truly be "natural," because it has been changed by human hands.[17]

Environmental restoration precedes current debates by many centuries. Marcus Hall demonstrates that the idea of converting "damaged lands into former ideal states is part of a tradition that is as old as maintaining a garden," and Richard Grove's research reveals that concern over the restoration of degraded forests dates from the earliest European colonization projects, particularly on tropical islands. The crucial point of both these writers is that humans have approached the restoration of despoiled environments differently over time. Hall notes that Americans have sought to return landscapes to a pre-European condition, where nature exists as an untouched wilderness, and Europeans have aimed at restoring landscapes of the past that incorporate humans. In essence, Americans seek to reinstate an ahistorical, mythic wilds that never existed, whereas Europeans attempt to "*renature historic* conditions."[18]

Following the American model of environmental restoration, the Park Board's post-1934 renovation of Stanley Park was an attempt to re-create an ideal version of nature, with the past in mind. After an inspection of the storm damage of December 1901, board chairman Robert Tatlow remarked that "it [would] cost a considerable amount of money to restore the park to its former condition," assuming that this was the most obvious course of action. His comment foreshadowed the board's future efforts, which aimed to return the park to some condition preceding a natural disturbance. Given the financial constraints on the board in its early years, it did not embark on a concerted restoration policy until after the 1934 storm.

In doing so, it solidified forestry policies that it had adopted in 1931. As discussed in Chapter 3, federal forest entomologists had promoted the clearance of dead trees, hemlock, spruce, and red alder and suggested the extensive planting of Douglas fir. James Swaine, chief of forest entomology, had also recommended "that for the sake of the scenic effect in the Park the dying tops of the cedars be cut off." The intent of these measures was to create what some ecologists call a climax forest, a stage of uninterrupted ecological succession during which the predominant trees "are not replaced by another set of plant species; they reproduce themselves for several or even many generations." In this case, the climax species, which was expected to retain its ascendancy as long as the site remained undisturbed, was the

Douglas fir. The board's policy would erase disturbance by eliminating the stages of ecological succession, replacing them with the appearance of stability, which was more in keeping with popular perceptions of Stanley Park.[19]

The disarray left by the windstorm of 1934 was worsened by a particularly harsh snowstorm in January 1935. By February, the board had done very little to remove the resulting debris, and Vancouverites became concerned. Public reaction to the storms in the 1930s was grounded in the belief that a natural forest should appear undisturbed and that the board had a responsibility to restore it. The *Vancouver Province* published an urgent plea for emergency funds to clean up the park. Although dismayed by the devastation, the *Province* remained optimistic, claiming that "it can be reclaimed; it can be restored; it can be made more glorious than ever." But with the dry summer season approaching, some feared that the debris would fuel a massive, destructive fire. The *Province*'s appeal launched the "Save the Park" campaign, which received broad support throughout the city. In endorsing it, former mayor Louis D. Taylor remarked, "In the past in times of great emergency Vancouver has always found a way to meet it. The same should hold true today and there should not be any delay in righting the menacing situation in the park." A joint delegation of city council and the Park Board secured $20,000 from the provincial government for a relief project to restore the park to its former condition contingent upon the City providing an additional $5,000. The board also produced a film, hoping to obtain more funding by displaying the destruction to the federal government.[20]

Expert foresters played a prominent role in the environmental restoration work of the 1930s. P.Z. Caverhill, chief forester of British Columbia, generated a report for the Park Board that embodied several key components of its 1931 forestry policy. He argued that the fallen trees posed a threat because they increased the risk of fire and provided breeding grounds for insects. They also diminished the visual appeal of the park, which Caverhill isolated as a chief concern:

> To my mind the question is not one of controversy as to the number of trees that have been destroyed, (I saw enough to state positively that they can be numbered in thousands) but how the esthetic value of the Park can best be restored, and it must be borne in mind that unless this debris is removed the depressing effect will grow worse instead of better.[21]

The "depressing effect" was the impact of a disturbed landscape on the public mind. By Caverhill's estimation, the park's value as a world-renowned

site was based on the appearance of an undisturbed wilderness. It was incumbent upon the board to reinstate this effect by clearing the debris and
reforesting with Douglas fir.

Even federal officials believed that the value of Stanley Park lay in its
identity as unspoiled. The minister of the interior wrote to the minister
of labour to seek federal dollars for the restoration effort, claiming that
"this area transcends in importance the value of an ordinary city park
because it contains one of the few remnants of virgin forest typical of
Pacific coast conditions." The funding agreement between the Park Board
and Ottawa embodied the goal of "preserving and restoring park values,"
those based on creating the appearance of an untouched wilderness.[22]

At its basic level, the board's approach to environmental restoration in
the 1930s amounted to a form of landscape gardening, similar to the facade
management practised earlier in the century. As it cleared the wreckage and
planted Douglas fir, the thought of leaving the fallen trees in place and permitting them to decompose never occurred to it. Perceiving the disturbance
as an aberration, it sought to speed up new growth rather than allowing
the forest to regenerate by natural means. According to Seth R. Reice, this
approach is consistent with an ecological equilibrium paradigm, or "balance
of nature" perspective. According to it, "climax communities are good and
disturbed communities are less desirable or somehow spoiled." The notion
of the ecological climax was based on the work of Frederic Clements, who
developed the model in the 1930s. Some ecologists today argue that disturbance can benefit an ecosystem and contribute to its long-term stability
by enhancing species diversity.[23]

In resisting the spontaneous forces of nature, the restoration work of
the Park Board combined elements of what Marcus Hall labels "reparative
naturalizing" and "maintenance gardening." Reparative naturalizing seeks
to return nature to a pristine condition and sees *cultural* forces as the
primary agent of ecological disturbance. Maintenance gardening sees
human intervention as essential to prevent the degeneration of the landscape by *natural* forces. In the case of Stanley Park, the board's restoration
policy sought to re-create a virgin forest that had been degraded not by
human activity but by natural processes. In effect, nature disappointed
Vancouverites by failing to meet their expectations of an ideal landscape.
Therefore, it was incumbent upon humans to compensate for its erratic
behaviour.[24]

In the 1930s, the public response to the restoration effort was largely
supportive. As mentioned above, it was fully endorsed by the Save the
Park campaign. "Let us preserve the natural beauty of Stanley Park by all

means," one editorial suggested in 1936, "but it is only reasonable to improve and beautify as much as we can of it without jeopardizing the illusion of natural wilderness." The editor also called on the public to "trust the eminently responsible citizens who compose the Park Board to safeguard the people's interests in that respect and take whatever measures they deem necessary."[25]

The board continued its restoration policy throughout the Second World War, though at a slower pace due to the financial limitations and labour shortages of wartime, but it reinvigorated its work in the late 1940s. Forestry experts encouraged it to launch an extensive reforestation program that saw thousands of Douglas fir seedlings planted every year. In a revealing moment, the superintendent remarked in 1949 that "strange as it may seem it takes quite a lot of work to keep a forest looking natural as a lack of such work soon allows the forest to get into a messy and untidy condition." As the program expanded in 1952, the superintendent revisited the subject: "It takes a considerable amount of work to keep a forest area looking as though it were just as nature intended. Obviously if it were a truly natural forest the trees would be lying in all directions and the picture would be decidedly untidy so it is our job to maintain a balance between naturalness and tidiness." His remarks almost buckle under the weight of the irony. The superintendent was fully aware that the "naturalness" of Stanley Park was entirely dependent on his labour. Like a shoemaker's elf, he covertly tidied the mess to produce a pleasing result. In doing so, he created the illusion that the work had been done, not by human hands, but by nature. The fiction of Stanley Park was that no one worked there.[26]

During the 1950s, the Park Board strove to limit public attention to its forest restoration program. After interviewing a number of park workers, a *Vancouver News-Herald* reporter attempted to reveal the truth in 1951, proclaiming, "contrary to first impressions, there is very little virgin timber in Stanley Park." His article portrayed the reforestation and landscape program as a ruse to create the impression of an unsullied forest. Chief Forester Harry Booth admitted, "we try to do our work so that the public won't know the forest is being touched." Booth strongly believed that human intervention was essential to the survival of the forest. "If we didn't put out new seedlings every year and keep the underbrush down," he confessed, "it would soon die."[27]

After Typhoon Freda struck Vancouver in 1962, the Park Board pursued its standard approach of removing fallen trees and reconstructing the forest. It closed the park for several days so that Superintendent Stuart Lefeaux and his assistant, W.C. Livingstone, could survey the damage. Stating that

Figure 5.4 After the 1962 storm, crews worked to re-open the causeway connector to Lions Gate Bridge and other park roadways. Their presence startled observers, who were unaccustomed to seeing human labour change the peninsula. Photograph Collection, CVA-392-540, City of Vancouver Archives

the "job of clearing up in Stanley Park alone is almost overpowering," Lefeaux was not optimistic about the work ahead. He recommended that immediate efforts should concentrate on opening up roadways and that clearing trails and the interior of the park could be delayed for several months (or years, as was the case). The board quickly removed fallen trees from the highway to Lions Gate Bridge. The estimated cost of repairs was $85,000. At first, both the provincial and federal governments refused to contribute, but eventually funds were transferred to the board through the joint federal-provincial winter works cost-sharing program.[28]

Although the cleanup effort of the 1960s resembled that of the 1930s, the same cannot be said for the public response. Due to the secretive character of the board's forest restoration work, people had forgotten both the regular occurrence of storms in the park and the constant labour required to maintain its forest. This time, there was no public campaign to save Stanley Park; there was only despair. In fact, some thought that the devastation was irreparable. In the days after the storm, as crews worked to re-open the roads, a *Vancouver Sun* journalist referred to the park as a "logging camp" (Figure 5.4). Commenting on the unusual sounds of power tools and snapping wood, he noted that the sight of logging crews cutting up trees and hauling out branches was "enough to make the Lost Lagoon willows weep." Unaware of the massive restoration effort of the 1930s and the subsequent reforestation program of the 1940s and 1950s, he inaccurately stated that such logging had not occurred on the peninsula since the nineteenth century. From his perspective, the park could be tidied up a little, "but it will never be quite the same." In the *Vancouver Province,* Pat Carney described the restoration efforts as "an eerie scene" but one that should be "a sharp reminder that Stanley Park is a living forest." The public found the situation jarring because it revealed that the forest was not untouched. The curtains were opened on the hidden work of Harry Booth and his forestry crew.[29]

As the cleanup continued into the next year, some saw it as an opportunity to make the park more serviceable. A *Vancouver Sun* editorial suggested to the Park Board that the newly cleared spaces be put to more general use. The natural forest had been destroyed and any attempt to preserve it as some kind of immaculate wilderness was "to a considerable extent a sentimental delusion." In 1964, when Mayor William Rathie reiterated this suggestion, noting that certain areas could be cleared to make them more usable and that the underbrush could be replaced with grass, his proposal was wildly unpopular and elicited sharp rebuke. An angry resident wrote that she "was horrified to read Mayor Rathie's remarks about Stanley Park" and added that she would "never vote for him again." Several *Vancouver Times* articles argued that "a park must be undisturbed," and they praised Stanley Park for its "1,000 acres of truly virgin forest full of rich lush growth," ignoring the fact that much of that growth had recently been flattened by Typhoon Freda.[30]

The Nature Myths of Stanley Park

The popular perception that Stanley Park was a static wilderness was informed by what Hall calls nature myths – the "collective beliefs and stories that help make sense of some crucial mystery of the natural world." For Americans, and I would argue Canadians as well, the prevailing nature myth is that of the virgin forest allegedly encountered by European explorers prior to colonization of the New World. This differs from perspectives regarding Europe, where the deep human history of the landscape has produced different myths. Despite the overwhelming evidence that Aboriginal peoples lived in North America for thousands of years and modified their environments prior to the arrival of Europeans, the myth persists. M.J. Bowden argues that its tenacity reveals that it has become an invented tradition, "a body of belief that is so deeply internalized by a nation/group that it is practically impervious to scholarship that shows it to be largely factitious." As Europeans pushed west, that tradition was modified to conform to newly encountered ecological zones. Their settlement of British Columbia produced its own set of nature myths.[31]

The nature myths of Stanley Park were produced and adjusted through decades of literature, art, and photography. George Vancouver's *Voyage of Discovery*, recounting his navigation of the Pacific, was one of the first widely read works that presented the Northwest Coast as a primeval wilderness. He described the landscape of Burrard Inlet as an "impenetrable wilderness of lofty trees, rendered nearly impassable by the underwood, which uniformly incumbers the surface." Vancouver's sentiments were echoed by dozens of early European colonizers, who assumed the land to be empty or, at best, thinly inhabited.[32]

During the late nineteenth century, people admired nature for its aesthetic qualities but saw it as requiring improvement. In 1888, the *Vancouver Daily News-Advertiser* described the park as a "wild natural beauty" that, aided by careful enhancement, would provide necessary relief for city-dwellers. It was not inherently beautiful, but it had the potential for greatness. In essence, it represented latent possibility for the city's *future,* a perspective that changed at the turn of the century as it became a representation of the city's *past.*[33]

In the 1910s, disputes over development projects such as the Deadman's Island sawmill, electric tramways, and road construction produced a new consciousness about the human role in the park, and writers began to describe it as an intact wilderness. During the 1920s, park admirers sought to curb human intrusions to prevent "the destruction of miles of trees and shrubbery which it has taken centuries to produce." The belief that nature needed improvement gradually faded in the 1920s and 1930s, as people became more reluctant to add adornments, such as the fountain in Lost Lagoon, which was built in 1936. The emphasis on inviolateness persisted throughout the decades: Like much souvenir literature of its day, Robert Allison Hood's 1929 book of "legends and reminiscences" described the park as a "tract of virgin forest." C. Roscoe Brown's 1937 pamphlet trumpeted it as invaluable for its "Virgin forest! Pristine beauty!" A mid-twentieth-century report admired its "1,000 acres of virgin timber." Now, disturbing it was perceived as undesirable, because its "natural charm and beauty must be kept unspoiled." This development reflected broader shifts in thinking. As historians have shown, the notion that the national parks

of North America should preserve wilderness did not emerge until the
early twentieth century. Parks such as Yellowstone and Banff were not
originally conceived as places where pristine wilderness was protected.
With time, however, public perceptions changed and parks became rep-
resentations of past natural landscapes worthy of preservation.[34]

The size and age of Stanley Park's largest trees authenticated its primeval
condition, and due to the work of Pauline Johnson, several became culturally produced monuments. Robert Allison Hood claimed that the preservation of the Seven Sisters "enables us to form an idea of what the original
stand of timber must have been before the hand of man depleted it."
Describing the "big tree" on Tatlow Walk, now known as the Hollow Tree,
Hood suggested that it could be a thousand years old. Catherine Mae
MacLennan wrote that "one feels very tiny standing beside the base of the
Big Tree, not only by comparison with its gigantic form but as one measures
his brief span of life with the long series of eventful centuries of whose
slow march it bears testimony." The admiration for the giant trees persisted
into the 1950s. For example, Allen Roy Evans commented that the Seven
Sisters "were splendid giants before Columbus caught sight of the New
World and they were close to their present proportions when the Pilgrims
landed at Plymouth." Nature in the park, represented by these trees, was
valuable for its perceived connection with the past. Claire Campbell notes
a similar phenomenon in Ontario, where "historical imagery was unusually
powerful in Georgian Bay because the archipelago *looked* like a wilderness,
and because of its associations with the explorers and frontiersmen of Canadian history." Where Georgian Bay was associated with Champlain,
Stanley Park was often linked to the voyages of Captain Vancouver.[35]

The cultural production of monumental trees in Stanley Park was a
revival of an older North American tradition of finding historical and
spiritual significance in nature. Since romantic poet William Cullen Bryant
ordained America's forests as "God's first temples," the towering height and
girth of their trees have stood as historical relics to rival the cathedrals and
castles of Europe. As Simon Schama points out, the sequoias of Yosemite
"proclaimed a manifest destiny that had been primordially planted; something which altogether dwarfed the timetables of conventional European
and even classical history." In this sense, as Michael Kammen suggests,
nature was "a surrogate for tradition" in American culture. Claire Campbell
argues that Canadians have also found solace and validation in the antiquity
of the Canadian Shield. Similarly, trees and other landscape features gave
Canadians not only a link to a distant past but also a spiritual connection
to the Creator. Emily Carr, perhaps the best-known artist to paint Stanley

Figure 5.5 Emily Carr's earliest work on the Northwest Coast includes watercolours of Stanley Park's deep woods, from the days when she lived in Vancouver. *Wood Interior*, 1909. Emily Carr Trust, VAG 42.3.86, Collection of the Vancouver Art Gallery

Park, chose to depict its giant trees because they were the holiest things she had ever experienced. According to Carr, "Stanley Park at that time was just seven miles of virgin forest." Her early watercolours reveal her struggle to capture the diffused light in the trees, which she felt revealed

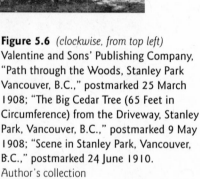

Figure 5.6 *(clockwise, from top left)*
Valentine and Sons' Publishing Company,
"Path through the Woods, Stanley Park
Vancouver, B.C.," postmarked 25 March
1908; "The Big Cedar Tree (65 Feet in
Circumference) from the Driveway, Stanley
Park, Vancouver, B.C.," postmarked 9 May
1908; "Scene in Stanley Park, Vancouver,
B.C.," postmarked 24 June 1910.
Author's collection

sublime and holy evocations (Figure 5.5). Carr's work popularized the
park's giant trees to the rest of the province and eventually the nation.[36]

Art and photography significantly influenced tourist perceptions of
parks. Of course, they are not neutral tools for the presentation of natural
environments. They represent particular ideological and social constructions, deliberately focusing on specific sites to set parks apart from industrial and urban environments. In the case of Jasper National Park, J. Keri
Cronin has found that, through popular photography and the construction
of what she calls National Park Nature, "the environmental actualities of
a place can become masked through dominant forms of visual representation." The same is true for Stanley Park; early postcards, such as those

published by Valentine and Sons, tend to emphasize the density of its forest and the height of its trees as a way of framing nature and excluding other landscapes (Figure 5.6). In portraying deep woods and large conifers, the postcards helped to associate them with the peninsula's admired wilderness qualities. In the vast photography collection of the City of Vancouver Archives, one of the most common images of Stanley Park is that of men and women standing at the base of a large conifer (Figure 5.7). The most famous example of this is the Hollow Tree, an enormous cedar stump in the middle of the park. Countless visitors have had their pictures taken inside it, even going so far as to park their carriages and automobiles within its depths (Figure 5.8). Standing next to large trees also illustrated their ancientness.

Figure 5.7 Charles S. Bailey, Bailey Brothers Studios, "Man Leaning against Cedar Tree, 50 Ft. in Circumference, Stanley Park," 1890[?]. Major Matthews Photograph Collection, SGN 102, City of Vancouver Archives

Figure 5.8 Posing for photographs inside the Hollow Tree has been a tourist tradition since the late nineteenth century. Charles S. Bailey, Bailey Brothers Studios, "Cedar Tree 80 Ft. Circumference, Stanley Park, Vancouver, BC," 1890[?]. Major Matthews Photograph Collection, St Pk P 1 9 N239, City of Vancouver Archives

Unlike photos of the Rocky Mountains parks, those of Stanley Park tended not to feature open landscape vistas, choosing instead to portray images deep within the forest. A photo series produced in 1912 by Rosetti Photographic Studios, a small company that operated in Vancouver from 1910 to 1915, provides a good example of this phenomenon. Focusing almost exclusively on large trees and thick forest cover, it emphasized the wilderness features of the park as a solitary experience, placing the viewer alone in dense woods. In an approach much like that of Emily Carr, Rosetti photographs such as "Among the 'Seven Sisters' in Stanley Park," "B.C. Jungle," and "A Beckoning Vista" attempted to capture the diffusion of light while emphasizing the evocative gloom of the woods (Figures 5.9, 5.10, 5.11). Photographs such as these shaped ways of seeing and understanding the park, reinforcing perceptions of an unblemished wilderness characterized by large, old trees.[37]

Vancouverites developed such strong sentimental attachments to the big trees that they almost forgot their impermanence. When some specimens died, the Park Board topped them, leaving only the tall trunks in an effort to preserve the remains. Perhaps the most extreme example of this

Figure 5.9 Rosetti Photographic Studios, "Among the 'Seven Sisters' in Stanley Park," 1912. Haweis Family fonds, box 18, no. 40, University of British Columbia Archives

Figure 5.10 *(top left)* Rosetti Photographic Studios, "B.C. Jungle," 1912. Haweis Family fonds, box 17, no. 14, University of British Columbia Archives

Figure 5.11 *(top right)* Rosetti Photographic Studios, "A Beckoning Vista," 1912. Haweis Family fonds, box 17, no. 42, University of British Columbia Archives

approach is the Hollow Tree, which the board fitted in 1965 with a steel truss, cables, and a cement base to prevent it from decaying. More recently, the tree has again become the subject of a public campaign to keep it standing. When large trees were toppled by windstorms or simply fell over, the press mourned them in arboreal obituaries. For instance, as the Seven

Sisters slowly rotted in the 1940s, a *Vancouver Sun* article lamented their imminent loss, predicting that the paper "will probably record that many of the hoary monarchs have had to be removed and 'tamer' trees substituted." Another report on a fallen cedar claimed that Vancouver had lost one of its "oldest inhabitants" and noted that "it was not cut down – that would have been sacrilege. Nor was it blown down, for there had been no gale. That moment in its age old life had arrived – as it does in many advanced human lives – when nature took an instantaneous toll and the monarch collapsed."[38]

Like Pauline Johnson, many writers sought to validate the antiquity of the park by associating it with the Coast Salish. Native legends and other tales were replicated in such tourist promotional literature as George H. Raley's *Our Totem Poles: A Souvenir of Vancouver* (1937) and B.A. McKelvie's *Legends of Stanley Park* (1941). The Art, Historical, and Scientific Association of Vancouver had long promoted the construction of totem poles in the park and once proposed to operate a model "Indian Village" to draw further connections between nature and Aboriginal people. The fact that the park had once housed a large Aboriginal settlement was also used to confirm its ancient status.[39]

In 1939, the *Vancouver News-Herald* had claimed that the park was necessary because "a city that has been carved out of the forest should maintain somewhere within its boundaries evidence of what it once was, and so long as Stanley Park remains unspoiled, that testimony to the giant trees which occupied the site of Vancouver in former days will remain." The nature myths of the park provided an imagined version of the past, which allowed Vancouverites to reflect on their own history. The park stood as a living metaphor for Vancouver's origins and progress. Eventually, it became a temple of atonement for the environmental destruction that was necessary to build the city and the province.[40]

The Limits of Growth

The shift in thinking about Stanley Park that postdated Typhoon Freda accompanied changing attitudes regarding consumption and the urban environment in Canada. Since the end of the Second World War, the Park Board had struggled to secure financing for an expansion of Vancouver's park system. The substantial increase of the city's population since the 1940s had placed a mounting burden on the commissioners to provide new facilities and services. As early as 1947, Superintendent Philip Bateman Stroyan explained the predicament in his annual report:

With the population of Vancouver growing steadily to the present figure of three hundred and fifty-four thousand for the city proper, public services generally are finding it increasingly difficult to keep pace with the requirements. The park and recreational services are no exception in this regard, part of the difficulty arising from the fact that, allowing for depression and war, we were fifteen years behind in the provision of facilities, without allowing for a fifty percent increase in population over the same period.[41]

Thus, in the late 1940s and the 1950s, the board pursued a significant expansion of the park system and launched major facility development projects in Stanley Park. It increased spending from $1,279,800 in 1946 to $4,869,312 in 1960.[42] During this period, the two biggest development projects for Stanley Park were the construction of a new zoo and an aquarium. In the mid-1940s, a growing constituency of animal advocates and park visitors became increasingly vocal about the conditions in which the zoo animals were kept. Newspaper editorials lamented the fact that "Vancouver has nothing to be proud of in its accommodation for wild life in Stanley Park." Others described the zoo as "a harrowing sight for animal lovers." The general opinion was that the zoo must be either abolished or improved. Even Superintendent Stroyan begrudgingly admitted that "the accommodation leaves much to be desired." He hoped that, when funding became available, the board would construct new facilities, because the zoo was one of the most valuable tourist attractions in the Lower Mainland.[43]

In 1949, the board secured additional funds to improve the zoo, but major renovations and expansion did not commence until 1950, when the City's ten-year civic plan allocated money for new facilities. The project started by renovating the bear cages and constructing a new monkey house. In 1952, the board secured a shipment of twelve penguins for a new penguin pool. The expansion continued to 1955, with the completion of a new bear pit, otter pool, pheasant display, and aviary.[44]

At the same time, the board was also engaged in building an aquarium. Since 1939, a private operator had leased the English Bay bathhouse for use as an aquarium, but it had become inadequate by the mid-1940s. As a result, an organization called the Public Aquarium Society formed to raise money for a new aquarium at Coal Harbour near the Vancouver Yacht Club. Garnering support from all levels of government, the society managed to contribute $300,000 toward the new attraction, but construction at Coal Harbour proved too expensive, so, in 1946, the Park Board decided to install the new aquarium adjacent to the expanded zoo. It opened to the public in May 1956.[45]

These two projects reflected the board's strategy for the growth of the park system. Popular tourist attractions, the zoo and the aquarium addressed the rising demand for greater recreational development in Vancouver. Although some detractors expressed concern over the confinement of animals, this type of development sparked little public opposition. Not until after Typhoon Freda did the public and the board begin to rethink infrastructure and development projects in an effort to eliminate human-induced disturbances in the park.

After the 1962 storm, the board faced a new urban development project that threatened to encroach on the park – a third bridge over Burrard Inlet. Returning to a stance that it had abandoned after the 1920s, the board resisted this undertaking. As in the first Lions Gate Bridge debate, it vigorously fought the proposed crossing, and it received generous amounts of public support; no longer would the compromises of the 1930s and 1940s be tolerated. In fact, the board even proposed to eliminate the causeway connector. In the context of increased public ambivalence toward major urban development projects and the expansion of Vancouver's suburban automobile culture, restoration would now be applied to past human degradation of the landscape.

Like other North American cities in the immediate post-war decades, Vancouver was subject to debates over the construction of new and elaborate freeway systems to better circulate automobile traffic from its distant suburbs to the downtown core. As Kay Anderson recounts, the story of the Vancouver "freeway began in the 1950s, when, in conjunction with the redevelopment plans for Strathcona, the city's civil servants began to tackle downtown congestion and circulation." But well before Vancouver's great freeway debate heated up in the late 1960s and early 1970s, the Park Board was already engaged in disputes with developers who envisioned another crossing at First Narrows. The third crossing, as it was called, was part of a broader plan for a network of high-speed freeways, which would convey traffic throughout the Lower Mainland. In the mid-1950s, City administrators began to conduct engineering studies to forecast future traffic pressures in Vancouver, particularly in the central business district. In 1965, the City obtained voter approval for the construction of a new Georgia Street Viaduct, intended as part of a waterfront freeway that would run through Chinatown and the Downtown Eastside. The construction of a third crossing was fundamental to linking the new freeway system to the Upper Levels Highway on the North Shore.[46]

The debate over the third crossing began with a number of proposals placed before city council and the Park Board in the late 1950s and early

1960s. F.C. Leighton, representing the Swan Wooster Engineering Company, played an important role in the issue. In 1960, Leighton proposed that Lions Gate Bridge be twinned and that a reconfigured eight-lane highway would run through Stanley Park. The new bridge would hold four lanes of traffic, and the old one would be reduced to two. The highway would feed across the peninsula, where a curved causeway, called the Ocean Parkway, would carry traffic across English Bay to the north shore of False Creek. Leighton claimed that the Ocean Parkway would be an attractive recreational area because it would be lined with beaches on both sides of the causeway and would create a new sheltered lagoon near Second Beach and the present-day English Bay bathing beach. The plan would remove the existing causeway connector and return the Georgia Street entrance, the site of significant traffic congestion, solely to park purposes. This, he believed, "would not create any additional severance within the park, and the net loss of parkland would be relatively small." Leighton's vision of recreational potential failed to convince the park commissioners, who rejected his scheme.[47]

Two years later, yet another crossing idea materialized. O.H. Bentzen, executive vice-president of Christiani and Nielsen of Canada, sketched out a fantastic plan to build a combination tunnel and bridge, which would traverse the inlet at Brockton Point, east of Lions Gate Bridge. Bentzen painted an incredible image of a small bridge connecting downtown to a land reclamation development on Burnaby Shoal, just to the east of Brockton Point, and a tunnel beneath the inlet. The plan called for the construction of high-rise apartments on Burnaby Shoal, to the east of the bridge, where upward of seventeen thousand people could live. The reclamation of Burnaby Shoal would add between 150 and 200 acres to Brockton Point. The park commissioners rejected this venture as well, passing a resolution on 7 October 1963 "that this Board is opposed to the taking of any more of Stanley Park for road purposes in connection with any future First Narrows Crossing." "We should make it plain," said Commissioner George Wainborn, "that we shall not tolerate any more of the park being taken for a highway." This resolution was a complete reversal of the board's 1930s stance, which had approved the construction of a bridge and a highway in hopes of stimulating the economy. In the 1960s, the need for economic growth conflicted with a strengthening public desire to protect and restore Stanley Park.[48]

Developers presented numerous other proposals to the board, all of which failed. In 1965, as pressure mounted to approve the construction of a third crossing, the board reiterated its anti-development position to city

council. Mayor Rathie, who had learned his lesson from the angry response
to his suggestion that park underbrush be replaced with grass, firmly opposed any further highway encroachments. Nonetheless, Philip Gaglardi,
minister of highways, approved provincial funding for a twin bridge at
First Narrows in 1966. When Vancouver electors chose the flamboyant
independent Thomas Campbell for mayor in 1967, he accepted the funding and moved ahead with the freeway plan, including the third crossing
of Burrard Inlet.[49]

F.C. Leighton reappeared before the Park Board in 1967 with another
bridge scheme. This time, he suggested a new causeway connector with
an entrenched double-deck eight-lane highway. Leighton also offered to
span the road with five wide pedestrian overpasses that would connect
the east and west sides of the peninsula. Mayor Campbell initially threw
his support behind this plan, claiming that it would "not cut one tree in
Stanley Park or remove one bulb." The board was not in agreement with
the mayor; Commissioner Andy Livingstone informed him that "you are
going to have a real fight on your hands if you try to put a freeway through
this park." Commissioner E.A. "Sandy" Robertson emphatically suggested
that the board should restate its 1963 resolution to assure that nothing be
allowed to "disturb any of the forest in Stanley Park." The board stood by
its policy of preventing further disturbance.[50]

Livingstone and Robertson were not alone in expressing reservations
about the bridge project. In the provincial legislature, the New Democratic
Party expressed concern that it would destroy the natural beauty of the
park. Alex Macdonald, NDP MLA for Vancouver East, suggested that the
road be sunk underground and covered with grass and trees, a measure that
he believed would "lead mother nature on a counter attack" and save the
park. Editorials and letters in the *Vancouver Times* voiced strong anxiety:
Stan Meadows, a long-time Vancouver resident, opposed the bridge
schemes and hoped the freeway promoters would "leave the park alone."
A *Times* reader insisted that "there must be no yielding an inch to the
builders of mis-called freeways," and an editorial asserted that "Mr.
Gaglardi's engineers must also be made to understand that the citizens of
Vancouver will not tolerate another great road sweeping through the park."
In a letter to Gaglardi, the Community Arts Council of Vancouver stated,
"we are opposed to the building of a second bridge next to the present
bridge because it would take away from the majesty of the present entry
to the harbour and further encroach on Stanley Park." The Vancouver
Civic Action Association sent a telegram to Prime Minster Lester Pearson,
pleading that "on behalf of the citizens of Vancouver, we strongly protest

any desecration of this jewel of nature." The Save Our Parkland Association joined a chorus of citizen groups that stood against the construction of the new road.[51]

Daunted by public disapproval and Park Board obstruction, Swan Wooster and city council turned their attention to Brockton Point as a possible site for a third crossing. The City hired Swan Wooster to present plans for bridge and tunnel options to be reviewed by the National Harbours Board. The company's schemes were remarkable engineering dreams that, had they been approved, would have dramatically altered the urban environment of Vancouver, obliterating what is now the Coal Harbour neighbourhood (Figure 5.12). The Brockton Point crossing proposals reflected an important modification of highway planning in Vancouver. In the 1930s, the city's highways had bent to conform to the park, but the Brockton Point scheme was designed to circumvent it (and the Park Board). Still, most board members, and some citizen groups, believed that the scheme would still have adverse aesthetic effects on the park.

In 1969, when the Park Board changed its strategy and presented its own twin bridge scheme for First Narrows, the situation became more complicated. Endorsed by many board supporters, this plan would connect the twin bridge to the city via a tunnel *beneath* Stanley Park, a feature that would enable the board to tear up the existing causeway connector and reforest it. As Commissioner George Puil explained, he "would much rather have seen the tunnel go under the present park causeway so Stanley Park could be restored to its old unity." Sandy Robertson, board vice-chairman, presented this plan to city council in August 1969, calling for a return to the full use of the park. "Vancouver's major tourist attraction, Stanley Park," Robertson reported, "is bleeding to death on the roadside and no one will stop to help it. Its problem is a wound that literally cuts it in half. A concrete hardened wound that is as noisy and dangerous as a snarling chain saw." He referred to the 1930s decision to build the connector as a "disaster," but like the disaster of Typhoon Freda, it could be reversed: "Give us back those 12 acres of concrete jungle and we will turn them back to nature." This was a "golden opportunity" to undo the most obvious human impact on the park.[52]

City council ultimately rejected Robertson's proposal, but the enormous public opposition to the freeway thwarted plans for the crossing (and nearly the entire freeway network). Taking their cue from other anti-freeway activists in Toronto and Calgary, a number of citizen groups allied to fight the third crossing and freeway construction, seeking to change

Figure 5.12 These remarkable images were presented as two alternative schemes to cross Burrard Inlet at Brockton Point with a bridge and a tunnel. Swan Wooster – CBA Consulting Engineers, "The Burrard Inlet Crossing: A Report to the National Harbours Board" (1970), 40, 122

transportation policy to provide for better public transit. In 1968, activists defeated schemes to route a freeway through Chinatown. Shortly afterward, Thomas Campbell lost the support of Ottawa, and the 1972 provincial election replaced W.A.C. Bennett's Social Credit government with the NDP. Campbell resigned from office and Art Phillips from The Electors' Action Movement (TEAM), a civic party formed to oppose the freeway, became the new mayor. In that year, the City abandoned the project. To substitute for the third crossing at Brockton Point, the Province launched a new commuter ferry service, known as the Seabus. The protection of Stanley Park played a significant role in the public opposition to freeways in Vancouver.[53]

Throughout the 1960s, Vancouverites became increasingly aware of the extent to which wilderness could be disturbed. This consciousness was partially influenced by environmental activism, which, as Frank Zelko demonstrates, emerged when "Vancouver's alternative culture met the city's mainstream society in Stanley Park." During the late 1960s and the 1970s, the city's various counter-culture movements staged protests, "be-ins," and other activities in the park to raise awareness of humanity's detrimental impact on the environment. Although Vancouver played a significant role in the birth of the environmental movement, particularly through the formation of Greenpeace, efforts to eliminate disturbance in Stanley Park were not driven primarily by either ecological awareness or the ecological sciences. Instead, they were fuelled by the popular memory of the peninsula and its connection to Vancouver's past. Following the third crossing debates, protests in the early 1970s against the construction of a Four Seasons Hotel and apartment complex near the entrance to Stanley Park were connected with the new environmental politics of the time. But they were grounded more in the anti-disturbance approach and in popular memory of the park's history than in ecological scientific management.[54]

This new politics of preservation set the stage for a confrontation in the late 1980s. In anticipation of the park's 1988 centennial, the forestry giant MacMillan Bloedel offered to donate $1.5 million toward a ten-year forest restoration program that would plant up to 250,000 Douglas fir and spruce seedlings. MacMillan Bloedel also intended to remove up to five thousand deciduous trees, mostly alders and maples, which were said to have invaded the park following Typhoon Freda. Company representatives, and most Park Board commissioners, saw the scheme as a means of returning the park to its 1888 condition. As a board spokesman said, "Stanley Park has been known as a coniferous forest since the 1870s, and we want to keep it that way." Local environmental groups vigorously opposed the project, criticizing its hubris and claiming that "people come from all over the world to see Stanley Park in its natural state, but we think we're going to fix nature by being better than nature." From their perspective, all efforts to improve nature should be abandoned. The debate continued until 1990, when the board finally bowed to public pressure and scrapped the restoration plan.[55]

Conclusion
Reconciliation with Disturbance

In the years after Typhoon Freda, the Park Board's foresters quietly restored Stanley Park once again. In a 1968 interview, Chief Forester Harry Hutchings assured readers of the *Vancouver Sun* that "the park's woodland is slowly being renewed. The people who tremble at the thought of even one tree being cut down have nothing to worry about." But an increasingly environmentally conscious (or self-conscious) citizenry had grown resistant to intrusions in the park. The depredations of Freda had made it all the more precious in the public mind and renewed a sense of responsibility to defend it against any kind of disturbance. Typhoon Freda constituted an opportunity to reconsider the role of disturbance in the park's past, but the board simply reinvigorated its pursuit of an elusive unsullied environment. And, just as in the 1930s, the erasure of Freda's impact served to cloud public memory. The twisted branches and splintered trunks of its collateral damage drifted quietly into the fog of the past, leaving no trace of nature's capacity to randomly frustrate our best intentions.[1]

No matter how hard the Park Board struggled to restore Stanley Park to a more desirable condition following Typhoon Freda, its task was as futile as that given to Sisyphus. As punishment for his hubris in believing that he was wiser than Zeus, Sisyphus was compelled to roll a large boulder up a hill, but the rock always escaped him before he reached the summit, and he would be forced to start again. Like Sisyphus, the board strove to undo the disorder brought by Freda, only to lose its grip on the boulder once again when several windstorms ripped through southwest BC in late 2006 and early 2007. They rivalled their predecessors of the past hundred years and gave Stanley Park a shakedown of a ferocity not known since the 1960s. Vancouverites stood in awe of the autonomy of nature and its capricious power.

In a reaction echoing that of 1962, shock and dismay filled the pages of local newspapers and magazines. The *Vancouver Sun* proclaimed that the 15 December 2006 storm was "one for the history books," and it was described as anomalous, or "freakish weather," just as in 1962 and 1934. In Stanley Park, "trees that had stood for centuries had their limbs ripped off. Hundreds more trees fell, from Garry oaks to giant cedars seeded before Captain George Vancouver's voyage of discovery in 1791." Reporters claimed that the city had lost many of its "ancient trees," despite the fact that very little old growth had remained.[2]

In the year following the storms, portions of the park were closed so that the board could carry out its latest restoration program. Through private and public contributions, it raised roughly $5.5 million for the Stanley Park Restoration Plan, but this time around, it did not simply erase evidence of the devastation. Instead, it strove to reconcile the interrelationship between nature and culture with persistent natural disturbance, stating that a "fundamental principle of the Stanley Park Restoration Plan was to ensure that all work be done in a manner that protects Stanley Park's natural and cultural environments, as well as park visitors, workers and volunteers." Its intent was to rebuild the park, recognizing both the natural and anthropogenic characteristics of its landscape and ecology, making evident the human labour required to construct and maintain it. Acknowledging the integrated and hybrid quality of the park, the restoration plan's vision statement called for the "forest [to] be a resilient coastal forest with a diversity of native tree and other species and habitats that allows park visitors to experience nature *in the city.*" This marked a turning point in board policy, establishing guidelines that recognized the fundamental connections between the park and its surrounding urban environment.[3]

During two years of restoration work, board staff worked closely with a group of experts to better understand the park's ecology and form a new forest management plan. Forestry scientists, biologists, and entomologists from the University of British Columbia as well as staff and volunteers from the Stanley Park Ecology Society conducted the most comprehensive scientific survey ever undertaken in the park, producing vast amounts of information about its ecology. They even discovered a species of rove beetle new to science, *Oxypoda stanleyi,* named for the park itself. In March 2009, the board approved a new forest management plan based on this exhaustive ecological review.[4]

The 2009 Stanley Park Forest Management Plan incorporates the main elements of the initial restoration program, including the overriding vision statement. Instead of seeking to reforest damaged sections with conifers and to wipe away the impact of the storms, the plan sets out the overall objective of encouraging the growth of "a diverse and resilient forest, with plant communities ideally suited to the underlying environmental conditions." Balancing public safety and the need to protect wildlife and plant habitats, it endorses the dispersal and retention of some damaged trees and debris for natural decay on the forest floor. It also recognizes that during the course of the longer restoration effort, "natural disturbances may occur at any time, and are expected to continue throughout the work." This awareness of persistent natural change, particularly from windthrow, is now embodied in a more flexible forest policy for Stanley Park. Finally, the plan acknowledges the human history of the peninsula, arguing that "the forest, while historically affected and manipulated by humans, remains a vibrant coastal rainforest of significant beauty with important ecological properties." By taking into account this history of natural and anthropogenic disturbance, the plan offers an encouraging new direction for the maintenance and development of this important Canadian urban forest.[5]

Far more than previous Park Board policies discussed in this book, the new management plan took ecological sciences into consideration. Richard West Sellars finds that this approach had been applied in US national parks since the 1960s and 1970s, influenced by the modern environmental movement, so the board was late in following suit. As mentioned above, though the environmental movement did play a role in the post-1962 approach to the park, its management was grounded more in popular memory than the ecological sciences.[6]

Not until the 1990s, following an acrimonious public debate regarding the Stanley Park Zoo did the board and the public begin to consider ecological sciences as a basis for management. In the early 1990s, responding to widespread criticism of the degrading conditions in the zoo, the board proposed to implement a new $9.1 million "interpretation and wildlife plan" to modernize the facilities once again: this time, a new conservation centre would be focused on the protection and rehabilitation of endangered indigenous species. At a public meeting, several Vancouverites voiced their opposition to the plan. Joe Arnaud, a West End resident, suggested that the board should "leave the park in its natural state. Stanley

Park is not an appropriate place for a zoo." Arnaud's remarks exemplified a new public attitude toward the management of animals in the park and the interrelationship between its "natural" conditions and its animal population. Despite very vocal opposition, the board approved the plan in 1993 by a five-to-two margin. Its chair, Nancy Chiavario, argued that what the board was "trying to do is make Stanley Park a place where people can learn about the wilds of the province and the habitats of animals who live there." She contended that the project would modernize the zoo and eliminate previous animal capture programs, focusing instead on rescue and rehabilitation.[7]

The subsequent uproar prompted city council to put the matter to a vote in a public referendum. Vancouverites were asked whether they wished to keep the petting zoo near the miniature railway and the children's farmyard and whether they supported "the first phase of replacing the existing animal exhibits around the miniature railway with British Columbia animal habitats focusing on endangered species, conservation and education." In the November 1993 referendum, 54.13 percent of voters rejected the upgrade proposal. This result left the newly elected Park Board with no choice but to dismantle and close the aging, inadequate zoo facilities. By 1996, most of the animals had been removed, leaving only Tuk, the thirty-five-year-old polar bear *(Ursus maritimus)* as the final resident in a site that had once housed specimens from across Canada and around the world.[8]

Voter rejection of the zoo upgrade obviously represented a diversity of interests, but it was clear that the public no longer approved the artificial introduction of new species, desiring instead that ecological sciences guide park policy. Even the board's proposed conservation and wildlife centre focused on fostering habitat and supporting native species. After the referendum, the former Stanley Park Zoological Society reconstituted as the Stanley Park Ecology Society and shifted its efforts toward conservation and nature education programs and providing ecological advice to the board.[9]

Stanley Park's history is filled with disturbance, as I hope this book has made plain. Not only have natural forces randomly altered the appearance and ecology of the peninsula, humans have been a part of that story for thousands of years. Their exploitation has brought many changes; as a village, as a logging camp, as a military site, and as a park, the park bears the legacies of its past. Even in its present incarnation as a protected space, it holds magnificent cultural value that has laid its own mark on the landscape. The preservation of any natural environment, including Stanley

Park, is both dependent on human intervention and beholden to alteration by non-human forces. Without the active human labour of the past century, the park would be very different today. Lost Lagoon would still be a muddy tidal flat; the forest would be littered with dead trees, which would periodically be consumed by summer fires; different animals would inhabit the woods and waters; there would be no sand at Second and Third Beaches; and shoreline erosion, without the protective seawall, would eventually change the shape of the peninsula. The human role in the park is inescapable.

Nonetheless, we must not naively assume that we can order nature as we please. Innumerable unforeseen consequences typically followed efforts to alter the park, as non-human forces produced feedback effects. Whether in the form of the rains that washed away the first road or the insects that defoliated the trees, material limits have always been placed on our capacity to manipulate natural surroundings. And no matter how much energy people expended in re-creating the park after Typhoon Freda, nature undid it all just forty-four years later and may do so again in the future.

If Stanley Park is a hybrid produced by a confluence of natural and cultural forces, its management policy must not rely on the assertion of control. Nor can it be guided by the illusory belief that nature can be kept undisturbed as long as humans are removed from the equation. What is needed is a critical realignment of human relations with the rest of nature, not just in park management but also in other areas of environmental policy. Carolyn Merchant suggests that we must adopt a new ethic of "partnership" with nature to "reinforce the idea that predictability, while still useful, is more limited than previously assumed and that nature, while in part a human construct and a representation, is also a real, material, autonomous agent." Environmental policy must account for the autonomy of nature as an irrational actor.[10]

This book also offers a constructive case for rethinking the ecological and social complexities of nature preservation and park policy by examining the interrelationship between nature, history, and memory. If we are to reconceptualize our place in Stanley Park, we must abandon the powerful nature myths that have guided our perceptions of it. This is a central challenge in preservation and park policy throughout North America. Nature can be a useful window into the past, but it is not a static representation of the past. Nature has a history. Inscribed in the landscape of Stanley Park, like words carved into a monument, are the values that human cultures have placed there at particular moments in history. Time has worn on these inscriptions, eroding parts of the message and covering the rest with a tangle of plant life. Environmental history enables us to clear away some of the overgrowth and attempt to decipher that inscription, understand the social and cultural forces that shaped its message, and determine the relationship between humans and the rest of nature that is reflected in the landscape.

Notes

Foreword: Between Art and Nature

1 Details of this office are limited. It was run by Thomas Mawson's second son, John William, with the assistance of Thomas's nephew Robert Mattocks, who was chief of staff. Thomas Mawson describes this venture in Thomas H. Mawson, *The Life and Work of an English Landscape Architect: An Autobiography by Thomas H. Mawson, FLS* (New York: Charles Scribner's Sons, 1927), 214: "I had gotten together the nucleus of a town-planning staff in Canada with a well-equipped office in Vancouver ... The help thus assured enabled us to work more expeditiously, and to check off our draft plans on the sites before submission to our clients, also to make such amendments as seemed desirable before returning these plans to our English office for final completion." Janet Waymark, *Thomas Mawson: Life, Gardens and Landscapes* (London: Francis Lincoln, 2009), 152, includes a photograph of the Vancouver office staff (including seven people) ca. 1913. John W. Mawson served with a Canadian regiment in the First World War, and the Vancouver office was closed in 1921. John W. later became the second director of town planning in New Zealand (1928-33). See Caroline Miller, "A Prophet in a Barren Land: The New Zealand Career of J.W. Mawson," in *The 21st Century City: Past/Present/Future, Proceedings of Seventh Australasian Urban History/Planning History Conference* (Geelong: Deakin University, 2004), 258-71.
2 For context, see Graeme Wynn, "The Rise of Vancouver," in *Vancouver and Its Region*, ed. Graeme Wynn and Timothy Oke (Vancouver: UBC Press, 1992), 69-145.
3 There is a portrait of Mawson in 1913, painted by Sir Hubert Herkomer, RA, as the frontispiece of Mawson, *The Life and Work of an English Landscape Architect*.
4 The quotations in this paragraph are drawn from Thomas H. Mawson, "Civic Art and Vancouver's Opportunity," *The Canadian Club of Vancouver: Addresses and Proceedings, 1911-1912*, 39-46.
5 The fullest account of Mawson's life is Waymark, *Thomas Mawson: Life, Gardens and Landscapes*.

6 Edward Hyams, *A History of Gardens and Gardening* (London: J.M. Dent and Sons, 1971), 299.

7 Thomas H. Mawson, *The Art and Craft of Garden Making* (London: B.T. Batsford, 1900).

8 Mawson, *The Life and Work of an English Landscape Architect,* 187.

9 Thomas H. Mawson, *Civic Art: Studies in Town Planning, Parks, Boulevards, and Open Spaces* (London: B.T. Batsford, 1911).

10 Details of itineraries from Mawson, *The Life and Work of an English Landscape Architect,* quote from 205.

11 Mawson, *The Life and Work of an English Landscape Architect,* 204.

12 Details of the different plans drawn up by Mawson, with some commentary on them, can be found in Thomas H. Mawson, "Vancouver: A City of Optimists," *Town Planning Review* 4 (1913): 7-12. During this pre–First World War period, Mawson also worked on town plans for Ottawa, Regina, Banff, and Calgary and was consulted on the designs for the universities of Saskatchewan, British Columbia, Dalhousie, and Calgary.

13 Fascination with unbuilt landscapes is on the rise. See Kathryn J. Oberdeck, "Archives of the Unbuilt Environment: Documents and Discourses of Imagined Space in Twentieth-Century Kohler, Wisconsin," in *Archive Stories: Facts, Fictions, and the Writing of History,* ed. Antoinette Burton (Chapel Hill: University of North Carolina Press, 2006), 251-74, and Jonathan Peyton, "Corporate Ecology: BC Hydro's Stikine-Iskut Project and the Unbuilt Environment," *Journal of Historical Geography* 37, 3 (2011): 358-69, as well as a continuing series of books from Dundurn Press of which Dorothy Mindenhall, *Unbuilt Victoria* (Toronto: Dundurn Press, 2012) and Stephanie White, *Unbuilt Calgary* (Toronto: Dundurn Press, 2012) are the most recent.

14 All quotations in this paragraph are from Mawson, "Civic Art and Vancouver's Opportunity."

15 Ibid. This account contains only a verbal description of Mawson's scheme; for later plans of versions of this preliminary word sketch, see Mawson, "Vancouver: A City of Optimists."

16 Waymark, *Thomas Mawson,* 164.

17 Terence Young, *Building San Francisco's Parks, 1850-1930* (Baltimore, MD: Johns Hopkins University Press, 2004), xi.

18 Anne Whiston Spirn, "Constructing Nature: The Legacy of Frederick Law Olmsted," in *Uncommon Ground: Rethinking the Human Place in Nature,* ed. William Cronon (New York: W.W. Norton, 1995), 91.

19 The use of the term *facade management* in this context traces back to Richard W. Sellars, *Preserving Nature in the National Parks: A History* (New Haven, CT: Yale University Press, 1997), 4-5.

20 Key contributions on these themes are William Cronon, "The Trouble with Wilderness: Or Getting Back to the Wrong Nature," in *Uncommon Ground,* ed. Cronon, 69-90; Louis S. Warren, *The Hunter's Game: Poachers and Conservationists in Twentieth-Century America* (New Haven, CT: Yale University Press, 1997); Karl Jacoby, *Crimes against Nature: Squatters, Poachers, Thieves, and the Hidden History of American Conservation* (Berkeley: University of California Press, 2001); and John Sandlos, *Hunters at the Margin: Native People and Wildlife Conservation in the Northwest Territories* (Vancouver: UBC Press, 2007).

21 Robert A.J. McDonald, "'Holy Retreat' or 'Practical Breathing Spot'? Class Perceptions of Vancouver's Stanley Park, 1910-1913," *Canadian Historical Review* 45, 2 (1984): 127-53; Jean Barman, *Stanley Park's Secret: The Forgotten Families of Whoi Whoi, Kanaka Ranch, and Brockton Point* (Madeira Park, BC: Harbour Publishing, 2004); Jean Barman, "Erasing

Indigeneity in Vancouver," in *Home Truths: Highlights from BC History,* ed. Richard Mackie and Graeme Wynn (Madeira Park, BC: Harbour Publishing, 2012), 171-205; W.C. McKee, "The History of the Vancouver Parks System, 1886-1929" (master's thesis, University of Victoria, 1976); and Diane Beverley Hinds, "The Evolution of Urban Public Park Design in Europe and America: Vancouver Adaptation to 1913" (master's thesis, University of British Columbia, 1979), the quote that follows is from Hinds's abstract.

22 Young, *Building San Francisco's Parks,* 1-4.

Introduction: Knowing Nature through History

1 "Powerless after the Storm," *Vancouver Sun,* 16 December 2006, B1.

2 The storms occurred on 15 December 2006, 5 January 2007, and 9 January 2007. Vancouver Board of Parks and Recreation, *Stanley Park Restoration Recommended Plan* (Vancouver: Vancouver Board of Parks and Recreation, 2007), 10.

3 Randy Shore, "The Pain in Our Heart," *Vancouver Sun,* 6 January 2007, A8.

4 Richard M. Steele, *The Stanley Park Explorer* (North Vancouver: Whitecap Books, 1985), 7.

5 See, for instance, "Vagrants Threat to 'Crown Jewel': Major Fire Could Destroy Stanley Park in an Hour," *Edmonton Journal,* 25 July 1992, C4; "Bryan Adams in Stanley Park? Forget It! Friends of Vancouver's Green Jewel Mount Stiff Opposition to the Project," *Edmonton Journal,* 25 July 1992, C4; "Vancouver's Crown Jewel Splintered," *Vancouver Province,* 7 September 2003, A4; "Logging Stanley Park; Board Announces Plan to Turn Toppled Trees into $1 Million Worth of Timber in City's Storm Damaged Crown Jewel," *Montreal Gazette,* 12 March 2007, A4.

6 Editorial, *Vancouver Sun,* 4 June 1936, 4; General Manager, Parks and Recreation, to Board of Parks and Recreation, "Stanley Park Causeway Staff Report" (10 July 2000), 2, http://former.vancouver.ca/parks/board/2000/000724/causerpt.pdf.

7 Alison Parkinson, ed., *Wilderness on the Doorstep: Discovering Nature in Stanley Park* (Surrey, BC: Harbour, 2006), 9; Terry Taylor, "Trees of Stanley Park," in ibid., 51; William F. Findlay, "Contemplated Improvements in Stanley Park May Disclose Another Siwash Rock," *Vancouver Province,* 7 February 1903, 14; "Stanley Park: City's Fine Heritage," *Vancouver Province,* 28 July 1906, 13; "Expert Says Park Best He Ever Saw," 20 December 1907, *Vancouver Province,* 1; "Stanley Park," *Vancouver Province,* 13 February 1915, 6; F.C. Wade, "Why Tramcars Should Not Be Allowed in Stanley Park," *Vancouver Province,* 1 December 1906, 12; "Lovers of Stanley Park Strongly Opposed to Lions' Gate Bridge," *Vancouver Province,* 17 October 1926, 8 (magazine section); *Stanley Park: World's Most Wonderful Natural Park* (n.p., 1936), PD289, City of Vancouver Archives (CVA); Ginny Evans and Beth Evans, *The Vancouver Guide Book* (Victoria, BC: Campbell's Publishing, 1980), 101; Paul Grant and Laurie Dickson, *The Stanley Park Companion* (Winlaw, BC: Bluefield Books, 2003), 8 (emphasis added).

8 "Storm and Restoration," in "Stanley Park: A Special Place," special issue, *British Columbia Magazine,* May 2007, 54.

9 For more on the meaning of wilderness and the social construction of nature, see Clarence Glacken, *Traces on the Rhodian Shore: Nature and Culture in Western Thought from Ancient Times to the End of the Eighteenth Century* (Berkeley: University of California Press, 1967); Max Oelschlaeger, *The Idea of Wilderness, from Prehistory to the Age of Ecology* (New Haven: Yale University Press, 1991); William Cronon, ed., *Uncommon Ground: Rethinking the Human Place in Nature* (New York: W.W. Norton, 1995); and Roderick Nash, *Wilderness and the American Mind,* 4th ed. (New Haven: Yale University Press, 2001).

10 Parks Canada and the Vancouver Board of Parks and Recreation, "Stanley Park National Historic Site: Commemorative Integrity Statement" (May 2004), 8.

11 Carl O. Sauer, "The Morphology of Landscape," in *Land and Life: A Selection from the Writings of Carl Ortwin Sauer,* ed. John Leighly (Berkeley: University of California Press, 1983), 321, originally published in *University of California Publications in Geography* 2, 2 (1925): 19-54.

12 Galen Cranz, *The Politics of Park Design: A History of Urban Parks in America* (Cambridge, MA: MIT Press, 1982).

13 Writing on the US National Park Service, Richard West Sellars refers to this as facade management, in *Preserving Nature in the National Parks: A History* (New Haven: Yale University Press, 1997), 4-5.

14 Marc Cioc and Char Miller, "Alfred Crosby," *Environmental History* 14, 3 (2009): 564; Donald Worster, "Appendix: Doing Environmental History," in *The Ends of the Earth: Perspectives on Modern Environmental History,* ed. Donald Worster (Cambridge: Cambridge University Press, 1988), 290. For an excellent discussion of nature as an autonomous agent, see Keekok Lee, "Is Nature Autonomous?" in *Recognizing the Autonomy of Nature: Theory and Practice,* ed. Thomas Heyd (New York: Columbia University Press, 2005), 54-74.

15 For more on the history of Canadian urban parks, see A.L. Murray, "Frederic Law Olmsted and the Design of Mount Royal Park," *Journal of the Society of Architectural Historians* 26 (1967): 163-71; Walter Van Nus, "The Fate of City Beautiful Thought in Canada, 1893-1930," *Canadian Historical Association, Historical Papers* 54 (1975): 191-210; Alan Metcalfe, "The Evolution of Organized Physical Recreation in Montreal, 1840-1895," *Histoire sociale/Social History* 11, 21 (1978): 144-66; Gene Howard Homel, "Sliders and Backsliders: Toronto's Sunday Tobogganing Controversy of 1912," *Urban History Review* 10, 2 (1981): 25-34; Robert A.J. McDonald, "Stanley Park: Vancouver's Forest Playground," *British Columbia Historical News* 15 (1982): 6-13; W.C. McKee, "The Vancouver Park System, 1886-1929: A Product of Local Businessmen," *Urban History Review* 7, 3 (1979): 33-49; George Woodcock, "Savage and Domestic: The Parks of Vancouver," *Journal of Garden History* 3, 3 (1983): 26-53; Robert A.J. McDonald, "'Holy Retreat' or 'Practical Breathing Spot'? Class Perceptions of Vancouver's Stanley Park, 1910-1913," *Canadian Historical Review* 45, 2 (1984): 127-53; Bruce Curtis, "The Playground in Nineteenth-Century Ontario: Theory and Practise," *Material History Bulletin* 22 (1985): 21-29; Barbara Schrodt, "Control of Sports Facilities in Early Vancouver: The Brockton Point Athletic Association at Stanley Park, 1880 to 1913," *Canadian Journal of History of Sport* 23, 2 (1992): 26-53; William Brennan, "Visions of a City Beautiful: The Origin and Impact of the Mawson Plans for Regina," *Saskatchewan History* 46 (1994): 19-33; Susan Mather, "One of Many Homes: Stories of Dispossession from 'Stanley Park'" (master's thesis, Simon Fraser University, 1998); John Selwood, John C. Lehr, and Mary Cavett, "'The Most Lovely and Picturesque City in All of Canada': The Origins of Winnipeg's Public Park System," *Manitoba History* 31 (1996): 21-29; David Bain, "The Early Pleasure Grounds of Toronto," *Ontario History* 91, 2 (1999): 165-82; Lyle Dick, "Commemorative Integrity and Cultural Landscapes: Two National Historic Sites in British Columbia," *Association for Preservation Technology Bulletin* 31, 4 (2000): 29-36; Ken Cruikshank and Nancy B. Bouchier, "'The Heritage of the People Closed against Them': Class, Environment, and the Shaping of Burlington Beach," *Urban History Review* 30, 1 (2001): 40-55; Michèle Dagenais, "Entre tradition et modernité: Espaces et temps de loisirs à Montréal et Toronto au xxe siècle," *Canadian Historical Review* 82, 2 (2001): 307-30; David Bain, "The Queen's Park and Its Avenues: Canada's First Public Park," *Ontario History* 95, 2 (2003): 192-215; Jean Barman, *Stanley Park's Secret: The Forgotten Families of*

Whoi Whoi, Kanaka Ranch and Brockton Point (Vancouver: Harbour, 2005); H.V. Nelles, "How Did Calgary Get Its River Parks?" *Urban History Review* 34, 1 (2005): 28-45; Sean Kheraj, "Restoring Nature: Ecology, Memory, and the Storm History of Vancouver's Stanley Park," *Canadian Historical Review* 88, 4 (2007): 577-612; and Sean Kheraj, "Improving Nature: Remaking Stanley Park's Forest, 1888-1931," *BC Studies* 158 (2008): 63-90.

16 The literature on Frederick Law Olmsted is extensive, but see Frederick Law Olmsted, *Public Parks and the Enlargement of Towns* (1870; repr., New York: Arno Press, 1970); Laura Wood Roper, *FLO: A Biography of Frederick Law Olmsted* (Baltimore: Johns Hopkins University Press, 1973); Cynthia Zaitzevsky, *Frederick Law Olmsted and the Boston Park System* (Cambridge: Belknap Press, 1982); and Charles E. Beveridge, *Frederick Law Olmsted: Designing the American Landscape* (New York: Rizzoli, 1995). It should be noted that British landscape architecture played only an indirect role in shaping Canadian urban park design. Although Olmsted and his followers were initially influenced by some of Britain's early landscape principles, including those of Capability Brown and Humphrey Repton, there is little evidence that their work had much impact in Canada. British landscape architect Thomas Mawson, who reappears in Chapter 3, provided a number of plans and visions for Canadian cities prior to 1914, most of which were never implemented.

17 Tina Loo, *States of Nature: Conserving Canada's Wildlife in the Twentieth Century* (Vancouver: UBC Press, 2006), 29-35; see also T.J. Jackson Lears, *No Place of Grace: Antimodernism and the Transformation of American Culture, 1880-1920* (New York: Pantheon, 1981); and Ian McKay, *The Quest of the Folk: Antimodernism and Cultural Selection in Twentieth-Century Nova Scotia* (Montreal and Kingston: McGill-Queen's University Press, 1994).

18 Terence Young, *Building San Francisco's Parks, 1850-1930* (Baltimore: Johns Hopkins University Press, 2004). Young's model of the four virtues succinctly synthesizes other writing on the American parks movement. For a discussion of an early-twentieth-century attempt to attract real estate investment, in this case through the use of San Diego's Balboa Park, see Mike Davis, "The Next Little Dollar: The Private Governments of San Diego," in Mike Davis, Kelly Mayhew, and Jim Miller, *Under the Perfect Sun: The San Diego Tourists Never See* (New York: New Press, 2005), 17-144.

19 Towns such as New York City, Worcester (in Massachusetts), St. Paul, San Francisco, San Diego, and Winnipeg serve as examples of this argument. See Roy Rosenzweig and Elizabeth Blackmar, *The Park and the People: A History of Central Park* (Ithaca: Cornell University Press, 1992); Roy Rosenzweig, "Middle-Class Parks and Working-Class Play: The Struggle over Recreational Space in Worcester, Massachusetts, 1870-1910," *Radical History Review* 21 (1979): 31-46; Andrew J. Schmidt, "Pleasure and Recreation for the People: Planning St. Paul's Como Park," *Minnesota History* 58, 1 (2002): 40-58; Young, *Building San Francisco's Parks;* G.E. Montes, "San Diego's City Park, 1868-1902: An Early Debate on Environment and Profit," *Journal of San Diego History* 23 (1977): 40-59; and Selwood, Lehr, and Cavett, "'The Most Lovely and Picturesque City,'" 21-29.

20 Most historians use this periodization. Cranz's seminal work, *The Politics of Park Design,* sharply draws the line at 1900 between what she calls the romantic park and the reform park. Terence Young builds upon Cranz's model, arguing that the transition occurs at different times in different US cities, though it first occurred during the late nineteenth century. An important distinction between the studies of Cranz and Young is that the latter focuses on cultural and environmental aspects, whereas the former employs a sociological approach. Also, Young uses the term "rationalistic" rather than "reform" for the second design phase, following Samuel P. Hays, *Conservation and the Gospel of Efficiency:*

The Progressive Conservation Movement (Cambridge, MA: Harvard University Press, 1959). Young sees the second phase as comparable to the progressive conservation movement in which planners sought a more efficient use and development of natural resources. David Schuyler also draws a similar comparison in *The New Urban Landscape: The Redefinition of City Form in Nineteenth-Century America* (Baltimore: Johns Hopkins Press, 1986). For an examination of nineteenth-century thought regarding the nervous stress caused by modern urban life, see Lears, *No Place of Grace.*

21 The playground movement was also current in Canadian cities such as Montreal and Vancouver. See Metcalfe, "The Evolution of Organized Physical Recreation in Montreal"; and W.C. McKee, "The History of the Vancouver Park System, 1886-1929" (master's thesis, University of Victoria, 1976). For more on working-class perspectives on leisure in urban parks, see Peter Bailey, *Leisure and Class in Victorian England: Rational Recreation and the Contest for Control, 1830-1885* (Toronto: University of Toronto Press, 1978); Rosenzweig, "Middle-Class Parks and Working-Class Play"; and McDonald, "'Holy Retreat' or 'Practical Breathing Spot'?"

22 W.C. McKee makes the case that American models largely influenced the park system in Vancouver. Others, such as George Woodcock and Robert A.J. McDonald, support his argument. See Woodcock, "Savage and Domestic"; McDonald, "'Holy Retreat' or 'Practical Breathing Spot'?" Although the parks of some Canadian cities, such as Toronto and Halifax, pre-dated the creation of Central Park, the larger movement for urban parks did not begin in Canada until the construction of Montreal's Mount Royal Park, which was landscaped and designed by Frederick Law Olmsted during the 1870s. Later examples, such as Assiniboine Park in Winnipeg, were designed by Frederick Todd, a Montreal landscape architect influenced by Olmsted.

23 In Canada and the United States, railway corporations played a prominent role in the promotion of the national park idea. See Leslie Bella, *Parks for Profit* (Montreal: Harvest House, 1987); Alfred Runte, *Yosemite: The Embattled Wilderness* (Lincoln: University of Nebraska Press, 1990); Alfred Runte, *National Parks: The American Experience,* 3rd ed. (Lincoln: University of Nebraska Press, 1997); and S.A. Germic, *American Green Class: Crisis and the Deployment of Nature in Central Park, Yosemite, and Yellowstone* (Lanham, MD: Lexington Books, 2001).

24 Alan MacEachern, "In Search of Eastern Beauty: Creating National Parks in Atlantic Canada, 1935-1970" (PhD diss., Queen's University, 1997), 20.

Chapter 1: Before Stanley Park

1 Al Birnie, "Time, Tide Wait for No Man – Seawall Battle Continues," *Vancouver Sun,* 24 July 1964, 14.

2 Board Minutes, 10 February 1915 and 15 September 1916, Board of Parks and Recreation fonds (Park Board), MCR 47-2, City of Vancouver Archives (CVA).

3 Ibid., 10 January 1917; 13 October 1920, MCR 47-4; 27 February 1967, MCR 47-9; 22 February 1921, MCR 47-4; 12 April 1921, MCR 47-4; W.D. Harvie, Secretary of the Vancouver Harbour Commission, to the Deputy Minister of Marine and Fisheries, 15 April 1921, Correspondence, Stanley Park, 1920-21, Park Board, 49-B-5, file 2, CVA.

4 "Toughest Section Remains in Building Park Seawall," *Vancouver Sun,* 3 October 1963, 41; "James Cunningham's Granite Monument," *Vancouver Province,* 4 October 1963, 4; Board Minutes, 11 July 1917, Park Board, MCR 47-3, CVA; Annual Reports, 1917, Park Board, PDS 12, CVA.

5 Mike Davis, *Dead Cities and Other Tales* (New York: New Press, 2002), 361; Roger Hooke, "On the History of Humans as Geomorphic Agents," *Geology* 28, 9 (2000): 843; Christopher Armstrong, Matthew Evenden, and H.V. Nelles, *The River Returns: An Environmental History of the Bow* (Montreal and Kingston: McGill-Queen's University Press, 2009), 389.

6 John Clague and Bob Turner, *Vancouver, City on the Edge: Living with a Dynamic Geological Landscape* (Vancouver: Tricouni, 2003), 39; O. Slaymaker et al., "The Primordial Environment," in *Vancouver and Its Region,* ed. Graeme Wynn and Timothy Oke (Vancouver: UBC Press, 1992), 20.

7 G.C. Rogers, "An Assessment of the Megathrust Earthquake Potential of the Cascadia Subduction Zone," *Canadian Journal of Earth Sciences* 25 (1988): 846; D.R. Muhs et al., "Pacific Coast and Mountain System," in *Geomorphic Systems of North America,* ed. W.L. Graf (Boulder, CO: Geological Society of America, 1987), 2:528; Clague and Turner, *Vancouver, City on the Edge,* 24; John E. Armstrong, *Vancouver Geology* (Vancouver: Geological Association of Canada, 1990), 28-29.

8 J.A. Roddick, *Capsule Geology of the Vancouver Area and Teacher's Field-Trip Guide* (Vancouver: Geological Survey of Canada, 2001), 13; Armstrong, *Vancouver Geology,* 40; R.J.W. Turner et al., *Vancouver Rocks,* Geological Survey of Canada, Miscellaneous Report no. 68 (n.p.: Geological Survey of Canada, 2000).

9 Clague and Turner, *Vancouver, City on the Edge,* 35; Slaymaker et al., "The Primordial Environment," 20; Muhs et al., "Pacific Coast and Mountain System," 533-38; Armstrong, *Vancouver Geology,* 49.

10 Clague and Turner, *Vancouver, City on the Edge,* 57; David M. Schaepe, "The Land and the People: Glaciation to Contact," in *A Stó:lō–Coast Salish Historical Atlas,* ed. Keith Thor Carlson (Vancouver: Douglas and McIntyre, 2001), 18; Slaymaker et al., "The Primordial Environment," 22.

11 Roy H. Blunden, "Vancouver's Downtown (Coal) Peninsula: Urban Geology" (B.Sc. thesis, University of British Columbia, 1971), 23-36.

12 Slaymaker et al., "The Primordial Environment," 32. V.J. Krajina describes biogeoclimatic zones as "geographical segments of the earth's climate, soil and biota that are characterized by the same general macroclimate and the same zonal soil and biota." V.J. Krajina, "Biogeoclimatic Zones and Classification of British Columbia," *Ecology of Western North America* 1 (1965): 3. See also Richard J. Hebda, "British Columbia Vegetation and Climate History with Focus on 6 KA BP," *Géographie Physique et Quaternaire* 49 (1995): 55-79; and Stanley Park Ecology Society, *State of the Park: Report for the Ecological Integrity of Stanley Park* (Vancouver: Stanley Park Ecology Society, 2010), 46.

13 Leland Donald, "The Northwest Coast as a Study Area: Natural, Prehistoric, and Ethnographic Issues," in *Emerging from the Mist: Studies in Northwest Coast Culture History,* ed. R.G. Matson, Gary Coupland, and Quentin Mackie (Vancouver: UBC Press, 2003), 296; Knut Fladmark, *A Paleoecological Model for Northwest Coast Prehistory,* National Museum of Man Mercury Series, Archaeological Survey of Canada, no. 43 (Ottawa: National Museum of Man, 1975).

14 British Columbia Ministry of Tourism, Sport and the Arts, Archaeology Branch, "Stanley Park, Resource Management Report" (2006), 43.

15 Susan Roy's insightful article in a recent special issue of *BC Studies* argues that early archaeologists, such as Charles Hill-Tout, refused to link the archaeological evidence from the Marpole Midden in South Vancouver to a continuous human occupation connected with the neighbouring Musqueam people. For most of the twentieth century, archaeologists in the Lower Mainland stubbornly held to the belief that Vancouver was first occupied by

an ancient Aboriginal race that was later displaced by the Native people of the historic period. This, of course, contributed to the process of dispossession. For more, see Susan Roy, "'Who Were These Mysterious People?' C'əsna:m, the Marpole Midden, and the Dispossession of Aboriginal Lands in British Columbia," *BC Studies* 152 (2006-07): 67-95; and Susan Roy, *These Mysterious People: Shaping History and Archaeology in a Northwest Coast Community* (Montreal and Kingston: McGill-Queen's University Press, 2010).

16 Robert Boyd, *The Coming of the Spirit of Pestilence: Introduced Infectious Diseases and Population Decline among Northwest Coast Indians, 1774-1874* (Vancouver: UBC Press, 1999), 265. Kenneth Ames and Herbert D.G. Maschner argue that the region's Aboriginal population peaked between AD 1000 and 1100, after which it steadily declined in response to climatic and vegetative changes. Kenneth M. Ames and Herbert D.G. Maschner, *Peoples of the Northwest Coast: Their Archaeology and Prehistory* (London: Thames and Hudson, 1999), 55.

17 Carlson, *A Stó:lō–Coast Salish Historical Atlas*, 76.

18 Randy Shore, "Before Stanley Park: First Nations Sites Lie Scattered Throughout the Area," *Vancouver Sun*, 17 March 2007, B1.

19 John C. Goodfellow, *The Totem Poles in Stanley Park* (Vancouver: Art, Historical, and Scientific Association of Vancouver, c. 1920), 13, 26-29, 42-43; "Fund for Park Curios Near $800," *Vancouver Sun*, 4 December 1921, 18; Robert Allison Hood, *By Shore and Trail in Stanley Park* (Toronto: McClelland and Stewart, 1929), 83-85; Harlan I. Smith, "A List of Petroglyphs in British Columbia," *American Anthropologist* 29, 4 (1927): 609. Known for a time as the Shelly Stone, this priceless petroglyph sat in Stanley Park near Lumbermen's Arch until it was relocated to the Vancouver Museum in 1992. Controversy arose when University of Victoria archaeologist Quentin Mackie recently discovered that it was kept outdoors in a museum courtyard garden, where it had been irreparably damaged due to exposure to the elements. See Quentin Mackie, "One More Update on the Museum of Vancouver's Petroglyph," 14 March 2012, Northwest Coast Archaeology, http://qmackie.wordpress.com/. Due to the efforts of the Stswecem'c Xgat'tem First Nation, Vancouver Museum staff, Professor Bruce Miller from the UBC Department of Anthropology, and archaeologist Chris Arnett, the petroglyph has since been returned to its indigenous territory. See Joan Seidl, "The Joy of Giving Back," *The Tyee*, 12 June 2012, http://thetyee.ca/.

20 George H. Raley, *Our Totem Poles: A Souvenir of Vancouver* (Vancouver, 1937), 5-6.

21 Susan Mather, "One of Many Homes: Stories of Dispossession from 'Stanley Park'" (master's thesis, Simon Fraser University, 1998); Jean Barman, *Stanley Park's Secret: The Forgotten Families of Whoi Whoi, Kanaka Ranch and Brockton Point* (Vancouver: Harbour, 2005); Renisa Mawani, "Imperial Legacies (Post) Colonial Identities: Law, Space and the Making of Stanley Park, 1859-2001," *Law Text Culture* 7 (2003): 98-141; Renisa Mawani, "Genealogies of the Land: Aboriginality, Law, and Territory in Vancouver's Stanley Park," *Social and Legal Studies* 14, 3 (2005): 315-39; Archaeology Branch, "Stanley Park, Resource Management Report."

22 James Skitt Matthews, *Early Vancouver* (1933; repr., Vancouver: City of Vancouver Archives, 2011), 2:1. The *Stó:lō–Coast Salish Historical Atlas* records eleven place names in Stanley Park. Carlson, *A Stó:lō–Coast Salish Historical Atlas*, 138.

23 For more on Andrew Paull, see E. Palmer Patterson, "Andrew Paull and the Early History of British Columbia Indian Organizations," in *One Century Later: Western Canadian Reserve Indians since Treaty 7*, ed. Ian A.L. Getty and Donald B. Smith (Vancouver: UBC Press, 1978), 43-54; and Brendan F.R. Edwards, "'I Have Lots of Help behind Me, Lots of Books

to Convince You': Andrew Paull and the Value of Literacy in English," *BC Studies* 164 (2009-10): 7-30.

24 Edwards, "'I Have Lots of Help behind Me,'" 30; Andy Paull, "The Battle-Ground of Stanley Park" *Vancouver Sun*, 26 March 1938, 4; Matthews, *Early Vancouver*, 2:20, 2:16C; J.S. Matthews, *Conversations with Khatsalano, 1932-1954* (Vancouver: City Archives, 1955), 8, 196-97; Matthews, *Early Vancouver*, 5:256; Barman, *Stanley Park's Secret*, 19. I want to thank Victor Guerin and his father, Delbert Victor Guerin, for helping to clarify some of the Aboriginal history, with particular attention to the pre-reserve era interconnections between the Musqueam and the Squamish, which persist to the present day.

25 Matthews chose this spelling, but it was sometimes given as xw'ay xway. According to his Squamish and Musqueam interviewees, Whoi Whoi means "place of masks." See Barman, *Stanley Park's Secret*, 21.

26 Matthews, *Early Vancouver*, 2:20, 2:111, 7:190.

27 Ibid., 2:252.

28 Ibid., 3:282.

29 Charles Hill-Tout, "Notes on the Skqomic [Squamish] of British Columbia, a Branch of the Great Salish Stock of North America," in Charles Hill-Tout, *The Salish People: The Local Contribution of Charles Hill-Tout*, vol. 2, *The Squamish and the Lillooet*, edited by Ralph Maud (Vancouver: Talonbooks, 1978), 51, originally published in *Report of the British Association for the Advancement of Science*, 70th meeting, 1900.

30 The studies cited in this chapter use uncalibrated radiocarbon dates unless otherwise indicated. Archaeology Branch, "Stanley Park, Resource Management Report," DhRs-3, 48.

31 Since 1955, there have been at least six archaeological investigations of DhRs-2. Ibid., DhRs-2, 17.

32 Matthews, *Conversations with Khatsalano*, 280.

33 Matthews, *Early Vancouver*, 3:282.

34 Matthews, *Conversations with Khatsalano*, 198.

35 David R. Croes, "Northwest Coast Wet-Site Artifacts: A Key to Understanding Resource Procurement, Storage, Management and Exchange," in Matson, Coupland, and Mackie, *Emerging from the Mist*, 51; Matthews, *Early Vancouver*, 4:48, 3:9; Archaeology Branch, "Stanley Park, Resource Management Report," DhRs-305, 71; Arnold H. Styrd and Vicki Feddemma, *Sacred Cedar: The Cultural and Archaeological Significance of Culturally Modified Trees*, A Report of the Pacific Salmon Forests Project (Vancouver: David Suzuki Foundation, 1998), 19.

36 Matthews, *Conversations with Khatsalano*, 2-3; Archaeology Branch, "Stanley Park, Resource Management Report," DhRs-79, 125.

37 Archaeology Branch, "Stanley Park, Resource Management Report," DhRs-7, 115, DhRs-303, 64; Matthews, *Early Vancouver*, 2:23-24.

38 Matthews, *Early Vancouver*, 2:17; Matthews, *Conversations with Khatsalano*, 27; Archaeology Branch, "Stanley Park, Resource Management Report," 106.

39 Matthews, *Early Vancouver*, 2:17; E. Pauline Johnson, *Legends of Vancouver* (1911; repr., Toronto: Douglas and McIntyre, 1997), 10.

40 Vancouver's depiction of Stanley Park as an island was not necessarily incorrect. The isthmus that joins downtown Vancouver to the park was originally so low lying that, at high tide, the waters of Coal Harbour washed across it and connected with English Bay, cutting off the peninsula from the rest of the Burrard uplands. The isthmus was raised with sand and landfill on a number of occasions during the early twentieth century.

41 George Vancouver, *A Voyage of Discovery to the North Pacific Ocean and round the World, 1791-1795,* edited by W. Kaye Lamb (London: Hakluyt Society, 1984), 2:582; R. Cole Harris, ed., *The Resettlement of British Columbia: Essays on Colonialism and Geographical Change* (Vancouver: UBC Press, 1997), 12.

42 Alfred Crosby, *The Columbian Exchange: Biological and Cultural Consequences of 1492* (Westport, CT: Greenwood, 1973), 3.

43 Boyd, *The Coming of the Spirit of Pestilence,* 22; Harris, *The Resettlement of British Columbia,* 4, 26.

44 "Report of the British Columbia Reserve Commission with Census Reports," Department of Indian Affairs, RG 10, vol. 3645, file 7936, Library and Archives Canada (LAC); Matthews, *Early Vancouver,* 2:20; Matthews, *Conversations with Khatsalano,* 25.

45 Hill-Tout, "Notes on the Skqomic Skqomic," 53-54.

46 Ibid., 22.

47 Matthews, *Early Vancouver,* 2:333.

48 Vancouver, *A Voyage of Discovery,* 2:543.

49 Governor James Douglas to Lord Stanley, M.P., 10 June 1858, Deadman's Island Land Use Privy Council Records Collection, Proceedings and Judgement, 1905-1906, Add. MSS. 202, 513-E-4, file 1 (Deadman's Island Land Use), CVA.

50 E.B. Lytton to Colonel R.C. Moody, 29 October 1858, Deadman's Island Land Use, CVA.

51 Colonel R.C. Moody to E.B. Lytton, 28 January 1859, Deadman's Island Land Use, CVA.

52 British Columbia, *Proclamations and Ordinances, 1858-1864* (Victoria and New Westminster, 1858-64); Colonel Moody to James Douglas, 13 December 1859, Deadman's Island Land Use, CVA; F.W Howay, "Early Settlement on Burrard Inlet," *British Columbia Historical Quarterly* 1, 2 (1937): 102-3; Barman, *Stanley Park's Secret,* 261.

53 E.B. Lytton to Colonel R.C. Moody, 29 October 1858, Deadman's Island Land Use, CVA.

54 "Report by Geo. H. Richards, Capt. of Survey Ship, 'Plumper' to H.E. Governor Douglas" (23 October 1858); Captain G.H. Richards to Governor James Douglas, 14 June 1859, Colonial Correspondence, GR-1372, B01349-1217, British Columbia Archives (BCA).

55 "Letter from Charles B. Wood to Captain Geo. H. Richards," 14 June 1859, Appendix 1 in Blunden, "Vancouver's Downtown (Coal) Peninsula"; Richards to Douglas, 14 June 1859.

56 Anne Burnaby McLeod and Pixie McGeachie, eds., *Land of Promise: Robert Burnaby's Letters from Colonial British Columbia, 1858-1863* (Burnaby: City of Burnaby, 2002), 101.

57 Ibid., 102.

58 Ibid., 104 (emphasis in original).

59 Ibid., 109 (emphasis in original).

60 Barman, *Stanley Park's Secret,* 26; H.P.P. Crease to Colonel Moody, 5 March 1860, Colonial Correspondence, GR-1372, B01322, item 392, BCA; R.C. Moody to W.R. Spalding, 20 January 1860, Department of Lands and Works, GR-1404, BCA.

61 Pre-emption Notices, 3 November 1862, GR-0567, box 2, file 28, BCA.

62 "Proceedings and Judgement, 1905-1906," Deadman's Island Land Use, CVA.

63 Bruce Macdonald, *Vancouver: A Visual History* (Vancouver: Talon Books, 1992), 14-15.

64 Pioneer Mills advertisement, *New Westminster British Columbian,* 18 July 1863, 3; 26 November 1862, 1; Robert A.J. McDonald, "Lumber Society on the Industrial Frontier: Burrard Inlet, 1863-1886," *Labour/Le Travail* 33 (1994): 78; Stephen Gray, "The Government Timber Business: Forest Policy and Administration in British Columbia, 1912-1928," *BC Studies* 81 (1989): 24-49.

65 T.A. Rickard, "Gilbert Malcolm Sproat," *British Columbia Historical Quarterly* 1, 1 (1937): 21; James Morton, *The Enterprising Mr. Moody, the Bumptious Captain Stamp: The Lives*

and Colourful Times of Vancouver's Lumber Pioneers (North Vancouver: J.J. Douglas, 1977), 25. I borrow the phrase "turning trees into dollars" from Gordon Hak, *Turning Trees into Dollars: The British Columbia Coastal Lumber Industry, 1858-1913* (Toronto: University of Toronto Press, 2000).

66 Edward Stamp to Arthur Birch, 17 May 1865, Colonial Correspondence, GR-1372, B01366, item 1643, BCA; *The British Columbia and Vancouver Island Spar Lumber and Saw Mill Company Limited Act of Incorporation,* 1865, Department of Lands and Works, GR-1404, file 5, BCA; A.N. Birch to Edward Stamp, 20 May 1865, Stamp's Mill Burrard Inlet, MS-0120, file 1, BCA; Edward Stamp to A.N. Birch, 30 May 1865, Hastings Sawmill Company fonds, box 1, University of British Columbia Special Collections (UBCSC).

67 J.B. Launders to A.N. Birch, 3 June 1865; Chartes Brew to A.N. Birch, 7 June 1865, both in Colonial Correspondence, GR-1372, B01343, item 969, BCA.

68 Edward Stamp to A.N. Birch, 18 July 1865, Hastings Sawmill Company fonds, box 1, UBCSC.

69 *The British Columbia and Vancouver Island Spar Lumber and Saw Mill Company Limited Act of Incorporation,* 1865.

70 Robert E. Cail, *Land, Many, and the Law: The Disposal of Crown Lands in British Columbia, 1871-1913* (Vancouver: UBC Press, 1974), 92.

71 A.N. Birch to H.P.P. Crease, 30 September 1865; Burrard Inlet Timber Lease, 13 January 1866, both in Stamp's Mill Burrard Inlet, MS-0120, file 1, BCA.

72 H.P.P. Crease to Joseph W. Trutch, 4 January 1867, Colonial Correspondence, GR-1372, B01322, item 392, BCA.

73 Edward Stamp to A.N. Birch, 24 January 1867, Hastings Sawmill Company fonds, box 1, UBCSC.

74 Charles Good to Joseph W. Trutch, 30 October 1867, Deadman's Island Land Use, CVA; Joseph W. Trutch to H.P.P. Crease, 23 December 1867, Stamp's Mill Burrard Inlet, MS-0120, file 1, BCA; Charles Good to Edward Stamp, 27 December 1867, Hastings Sawmill Company fonds, box 1, UBCSC.

75 Joseph W. Trutch to Edward Stamp, 11 January 1868, Hastings Sawmill Company fonds, box 1, UBCSC; Morton, *The Enterprising Mr. Moody,* 81; Editorial, *New Westminster British Columbian,* 2 May 1868, 2; 11 July 1868, 1 (emphasis in original).

76 Editorial, *New Westminster British Columbian,* 5 August 1868, 2.

77 W.A.C. Young to Edward Stamp, 25 November 1868, Hastings Sawmill Company fonds, box 1, UBCSC; Cail, *Land, Many, and the Law,* 93-94.

78 Copy of Timber Lease Granted to Mr. Rogers, Deadman's Island Land Use, CVA; "Council Asked to Resign," *Victoria Daily-Colonist,* 29 April 1899, 2; Cail, *Land, Many, and the Law,* 96; Richard Rajala, "The Forest as Factory: Technological Change and Worker Control in the West Coast Logging Industry, 1880-1930," *Labour/Le Travail* 32 (1993): 77.

79 For more on Bailey and his work, see David Mattison, *Eyes of a City: Early Vancouver Photographers, 1868-1900* (Vancouver: City of Vancouver Archives, 1986).

80 Margaret A. Ormsby, *British Columbia: A History* (1958; repr., Toronto: Macmillan of Canada, 1976), 107.

81 Alfred Crosby, *Ecological Imperialism: The Biological Expansion of Europe, 900-1900* (Cambridge: Cambridge University Press, 1986), 2.

82 Virginia DeJohn Anderson, *Creatures of Empire: How Domestic Animals Transformed Early America* (Oxford: Oxford University Press, 2004), 38. Although Northwest Coast Native people did have traditions of proprietorship over fishing sites, they did not perceive living creatures as property.

83 Vancouver, *A Voyage of Discovery,* 2:548; Matthews, *Conversations with Khatsalano,* 34; John Keast Lord, *The Naturalist in Vancouver Island and British Columbia* (London: R. Bentley, 1866), 2:217; Anderson, *Creatures of Empire,* 34.

84 For more on the European settlers at Brockton Point, see Jean Barman, *The Remarkable Adventures of Portuguese Joe Silvey* (Madeira Park, BC: Harbour, 2004); and Barman, *Stanley Park's Secret.*

85 Park 1923, Maps Collection, Map 06, CVA; Mather, "One of Many Homes," 80; *Attorney General of Canada and City of Vancouver v. Alfred Gonzalves,* 971.133 v22ca, Vancouver Public Library Special Collections.

86 Douglas C. Harris, *Fish, Law, and Colonialism: The Legal Capture of Salmon in British Columbia* (Toronto: University of Toronto Press, 2001), 15; Dianne Newell, *Tangled Webs of History: Indians and the Law in Canada's Pacific Coast Fisheries* (Toronto: University of Toronto Press, 1993), 46-47.

87 Matthews, *Conversations with Khatsalano,* 62, 252; Macdonald, *Vancouver: A Visual History,* 24.

88 Matthews, *Conversations with Khatsalano,* 18.

89 Ibid., 36. Wayne Suttles has documented the early adoption of potatoes from Fort Langley among the Coast Salish as evidence of a pre-existing Aboriginal agricultural knowledge. Wayne Suttles, "Coast Salish Resource Management: Incipient Agriculture?" in *Keeping It Living: Traditions of Plant Use and Cultivation on the Northwest Coast of North America,* ed. Douglas Deur and Nancy J. Turner (Vancouver: UBC Press, 2005), 183-91.

90 Matthews, *Conversations with Khatsalano,* 36.

91 Ibid., 114.

92 Ibid.; "Report of the British Columbia Reserve Commission."

93 R. Cole Harris, *Making Native Space: Colonialism, Resistance, and Reserves in British Columbia* (Vancouver: UBC Press, 2002), xxviii, 98-99.

94 Ibid., 87.

95 Alexander Caulfield Anderson, *The Dominion at the West: A Brief Description of the Province of British Columbia, Its Climate and Resources* (Victoria: R. Wolfenden, 1872), 60, 80.

96 Gilbert Malcolm Sproat, *Scenes and Studies of Savage Life* (London: Smith, Elder, 1868), 7-8.

97 James Douglas to the Colonial Secretary, 14 March 1859, Colonial Correspondence, 1857-1872, GR-1372, B01325, item 485, BCA; Sproat, *Scenes and Studies of Savage Life,* 8.

98 Gilbert Malcolm Sproat, *British Columbia; Information for Emigrants* (London: W. Clowes, 1873), 7.

99 "Commission to Fix and Determine the Number, Extent, and Locality of the Reserve or Reserves to Be Allowed to the Indians of British Columbia," Gilbert Malcolm Sproat to the Minister of the Interior, 27 November 1876, *Canadian Royal Commission Reports* (Ottawa, 1876), n.p.

100 "Report of the British Columbia Reserve Commission."

101 Diary of Archibald McKinley, 1876-1877, Archibald McKinley fonds, E/C/M21, BCA.

102 G.M. Sproat to A.C. Elliot, 27 November 1876, Indian Reserve Commission, 1876-1878, GR-0494, box 1, file 4, BCA.

103 Diary of Archibald McKinley; "Report of the British Columbia Reserve Commission."

104 "Commission to Fix and Determine"; Sproat to Elliot, 27 November 1876; Barman, *Stanley Park's Secret,* 40.

105 Diary of Archibald McKinley; Archibald McKinley and G.M. Sproat to F.G. Vernon, Chief Commissioner of Lands and Works, 27 November 1876, Joint Reserve Commission, GR-2982, box 1, file 1 2935/76, BCA; Sproat to Elliot, 27 November 1876.

Chapter 2: Making the Park Public

1 I borrow the term "non-consumptive use" from Tina Loo's *States of Nature,* in which she argues that Canadian wildlife conservation at the turn of the century sought to manage wildlife for non-consumptive purposes and to eliminate the use of wild animals for food and individual trade. Tina Loo, *States of Nature: Conserving Canada's Wildlife in the Twentieth Century* (Vancouver: UBC Press, 2006). Similarly, park advocates in Vancouver strove to protect Stanley Park solely for recreational purposes by outlawing the consumptive uses of its resources. Although tourism has had a direct ecological impact on the park, which could be described as recreational consumption, I make a distinction on this point because tourist use is not for private profit and is conducted under the authority of the Vancouver Park Board.

2 For use of the term "emparkment," see Joe Hermer, *Regulating Eden: The Nature of Order in North American Parks* (Toronto: University of Toronto Press, 2002).

3 Ari Kelman, *A River and Its City: The Nature of Landscape in New Orleans* (Berkeley: University of California Press, 2003), 12.

4 Jacoby derives his terminology from E.P. Thompson's notion of a moral economy among the English working class in its struggle over the repeal of the corn laws. Karl Jacoby, *Crimes against Nature: Squatters, Poachers, Thieves, and the Hidden History of American Conservation* (Berkeley: University of California Press, 2001).

5 Irene Spry, "The Great Transformation: The Disappearance of the Commons in Western Canada," in *Man and Nature on the Prairies,* Canadian Plains Studies 6, ed. Richard Allen (Regina: Canadian Plains Research Center, 1976), 21-45.

6 Jean Barman, *Stanley Park's Secret: The Forgotten Families of Whoi Whoi, Kanaka Ranch and Brockton Point* (Vancouver: Harbour, 2005), 12. This case study builds upon the findings in Theodore Binnema and Melanie Niemi, "'Let the Line Be Drawn Now': Wilderness, Conservation, and the Exclusion of Aboriginal People from Banff National Park in Canada," *Environmental History* 11, 4 (2006): 724-50, in which they argue that the construction of an uninhabited wilderness was not always the central concern of park authorities.

7 Norbert MacDonald, *Distant Neighbours: A Comparative History of Seattle and Vancouver* (Lincoln: University of Nebraska Press, 1987), 2; Robert A.J. McDonald, *Making Vancouver: Class, Status and Social Boundaries, 1863-1913* (Vancouver: UBC Press, 1996), 4.

8 Apart from reserve lands for the military, government, and Indians, land could be pre-empted in 160-acre lots at $1 per acre. MacDonald, *Distant Neighbours,* 9.

9 McDonald, *Making Vancouver,* 37.

10 MacDonald, *Distant Neighbours,* 29.

11 Bruce Macdonald, *Vancouver: A Visual History* (Vancouver: Talonbooks, 1992), 24.

12 Vancouver City Council Minutes, 12 May 1886, vol. 1, MCR 1-1, City of Vancouver Archives (CVA).

13 McDonald, *Making Vancouver,* 37.

14 W.C. McKee, "The Vancouver Park System, 1886-1929: A Product of Local Businessmen," in *Recreational Land Use: Perspectives on Its Evolution in Canada,* ed. Geoffrey Wall and John Marsh (Ottawa: Carleton University Press, 1982), 302.

15 A.W. Ross to Adolphe Caron, Minister of Militia and Defence, 24 March 1886, in Canada, Secretary of State, *Correspondence and Papers in Reference to Stanley Park and Deadman's Island, British Columbia* (Ottawa: S.E. Dawson, 1899), 12 *(Correspondence and Papers).*

16 Vancouver City Council Minutes, 12 May 1886. Hamilton's motion was seconded by Alderman Coldwell.

17 W.C. Van Horne to D.L. MacPherson, Minister of Interior, 14 March 1885, in *Correspondence and Papers*, 10-11.

18 Henry Beatty to W.C. Van Horne, 9 July 1885; W.C. Van Horne to L.A. Hamilton and Henry Beatty, 12 January 1885, both in Canadian Pacific Railway Company fonds, Add. MSS. 42, 582-B-1, file 5, CVA.

19 Prior to the CPR acquisitions in the West End, Sam Brighouse, George Byrnes, Charles Dupont, William Hailstone, John Morton, Isaac Oppenheimer, and John Robson were the major landowners there. Brighouse, Hailstone, and Morton, who had once owned the entire West End, started selling portions of their property in the 1880s. Macdonald, *Vancouver: A Visual History,* 22.

20 Terence Young, *Building San Francisco's Parks, 1850-1930* (Baltimore: Johns Hopkins University Press, 2004), 3. Rosenzweig and Blackmar recount the myth of an unnamed gentleman who, inspired by the green spaces of European cities, had called for a grand urban park in New York City. Roy Rosenzweig and Elizabeth Blackmar, *The Park and the People: A History of Central Park* (Ithaca: Cornell University Press, 1992), 17; John Selwood, John C. Lehr, and Mary Cavett, "'The Most Lovely and Picturesque City in All of Canada': The Origins of Winnipeg's Public Park System," *Manitoba History* 31 (1996): 23.

21 McKee, "The Vancouver Park System, 1886-1929."

22 J.S. Matthews, "The Naming, Opening and Dedication of Stanley Park," *Vancouver Historical Journal* 2 (January 1959): 13.

23 *Attorney General of Canada and City of Vancouver v. Alfred Gonsalves,* 165, 971.133 v22ca, Vancouver Public Library Special Collections.

24 Ibid.

25 The contract for constructing the bridge, which estimated its cost at $816, was awarded to Leatherdale and McDonald. According to city archivist J.S. Matthews, the bridge was intended to give access to a pest house that was built on the island during a smallpox epidemic in 1892. However, because the bridge pre-dated the epidemic by two years, its purpose was probably to convenience picnickers and other park visitors. Board Minutes, 7 June 1890, Board of Parks and Recreation fonds (Park Board), MCR 47-1, CVA.

26 "Early Morning Invasion," *Vancouver Province,* 24 April 1899, 3.

27 Many historians have referred to Ludgate as an American, but he was born in Ontario and later worked in the United States. He has also been described as a resident of Seattle. Ludgate moved to Vancouver from Chicago in 1899 and lived with his wife, Catherine, on Burrard Street. After the Deadman's Island debate and litigation, the Ludgates relocated to Seattle. The error regarding Ludgate's nationality probably originated in the newspapers of the time, which casually refer to him as an American businessman, hoping to incite anti-American sentiment in rallying opposition to the Deadman's Island lease. "Deadman's Island," *Vancouver Daily News-Advertiser,* 17 February 1899, 5; *Henderson's British Columbia Gazetteer and Directory and Mining Companies for 1899-1900,* vol. 6 (Vancouver: Henderson, 1900).

28 Joseph Martin to F.W. Borden, Minister of Militia and Defence, 20 January 1899; Theodore Ludgate to F.W. Borden, Minister of Militia and Defence, 3 February 1899; George Maxwell, M.P., to F.W. Borden, Minister of Militia and Defence, 3 February 1899, all in *Correspondence and Papers,* 23.

29 Gordon Hak, *Turning Trees into Dollars: The British Columbia Coastal Lumber Industry, 1858-1913* (Toronto: University of Toronto Press, 2000), 21.

30 Major-General Edward T.H. Hutton, Commanding Canadian Militia, to Colonel C.E. Panet, Deputy Minister of Militia and Defence, 8 February 1899, in *Correspondence and Papers*, 24.

31 Lieutenant Colonel D.A. Macdonald to Colonel C.E. Panet, Deputy Minister of Militia and Defence, 6 February 1899, in *Correspondence and Papers*, 24. The lease, which was good for the next twenty-five years, made Ludgate's company responsible for the continued maintenance of the island and permitted it to "cut down and remove such timber as may be necessary to provide space for the erection of all buildings in connection with their industry." No terms of renewal were mentioned, an omission that was addressed on 4 April 1900, when Ludgate and Borden signed an amended lease; this included a clause for renewal after twenty-five years, and it removed all prior restrictions on what Ludgate could do with the island. The Privy Council approved the original lease in 1899 but never officially approved the amended version. City of Vancouver vs. Ludgate, 1899-1911, George Henry Cowan fonds, Legal Files, Add. MSS. 800, 588-C-4, file 3, CVA.

32 "Deadman's Island," *Vancouver Daily News-Advertiser*, 21 February 1899, 5.

33 Ibid.; "Many Oppose It," *Vancouver Province*, 21 February 1899, 5; Angus Everett Robertson, "The Pursuit of Power, Profit and Privacy: Study of Vancouver's West End Elite, 1886-1914" (master's thesis, University of British Columbia, 1977).

34 Mark Leier, *Red Flags and Red Tape: The Making of a Labour Bureaucracy* (Toronto: University of Toronto Press, 1995), 58.

35 Ibid., 61.

36 "Deadman's Island," *Vancouver Daily News-Advertiser*, 17 February 1899, 5; "Deadman's Island," *Vancouver Daily News-Advertiser*, 19 February 1899, 5; "Deadman's Island Deal," *Vancouver Daily News-Advertiser*, 21 February 1899, 4.

37 Canada, *House of Commons Debates* (19 May 1899), 3503.

38 It is important to remember that Aboriginal title was never legally extinguished in most of British Columbia, even though the Native inhabitants of Stanley Park were officially dispossessed in 1876.

39 "The Passing Show," *Vancouver Province*, 2 May 1899, 4; "Ludgate Has It," *Vancouver Province*, 8 May 1899, 1; "The Situation Changed," *Vancouver Daily News-Advertiser*, 2 May 1899, 4; "An Overt Act," *Vancouver Daily News-Advertiser*, 9 May 1899, 5. Francis Carter-Cotton was also the publisher and editor of the *Vancouver Daily News-Advertiser*, one of the most vocal newspapers opposed to the lease of Deadman's Island. His intervention in this case was one of several politically intriguing episodes in the history of the somewhat fractured government of Charles Semlin. Carter-Cotton and Martin led two factions within the ultimately unstable coalition. The rivalry between the two men flared up during a number of different occasions, including the battle for Deadman's Island.

40 "Axes Laid Down," *Vancouver Province*, 9 May 1899, 1; "An Overt Act," *Vancouver Daily News-Advertiser*, 9 May 1899, 5.

41 "Riot Act Was Read," *Vancouver Province*, 15 May 1899, 1.

42 When Ottawa sought to acquire all former military lands from the British government during the 1870s and 1880s, the Colonial Office scrambled to determine what lands it had reserved for military purposes in British Columbia. The colonial records were sparse, unorganized, and incomplete. The War Office compiled a schedule of lands to be turned over to the Dominion of Canada, which inaccurately recorded the Stanley Park peninsula reserve as consisting of six hundred acres. For a detailed analysis of the 1884 transfer of BC military reserves to the Dominion, see Barman, *Stanley Park's Secret*, 85-88.

43 A.M. Burgess, Deputy Minister of the Interior, to Grant Powell, Under Secretary of State, 19 April 1886; Adolphe P. Caron, Minister of Militia and Defence, to J.W. Trutch, Dominion government agent, 20 April 1886, both in *Correspondence and Papers*, 12, 14.

44 F. Carter-Cotton, Chief Commissioner of Lands and Works, to F.W. Borden, Minister of Militia and Defence, 22 April 1899, in *Correspondence and Papers*, 40.

45 Lieutenant Colonel L.F. Pinault, Deputy Minister of Militia and Defence, to F. Carter-Cotton, Chief Commissioner of Lands and Works, 12 May 1899, in *Correspondence and Papers*, 41-42.

46 F. Carter Cotton, Chief Commissioner of Lands and Works, to Lieutenant Colonel L.F. Pinault, Deputy Minister of Militia and Defence, 23 May 1899, in *Correspondence and Papers*, 44.

47 *The Attorney General of British Columbia v. Ludgate and the Attorney General of Canada*, [1900-01] 8 B.C.R. 242.

48 Section 109 guarantees the land and mineral rights of the provinces, and section 117 allows provinces entering Confederation to retain "all their respective Public Property not otherwise disposed of in this Act, subject to the Right of Canada to assume any Lands or Public Property required for Fortifications or for the Defence of the Country." *British North America Act, 1867*, 30 & 31 Vict., c. 3, ss. 109, 117 (U.K.).

49 Both Jean Barman and F.W. Howay have scoured British Columbia's colonial records in the BC Archives in Victoria and the National Archives (formerly the Public Record Office) in London to determine the early land history of Vancouver. Neither discovered any official declaration of the reserve made through public gazette or signed maps. The evidence is, at best, vague. F.W. Howay, "Early Settlement on Burrard Inlet," *British Columbia Historical Quarterly* 1, 2 (1937): 101-43.

50 *The Attorney General of British Columbia v. Ludgate and the Attorney General of Canada* at 249.

51 Ibid. at 257.

52 *The Attorney General of British Columbia v. Ludgate and the Attorney General of Canada*, [1904-05] 11 B.C.R. 258.

53 Ibid. at 269.

54 *Attorney General of British Columbia v. Attorney General of Canada*, [1906] Law Reports Appeal Cases 553. Jean Barman argues that the Privy Council decision merely affirmed the status quo, which was based on a fabricated construction of the past. See Barman, *Stanley Park's Secret*, 162-66.

55 Vancouver had been seeking this concession for several years. On behalf of city council, Mayor David Oppenheimer had petitioned the minister of militia and defence as early as 1889 to grant the City an official lease. David Oppenheimer, Mayor of Vancouver, and Thomas F. McGuigan, City Clerk, to A.P. Caron, Minister of Militia and Defence, 9 January 1889, in *Correspondence and Papers*, 18.

56 "To Secure Lease of Stanley Park," *Vancouver Daily Province*, 11 February 1904, 4.

57 "Stanley Park Is Leased to City," *Vancouver Daily Province*, 15 August 1904, 1.

58 "Lease of Stanley Park," *Vancouver Daily Province*, 15 March 1905, 6; City of Vancouver vs. Ludgate.

59 *The King v. Vancouver Lumber Co.*, [1918] 41 D.L.R. 617.

60 Board Minutes, 26 November 1919, Park Board, MCR 47-4, CVA.

61 "Superintendent's Interim Annual Report and Resume of Work of Park System for the Year Ending December 31, 1929," Correspondence, Annual Reports, Park Board, 49-C-7, file 17, CVA.

62 *Statutes of British Columbia: Consolidated Acts* (N.p.: Richard Wolfenden, 1888), 1:819, see also 1:810-11, 1:819-20.

63 Vancouver City Council Minutes, 20 August 1888, MCR 1-2, vol. 2, CVA.

64 *A by-law to govern and regulate the public parks,* 26 September 1888, City of Vancouver By-Laws, By-law no. 68, CVA.

65 *An act to amend the "Vancouver Incorporation Act, 1886" and the "Vancouver Incorporation Amendment Act, 1887,"* S.B.C. 1889, c. 40.

66 *A by-law respecting the election of Park Commissioners,* 28 April 1890, City of Vancouver By-Laws, By-law no. 96, CVA; *A by-law to amend the by-law regulating the election of Park Commissioners,* 7 December 1904, City of Vancouver By-Laws, By-law no. 461, CVA; *A by-law to provide for, and regulate, the election of the Board of Park Commissioners, or the Park Board, for the City of Vancouver,* 2 July 1929, City of Vancouver By-Laws, By-law no. 2007, CVA. The first Park Board was composed of three elected commissioners. Their number was increased to five in 1904 and to seven in 1929 in anticipation of the amalgamation of South Vancouver and Point Grey.

67 Henry Avison, Major Matthews Collection, Topical and Categorical Files, AM0054.013.00126, CVA; Board Minutes, 23 October 1890, Park Board, MCR 47-1, CVA.

68 *An act to amend the "Vancouver Incorporation Act, 1886" and the "Vancouver Incorporation Amendment Act, 1887,"* 290; Board Minutes, 8 August 1896, Park Board, MCR 47-1, CVA.

69 George Eldon, Major Matthews Collection, Topical and Categorical Files, AM0054.013. 01347, CVA; Board Minutes, 27 June 1902, Park Board, MCR 47-1, CVA.

70 Rosenzweig and Blackmar, *The Park and the People,* 238, 80.

71 Jacoby, *Crimes against Nature,* 2.

72 Rosenzweig and Blackmar, *The Park and the People,* 239.

73 Board Minutes, 7 November 1906, Park Board, MCR 47-1, CVA.

74 James Skitt Matthews, *Early Vancouver* (1933; repr., Vancouver: City of Vancouver Archives, 2011), 2:228; Animals – Beaver, Major Matthews Collection, Topical and Categorical Files, AM0054.013.06014, CVA; Board Minutes, 11 May 1904, Park Board, MCR 47-1, CVA.

75 "Trapped Game in Vancouver's Stanley Park," *Victoria Daily Colonist,* 7 April 1910, 3; "Trapper Lives in Stanley Park," *Vancouver Daily Province,* 4 April 1910, 1; 26 October 1911, 1. Uncovering the history of the park's homeless inhabitants is particularly challenging. Like most marginal or subaltern groups, they often seek to evade state surveillance, with the result that they are largely absent from historical records. The Vancouver Park Board has never kept records of the homeless population in Stanley Park for this very reason.

76 Thos. H. Ingram to Charles E. Tisdall, Mayor of the City of Vancouver, 20 February 1922, Park Board, Correspondence, Stanley Park, 1922, 49-C-5, file 6, CVA.

77 M.C. Schwaber to W.R. Owen, Chairman of the Board of Park Commissioners, 11 April 1914, Park Board, Correspondence, Requests and Complaints, 1913-1915, 48-C-5, file 8, CVA.

78 For more on the separation of passive and active recreation in large urban parks, see Young, *Building San Francisco's Parks.*

79 Robert A.J. McDonald, "'Holy Retreat' or 'Practical Breathing Spot'? Class Perceptions of Vancouver's Stanley Park, 1910-1913," *Canadian Historical Review* 45, 2 (1984): 127-53.

80 Board Minutes, 7 November 1906, Park Board, MCR 47-1, CVA.

81 Barbara Schrodt, "Control of Sports Facilities in Early Vancouver: The Brockton Point Athletic Association at Stanley Park, 1880 to 1913," *Canadian Journal of History of Sport* 23, 2 (1992): 45.

82 "A By-law to provide for the Use, Regulation, Protection and Government of Public Parks and Places within the Jurisdiction of the Park Board," 1915, City of Vancouver Board of Park Commissioners, Public Documents, PDS 14, CVA.

83 "A By-law to provide for the Use, Regulation, Protection and Government of Public Parks and Places within the Jurisdiction of the Park Board," 1934, City of Vancouver Board of Park Commissioners, Public Documents, PDS 7-55, CVA.

84 Board Minutes, 7 November 1906, Park Board, MCR 47-1, CVA.

85 Barman, *Stanley Park's Secret,* 170.

86 Theodore Catton, *Inhabited Wilderness: Indians, Eskimos, and National Parks in Alaska* (Albuquerque: University of New Mexico Press, 1997), 3. See also Shepard Krech, *The Ecological Indian: Myth and History* (New York: W.W. Norton, 1999); Nancy B. Bouchier and Ken Cruikshank, "The War on the Squatters, 1920-1940: Hamilton's Boathouse Community and the Re-Creation of Recreation on Burlington Bay," *Labour/Le Travail* 51 (2003): 9-46; and Binnema and Niemi, "'Let the Line Be Drawn Now.'"

87 Matthews, "The Naming, Opening and Dedication of Stanley Park," 34.

88 There was also a community of Hawaiians who lived at a settlement called Kanaka Ranch along the south shore of Coal Harbour, just outside the park.

89 Board Minutes, 20 October 1888, Park Board, MCR 47-1, CVA; Thomas F. McGuigan, City Clerk, to A.P. Caron, Minister of Militia and Defence, 9 March 1888; Thomas F. McGuigan, City Clerk, to A.P. Caron, Minister of Militia and Defence, 9 March 1888; James F. Garden, Mayor, to G.R. Maxwell, 15 August 1898, both in *Correspondence and Papers,* 16-17, 20.

90 Board Minutes, 30 May 1889, Park Board, MCR 47-1, CVA.

91 Henry Avison, AM0054.013.00126, CVA.

92 For more on the treatment of Asian people in Vancouver during the late nineteenth and early twentieth centuries, see Patricia Roy, "The Preservation of the Peace in Vancouver: The Aftermath of the Anti-Chinese Riot of 1887," *BC Studies* 31 (1976): 44-59; Patricia Roy, *A White Man's Province: British Columbia Politicians and Chinese and Japanese Immigrants, 1858-1914* (Vancouver: UBC Press, 1989); and Kay J. Anderson, *Vancouver's Chinatown: Racial Discourse in Canada, 1875-1980* (Montreal and Kingston: McGill-Queen's University Press, 1991).

93 City of Vancouver vs. Ludgate, 1899-1911, George Henry Cowan fonds, Legal Files, Add. MSS. 800, 588-C-4, file 3, CVA; *Rex v. Vancouver Lumber Co. et al.,* [1924] 2 D.L.R. 482.

94 Mike Steele, *Stanley Park: The Year-Round Playground* (Surrey, BC: Heritage House, 1993), 35; Jean Barman, *The Remarkable Adventures of Portuguese Joe Silvey* (Madeira Park, BC: Harbour, 2004), 17; William T. Cummings, Major Matthews Collection, Topical and Categorical Files, 504-B-3, file 386, CVA; *The Attorney-General of Canada and The City of Vancouver v. Cummings,* [1924-25] 34 B.C.R. 433.

95 Some treaties were signed on Vancouver Island by Governor Douglas in the 1850s, and part of the Peace River District was covered by Treaty 8 in 1899.

96 R.M. Galois, "The Indian Rights Association, Native Protest Activity and the 'Land Question' in British Columbia, 1903-1916," *Native Studies Review* 8, 2 (1992): 7.

97 Board Minutes, 22 May 1913, Park Board, MCR 47-2, CVA; Secretary of the Park Board to the Secretary of the Indian Commission, Victoria, BC, 29 May 1913; J.G.H. Bergeron, Secretary for the Royal Commission on Indian Affairs for the Province of British Columbia, to the Secretary of the Board of Park Commissioners, Vancouver, BC, 3 July 1913, both in Park Board, Correspondence, Requests and Complaints, 1913-1915, 48-C-5, file 8, CVA; S.J. Montgomery, Secretary of the Water Committee, to W.S. Rawlings, Superintendent

of Parks, 29 January 1918, Park Board, Correspondence, Stanley Park, 1914-1919, 49-A-5, file 3, CVA.

98 T.B. Jones to the Minister of Lands, 5 June 1919; W.E. Ditchburn to Duncan Campbell Scott, 28 July 1919, both in Indian Affairs, RG 10, vol. 4089, file 521, Library and Archives Canada. The term "authentic Indian" is borrowed from Paige Raibmon, *Authentic Indians: Episodes of Encounter from the Late Nineteenth-Century Northwest Coast* (Durham, NC: Duke University Press, 2005).

99 E.F. Jones, City Solicitor, to A.S. Wootton, Acting Superintendent of Parks, 7 October 1921, Park Board, Correspondence, Stanley Park, 1920-1921, 49-B-5, file 2, CVA.

100 Board Minutes, 13 December 1921, Park Board, MCR 47-4, CVA.

101 "Aunt Sally Dies on Eve of Eviction from Her Squatter's Home," *Vancouver Sun,* 21 April 1923, 1, 3.

102 *Attorney-General of Canada v. Gonzalves* (1924), 4 D.L.R. 474; "Vancouver Squatter Wins Lawsuit," *Victoria Daily Colonist,* 14 November 1923, 1. Aunt Sally, as she was known, was roughly a hundred years old when she died. Her home was near Whoi Whoi. Her claim to adverse possession was recognized by the court, but her daughter soon sold her land to the City.

103 *The Attorney-General of Canada and The City of Vancouver v. Gonsalves,* [1924-25] 34 B.C.R. 360.

104 Ibid. at 363.

105 Constance Backhouse, *Colour-Coded: A Legal History of Racism in Canada, 1900-1950* (Toronto: University of Toronto Press, 1999), 114.

106 *Attorney-General of Canada v. Gonzalves* (1924), 4 D.L.R. 474; *Attorney-General of Canada v. Gonzalves* (1924), 1 D.L.R. 605; *Attorney-General of Canada et al v. Cummings et al* (1925), 1 D.L.R. 52.

107 *The Attorney-General of Canada and The City of Vancouver v. Cummings* at 440.

108 *Attorney-General of Canada v. Gonzalves* at 479.

109 Renisa Mawani, "Imperial Legacies (Post) Colonial Identities: Law, Space and the Making of Stanley Park, 1859-2001," *Law Text Culture* 7 (2003): 100. Ironically, the totem poles for the model Indian village were erected on the site of Whoi Whoi and on the former property of Aunt Sally. "Stanley Park to Be Minus Indians," *Vancouver Sun,* 12 May 1933, 22.

110 Superintendent of Parks to Geo. E. McCrossan, Corporation Counsel, 24 January 1924, Park Board, Correspondence, General, 1924, 49-C-6, file 18, CVA; Board Minutes, 26 November 1925, Park Board, MCR 47-5, CVA.

111 Chairman of the Board of Park Commissioners to F. Burd, November 1924, Park Board, Correspondence, General, 1924, 49-C-6, file 18, CVA.

Chapter 3: Improving Nature

1 "Stanley Park," *Vancouver Daily News-Advertiser,* 28 September 1888, 8; J.S. Matthews, *The Naming, Opening, and Dedication of Stanley Park, Vancouver, Canada, 1888-1889* (Vancouver: Archives of Vancouver Society, 1964).

2 Richard Walker, *Country in the City: The Greening of the San Francisco Bay Area* (Seattle: University of Washington Press, 2009), 61.

3 Paul S. Sutter, *Driven Wild: How the Fight against Automobiles Launched the Modern Wilderness Movement* (Seattle: University of Washington Press, 2002), 10; William Cronon, "The Trouble with Wilderness; or, Getting Back to the Wrong Nature," in *Uncommon Ground: Rethinking the Human Place in Nature,* ed. William Cronon (New York: W.W. Norton,

1995), 69; Clarence Glacken, *Traces on the Rhodian Shore: Nature and Culture in Western Thought from Ancient Times to the End of the Eighteenth Century* (Berkeley: University of California Press, 1967), 4.

4   Anne Whiston Spirn, "Constructing Nature: The Legacy of Frederick Law Olmsted," in Cronon, *Uncommon Ground,* 91; Richard West Sellars, *Preserving Nature in the National Parks: A History* (New Haven: Yale University Press, 1997), 70; Linda Flint McClelland, *Building the National Parks: Historic Landscape Design and Construction* (Baltimore: Johns Hopkins University Press, 1998).

5   For more on the reconstruction of the sand dunes in Golden Gate Park, see Terence Young, *Building San Francisco's Parks, 1850-1930* (Baltimore: Johns Hopkins University Press, 2004), 74-87.

6   This understanding of the relationship between human-induced landscape change and autonomous non-human forces builds on arguments in Thomas Heyd, ed., *Recognizing the Autonomy of Nature: Theory and Practice* (New York: Columbia University Press, 2005).

7   *A by-law for making improvements and constructing a public road or drive around the Government Reserve or ground set apart for a Public Park by the Corporation of the City of Vancouver and for providing funds for the making or construction of said road,* 10 October 1887, City of Vancouver By-Laws, By-law no. 44, City of Vancouver Archives (CVA).

8   Vancouver Board of Works Minutes, 1886-1951, 14 November 1887 and 25 November 1887, City Engineering Services fonds, 116-D-4, MCR 36-1, CVA; J.S. Matthews, *Early Vancouver* (1932; repr., Vancouver: City of Vancouver Archives, 2011), 1: 217; Report of the Board of Works, 1888, Major Matthews Collection, Topical and Categorical Files, AM0054.013.04360, Add. MSS. 54, 505-C-6, file 312, CVA.

9   Roy Rosenzweig and Elizabeth Blackmar, *The Park and the People: A History of Central Park* (Ithaca: Cornell University Press, 1992), 121; McClelland, *Building the National Parks,* 28.

10   The roads of Mount Royal Park in Montreal, Queen's Park and Mount Pleasant Cemetery in Toronto, and Assiniboine Park in Winnipeg were also patterned after this tradition. For more, see A.L. Murray, "Frederic Law Olmsted and the Design of Mount Royal Park," *Journal of the Society of Architectural Historians* 26 (1967): 163-71; David Bain, "The Early Pleasure Grounds of Toronto," *Ontario History* 91, 2 (1999): 165-82; and John Selwood, John C. Lehr, and Mary Cavett, "'The Most Lovely and Picturesque City in All of Canada': The Origins of Winnipeg's Public Park System," *Manitoba History* 31 (1996): 21-29.

11   Vancouver City Council Minutes, 1 October 1888, MCR 1-2, CVA.

12   Editorial, *Vancouver Daily News-Advertiser,* 7 February 1888, 2; "By-Law," *Vancouver Daily News-Advertiser,* 5 May 1888, 5; untitled article, *Vancouver Daily News-Advertiser,* 10 June 1888, 6.

13   Matthews, *Early Vancouver,* 2:294.

14   "Brockton Point, Stanley Park," *Vancouver Province,* 15 June 1901, 9.

15   Board Minutes, 31 January 1889, 30 May 1889, 23 October 1890, 7 August 1891, 2 November 1891, Board of Parks and Recreation fonds (Park Board), MCR 47-1, CVA.

16   Mike Davis, *Dead Cities and Other Tales* (New York: New Press, 2002), 362.

17   David Louter, *Windshield Wilderness: Cars, Roads, and Nature in Washington's National Parks* (Seattle: University of Washington Press, 2006), 12; Sutter, *Driven Wild;* "Auto-Owner Is Made Defendant," *Vancouver Daily Province,* 13 June 1905, 1; Board Minutes, 11 August 1909, Park Board, MCR 47-1, CVA.

18   "Will Widen Roads of Stanley Park," *Vancouver Province,* 13 March 1906, 2; "Heavier Roads for Stanley Park," *Vancouver Daily Province,* 11 February 1907, 1; "Park Roads Closed

Indefinitely," *Vancouver Daily Province,* 7 February 1908, 7. Road troubles were not uncommon in other Canadian and American cities. Canadian roads were rarely paved and often difficult to travel during the winter. In 1934, nearly half of BC roads were still unpaved, and the majority of paved roads were simple gravel surfaces. Most US cities had some form of paving by the late nineteenth century, and by the 1920s, they used asphalt surfaces or some other form of bituminous road surfacing. Clay McShane argues that the shift in road-surfacing technology can be attributed to several factors, such as the rise of the automobile, but larger social and cultural forces lay behind the trend. He finds that early suburbanization in American cities, the extension of horse-drawn streetcars, and, later, electric street railways constituted a social and cultural shift in thinking about streets. By the early twentieth century, city engineers and suburban developers had forgotten the traditional uses of urban streets as social public spaces for gathering, commerce, and play; streets became transportation corridors to outlying suburbs. For more on early roads in eastern British North America, see Robert Mackinnon, "Roads, Cart Tracks, and Bridle Paths: Land Transportation and the Domestic Economy of Mid-Nineteenth-Century Eastern British North America," *Canadian Historical Review* 84, 2 (2003): 177-216. Complete statistics for road surfacing in all provinces can be found in George P. de T. Glazenbrook, *A History of Transportation in Canada* (Toronto: Ryerson Press, 1938), 446. For a critical look at the social and cultural forces propelling changes in road-surfacing technology, see Clay McShane, "Transforming the Use of Urban Space: A Look at the Revolution in Street Pavements, 1880-1924," *Journal of Urban History* 5, 3 (1979): 279-307.

19 "Park Engineer's Report on Roads in Stanley Park," Board Minutes, 25 March 1914, Park Board, MCR 47-2, CVA.

20 Board Minutes, 9 August 1911, Park Board, MCR 47-1, CVA; Secretary of the Park Board to the Clerk to the Municipality of Burnaby, 28 June 1912, Park Board, Correspondence, Stanley Park Plants, 48-C-5, file 7, CVA; Board Minutes, 25 June 1913 and 23 July 1913, Park Board, MCR 47-2, CVA; Report to the Board of Park Commissioners by A.S. Wootton, Park Engineer, 28 April 1915, Park Board, Correspondence, Stanley Park Plants, 48-C-5, file 7, CVA.

21 Board Minutes, 10 March 1909, Park Board, MCR 47-1, CVA.

22 "Park Protest," *Vancouver Daily Province,* 7 April 1910, 16; "Lovers of Stanley Forest Form a Society," *Vancouver Daily Province,* 12 April 1910, 1; Robert A.J. McDonald, *Making Vancouver: Class, Status and Social Boundaries, 1863-1913* (Vancouver: UBC Press, 1996), 171. F.C. Wade's attempt to protect the trees foreshadowed 1930s efforts, made in response to road construction, to establish wilderness areas in US national parks. For details, see Sutter, *Driven Wild;* and Louter, *Windshield Wilderness.*

23 Young, *Building San Francisco's Parks,* 103; Andrew J. Schmidt, "Pleasure and Recreation for the People: Planning St. Paul's Como Park," *Minnesota History* 58, 1 (2002): 40-58; "Tram Extension to Stanley Park," *Vancouver Province,* 25 August 1905, 13; Board Minutes, 11 July 1906, 10 August 1910, and 24 August 1910, Park Board, MCR 47-1, CVA; Chairman J.W. Wilkinson and Secretary J.H. McVety of the Vancouver Trades and Labor Council to the Board of Park Commissioners, 16 August 1911, Park Board, Correspondence, Stanley Park, Proposed Railway, December 1906–June 1913, 48-C-3, file 1, CVA; Robert A.J. McDonald, "'Holy Retreat' or 'Practical Breathing Spot'? Class Perceptions of Vancouver's Stanley Park, 1910-1913," *Canadian Historical Review* 45, 2 (1984): 127-53; Record of Nominations and Elections, 1886-1949, 11 January 1912, MCR 4-1, CVA.

24 F.C. Wade, "Why Tramcars Should Not Be Allowed in Stanley Park," *Vancouver Province,* 1 December 1906, 12.

25 E. Pauline Johnson, *Legends of Vancouver* (1911; repr., Toronto: Douglas and McIntyre, 1997), 96. Coal Harbour's muddy tidal flat is comparable to the eastern basin of Burrard Inlet at Rocky Point in Port Moody today.

26 "New Bathing Beach," *Vancouver Province,* 13 September 1900, 2; Board Minutes, 11 May 1904, 10 April 1907, 12 May 1914, and 8 July 1914, Park Board, MCR 47-1, CVA; Annual Reports, 1914, Park Board, PDS 12, CVA.

27 In 1908, prior to the bridge closure, city taxpayers approved funds for improvements to the park's Coal Harbour entrance. "Park Bridge Is Closed," *Vancouver Daily Province,* 9 August 1909, 9; Board Minutes, 24 August 1910, Park Board, MCR 47-1, CVA; "Hands Off Stanley Park," *Vancouver Province,* 27 August 1902, 4.

28 Board Minutes, 9 November 1910, Park Board, MCR 47-1, CVA; Elliott S. Rowe, Manager of the Vancouver Tourist Association, to A.E. Lees, Chairman of the Board of Park Commissioners, 10 November 1910; Arthur D. Monteith, Civil and Hydraulic Engineer, to Chairman of the Board of Park Commissioners, 17 November 1910; J.J. Blackmore, Architect, to the Board of Park Commissioners, 29 December 1910, all in Park Board, Correspondence, September-December 1910, 48-C-1, file 6, CVA.

29 Board Minutes, 17 January 1911, 22 November 1911, 20 March 1912, Park Board, MCR 47-1, CVA; Thomas H. Mawson, *The Life and Work of an English Landscape Architect: An Autobiography by Thomas H. Mawson* (New York: Charles Scribner's Sons, 1927), 187.

30 McDonald, "'Holy Retreat' or 'Practical Breathing Spot'?" 138; Mawson, *Life and Work,* 204. Mawson actually prepared four proposals, but the third and fourth were slight variations on the same idea.

31 Thomas H. Mawson, "Report on Alternative Schemes for the Improvement of Coal Harbour and Stanley Park, Vancouver, B.C." (1912), Corporation of Point Grey fonds, Reeve's Office, 6-B-7, file 8, CVA.

32 Ibid.; Thomas H. Mawson, *Civic Art: Studies in Town Planning, Parks, Boulevards and Open Spaces* (London: B.T. Batsford, 1911), 161.

33 Mawson, *Civic Art,* 185; Mawson, *Life and Work,* 205.

34 Wade's rejection of Mawson's plan was similar to the nineteenth-century debate over Richard Morris Hunt's entrance gate for Central Park. In 1863, the park commissioners for New York City adopted Hunt's proposal for a grand neoclassical entrance to Central Park, which would be located at Sixtieth Street and Fifth Avenue. The plan so offended the naturalistic sensibilities of Olmsted and Vaux that they resigned from the commission. Ultimately, the plan was dropped and never implemented. For more, see David Schuyler, *The New Urban Landscape: The Redefinition of City Form in Nineteenth-Century America* (Baltimore: Johns Hopkins Press, 1986), 98.

35 Mawson, "Report on Alternative Schemes for the Improvement of Coal Harbour and Stanley Park, Vancouver, B.C."

36 Secretary of the Park Board to Colonel Sam Hughes, Honourable Minister of Militia and Defence, 27 December 1912, Park Board, Correspondence, Coal Harbour, 1911-1919, 48-E-1, file 11, CVA; Thomas H. Mawson, Landscape Architect, to W.R. Owen, Park Commissioner, 7 May 1913, Park Board, Correspondence, Coal Harbour, 1911-1922, 48-E-1, file 10, CVA. Mawson and Hughes were already acquainted, having attended a social function in Ottawa two years earlier while Mawson was giving a lecture tour across the country. Mawson described Hughes as "a jolly good fellow" who "evidently could not string two sentences together without some amusing *faux pas.*" Mawson, *Life and Work,* 193 (emphasis in original).

37 Mawson, *Life and Work*, 227.
38 "Stadium for Park Adopted by Council After Warning Note," *Vancouver Sun*, 17 December 1912, 1.
39 "Lovers of Stanley Forest Form a Society," *Vancouver Daily Province*, 12 April 1910, 1.
40 Editorial, *Vancouver Daily News-Advertiser*, 18 August 1888, 4; Editorial, *Vancouver Daily News-Advertiser*, 19 August 1888, 4; Editorial, *Vancouver Daily News-Advertiser*, 4 September 1888, 8; Editorial, *Vancouver Daily News-Advertiser*, 6 September 1888, 8; Vancouver City Council Minutes, 20 August 1888, MCR 1-2, vol. 2, CVA.
41 Stephen J. Pyne, Patricia L. Andrews, and Richard D. Laven, *Introduction to Wildland Fire*, 2nd ed. (New York: Wiley and Sons, 1996), 209; Douglas J. Hallett et al., "11,000 Years of Fire History and Climate in the Mountain Hemlock Rainforests of Southwestern British Columbia Based on Sedimentary Charcoal," *Canadian Journal of Forest Research* 32, 2 (2003): 292-312; Sally Hermansen and Graeme Wynn, "Reflections on the Nature of an Urban Bog," *Urban History Review* 34, 1 (2005): 9-27; Robert Boyd, "Introduction," in *Indians, Fire, and the Land in the Pacific Northwest*, ed. Robert Boyd (Covallis: Oregon University Press, 1999), 2; Nancy J. Turner, "'Time to Burn': Traditional Use of Fire to Enhance Resource Production by Aboriginal Peoples in British Columbia," in Boyd, *Indians, Fire, and the Land*, 187.
42 For more on the history of fire prevention in British Columbia, see John Vye Parminter, "An Historical Review of Forest Fire Management in British Columbia" (master's thesis, University of British Columbia, 1978).
43 Stephen J. Pyne, *Fire in America: A Cultural History of Wildland and Rural Fire* (Princeton: Princeton University Press, 1982), 27.
44 Board Minutes, 7 November 1906, Park Board, MCR 47-1, CVA.
45 Ibid., 14 September 1904; City of Vancouver vs. Ludgate, 1899-1911, George Henry Cowan fonds, Legal Files, Add. MSS. 800, 588-C-4, file 3, CVA; Richard A. Rajala, *Feds, Forests, and Fire: A Century of Canadian Forestry Innovation* (Ottawa: Canada Science and Technology Museum, 2005).
46 Board Minutes, 8 September 1920, Park Board, MCR 47-4, CVA.
47 Ibid., 9 November 1910, 8 September 1920, MCR 47-1; Board of Park Commissioners, "Estimate of Cost of Watermains and Hydrants for Fire Protection in Stanley Park," 13 September 1920, Park Board, Correspondence, 49-C-5, file 7, CVA; Annual Reports, 1921, Park Board, PDS 12, CVA.
48 "Memorandum by Dominion Botanist Re: Conditions of Health of the Trees, Stanley Park, B.C." (1913) Park Board, Correspondence, Entomological Dept. re insect pests, 48-C-5, file 3, CVA.
49 Robert Glen, comp., "Entomology in Canada Up to 1956: A Review of Developments and Accomplishments," *Canadian Entomologist* 88, 7 (1956): 290-371. For more on the centralization of entomological research in Canada, see Stéphane Castonguay, "The Emergence of Research Specialties in Economic Entomology in Canadian Government Laboratories after World War II," *Historical Studies in the Physical and Biological Sciences* 32, 1 (2001): 19-40; and Stéphane Castonguay, "Naturalizing Federalism: Outbreaks and the Centralization of Entomological Research in Canada, 1884-1914," *Canadian Historical Review* 84, 1 (2004): 1-34.
50 "Preliminary Report on Insect Conditions in Stanley Park, Vancouver, BC" (January 1914), Park Board, Correspondence, 48-C-5, file 2, CVA.
51 "Report on Silvicultural Conditions in Stanley Park" (March 1914), Park Board, Correspondence, Entomological Dept. re insect pests, 48-C-5, file 3, CVA.

52 Ibid.
53 Ibid.; George M. Cook, "'Spray, Spray, Spray!' Insecticides and the Making of Applied Entomology in Canada, 1871-1914," *Scientia Canadensis* 22-23, 51 (1998-99): 7-50. Cook argues that British Columbia did not play a significant role in the development of entomology in Canada, but the case of Stanley Park refutes this claim, particularly with regard to the application of chemical pesticides by pumps and aerial spraying – early experiments in forest entomology. Cook's oversight is probably due to the fact that his research (and most research on entomology in Canada) is limited to the horticultural and agricultural application of pesticides.
54 Editorial, "Preservation of Stanley Park," *Vancouver Sun,* 17 February 1914, 6.
55 "Must Preserve Trees Growing in the Park," *Vancouver Sun,* 9 April 1914, 2.
56 "Report on Silvicultural Conditions in Stanley Park" (March 1914), Park Board, Correspondence, Entomological Dept. re insect pests, 48-C-5, file 3, CVA.
57 Ibid.
58 "Memorandum by Dominion Entomologist on Damage Due to Insects in Stanley Park, Vancouver, B.C.," (January 1914) Park Board, Correspondence, Entomological Dept. re insect pests, 48-C-5, file 3, CVA.
59 Ibid.; J.M. Swaine, Assistant Entomologist for Forest Insects, Division of Entomology, Central Experimental Farm, to W.S. Rawlings, Superintendent of Parks, 19 March 1914 (emphasis in original), Park Board, Correspondence, Entomological Dept. re insect pests, 48-C-5, file 3, CVA.
60 "Report on Condition of Stanley Park, July 1914," Park Board, Correspondence, Forestry, Stanley Park, October 1913–September 1919, 48-C-5, file 2, CVA; Entomological Branch, "Forest Insect Investigations in British Columbia," *Agricultural Gazette of Canada* 1, 9 (1914): 698.
61 "Forestry in Stanley Park: Extracts from Superintendent's Annual Reports" (1915), Park Board, Correspondence, 49-B-5, file 2, CVA; "Monarchs in Forest Cut Down," *Vancouver Sun,* 9 February 1915, 1, 2.
62 "Forestry in Stanley Park: Extracts from Superintendent's Annual Reports."
63 Ibid.
64 "Report on Present Condition of Tree Growth in Stanley Park, Vancouver, August 1919," Park Board, Correspondence, 48-C-5, file 3, CVA.
65 Superintendent of Parks to J.M. Swaine, Chief, Division of Forest Insects, Entomological Branch, Department of Agriculture, Ottawa, 5 July 1921, Park Board, Correspondence, 49-B-5, file 6, CVA.
66 Annual Reports, 1921, Park Board, PDS 12, CVA.
67 Annual Reports, 1930, Park Board, PDS 12, CVA.
68 Editorial, *Vancouver Daily Province,* 24 April 1930, 6.
69 "Triumphant," *Vancouver Sun,* 24 March 1914, 1. In North America, arsenic-based insecticides were used extensively for agriculture and horticulture during the late nineteenth and early twentieth centuries, but at the turn of the century, public health officials in the United States and Europe became aware of the long-term health effects of exposure to them. Britain has applied strict limitations to their use since 1903, following a public health crisis related to arsenic traces in the food supply. Canada and the United States resisted efforts to legislate similar restrictions. Lead arsenate was still widely used during the 1930s, even though its adverse health effects were well known. See James C. Whorton, "Insecticide Spray Residues and Public Health, 1865-1938," *Bulletin of the History of Medicine* 45, 3 (1971): 219-41.
70 Board Minutes, 14 January 1931, Park Board, MCR 47-5, CVA.

71 Annual Reports, 1958-61, Park Board, PDS 12, CVA.

72 Major Matthews Collection, Topical and Categorical Files, Stanley Park, Trees, AM0054. 013.04370, CVA; Board Minutes, 19 November 1931, MCR 47-5, Park Board, CVA.

73 For more on the changing animal landscape of Stanley Park, see Sean Kheraj, "Demonstration Wildlife: Negotiating the Animal Landscape of Vancouver's Stanley Park, 1888-1996," *Environment and History* 18, 4 (2012): 1-31.

74 Anne Whiston Spirn argues that the urban environment offers new habitats for wildlife species but usually in reduced numbers due to their diminished greenspaces: "Scattered, fragmented remnants of woodland, meadow, and marsh embedded within the urban fabric are islands surrounded by a sea of buildings and pavement." Anne Whiston Spirn, *The Granite Garden: Urban Nature and Human Design* (New York: Basic Books, 1984), 207; Patricia H. Partnow, "Ursine Urges and Urban Ungulates: Anchorage Asserts Its Alaskaness," *Western Folklore* 58, 1 (1999): 39; Matthews, *Early Vancouver*, 2:182.

75 "An Observer" to the Board of Park Commissioners, n.d., Park Board, Correspondence, Stanley Park, 1916-1919, 49-A-5, file 2, CVA.

76 Tina Loo argues that Canadian wildlife policies were intended to produce a "modernized wilderness," where principles of practical sciences were applied to the breeding of certain species and the construction of new habitats for game preserves. Tina Loo, "Making Modern Wilderness: Conserving Wildlife in Twentieth-Century Canada," *Canadian Historical Review* 82, 1 (2001): 91-120.

77 "Beautiful Black Swans," *Vancouver Province*, 19 May 1900, 2; "The Swan Pond, Stanley Park," *Vancouver Province*, 1 August 1901, 8; Secretary of Public Parks Board for Victoria to Charles Tisdall, Chairman of the Board of Park Commissioners, 26 August 1908, Park Board, Correspondence, January–December 1908, 48-C-1, file 2, CVA. As part of the Pacific Flyway, the Stanley Park wetlands host varying seasonal populations of wildfowl, including species of ducks, geese, and herons. The park is home to one of North America's largest urban heronries, and its coastline has been designated an Important Bird Area (IBA) of Canada. Stanley Park Ecology Society, *State of the Park: Report for the Ecological Integrity of Stanley Park* (Vancouver: Stanley Park Ecology Society, 2010), 96.

78 "An Observer" to the Board of Park Commissioners; Henry Smith, Commissioner of Parks, Boroughs of Manhattan and Richmond, to Charles E. Tisdall, Chairman of the Board of Park Commissioners, Vancouver, B.C., 29 March 1909; William S. Manning, General Superintendent, Department of Public Parks and Squares, City of Baltimore, to Charles E. Tisdall, Chairman of the Board of Park Commissioners, Vancouver, B.C., 23 April 1909; Invoice from Wenz and Mackensen, Naturalists, Yardley, Pa., proprietors of the Pennsylvania Pheasantry and Game Park, to Charles Tisdall, Vancouver, B.C., 3 January 1910; Wenz and Mackensen, Naturalists, Yardley, PA., to Mr. A. Hauchet, 22 June 1910, in Park Board, Correspondence, Stanley Park, 1916-1919, 48-C-1, file 3, CVA; Wenz and Mackensen, Naturalists, Yardley, PA., to Charles E. Tisdall, Chairman of the Board of Park Commissioners, 29 December 1910, in Park Board, Correspondence, September–December 1910, CVA. In 1951, Donald Joseph Robinson, a zoology graduate student from the University of British Columbia, studied the interrelationship between the grey and Douglas squirrels in Stanley Park. He found that the grey squirrels had successfully established a stable population by the 1920s and were able to co-exist with the Douglas squirrels, because the two species occupied different habitats in the park, reducing competition. For more, see Donald Joseph Robinson, "The Inter-Relations of the Introduced Gray Squirrel *(Sciurus carolinensis)* with the Ecological Conditions in Stanley Park" (master's thesis, University of British Columbia, 1951).

79 William S. Manning, General Superintendent, Department of Public Parks and Squares, City of Baltimore, to Charles E. Tisdall, Chairman of the Board of Park Commissioners, Vancouver, B.C., 23 April 1909, Park Board, Correspondence, January–December 1909, 48-C-1, file 3, CVA; "The Swan Pond, Stanley Park," *Vancouver Province*, 1 August 1901, 8; Henry Avison, 10 January 1912, Major Matthews Collection, Topical Files, AM0054.013.00126, CVA; Annual Reports, 1916, Park Board, PDS 12, CVA.

80 Spirn, *The Granite Garden,* 208; Mr. M.W. Woods to the Chairman of the Board of Park Commissioners, 2 July 1908; M.G. Johnson to the Board of Park Commissioners, 12 February 1909, both in Park Board, Correspondence, January–December 1909, 48-C-1, file 2, CVA; "An Observer" to the Board of Park Commissioners; Board Minutes, 9 March 1910, Park Board, MCR 47-1, CVA; "Ancient Elk, Bison and Marauding Owls Sentenced to Death," *Vancouver Sun,* 28 December 1916, 10. One year, the Park Board invited the Vancouver Gun Club to shoot horned owls in Stanley Park.

81 Ronald C. Campbell Johnson, letter to the editor, *Vancouver Daily News-Advertiser,* 19 March 1914, 10; Editorials, *Vancouver Sun,* 20 March 1914, 6, 25 March 1914, 6.

82 "Stanley Park Crow Shooting Ends This Year," *Vancouver Province,* 31 May 1961, 2; George Colpitts, *Game in the Garden: A Human History of Wildlife in Western Canada to 1940* (Vancouver: UBC Press, 2002).

83 "Big Game Hunters in Stanley Park," *Vancouver Daily Province,* 20 October 1911, 1; "Cougar Is Being Tracked to His Lair," *Vancouver Daily Province,* 23 October 1911, 1; "Different Ways of Killing a Cougar," *Vancouver Daily Province,* 26 October 1911, 1; "Park Marauder Meets His Fate," *Vancouver Daily News Advertiser,* 27 October 1911, 15. See also Richard Mackie, "Cougars, Colonists, and the Rural Settlement of Vancouver Island," in *Beyond the City Limits: Rural History in British Columbia,* ed. Ruth Sandwell (Vancouver: UBC Press, 1999), 120-141.

84 "The Cougar," *Vancouver Daily Province,* 28 October 1911, 6; "Different Ways of Killing a Cougar," 1.

85 A.H. Peters, letter to the editor, "The Cougar and Stanley Park," *Vancouver World,* 31 October 1911, 5.

86 Tina Loo, "Of Moose and Men: Hunting for Masculinities in British Columbia," *Western Historical Quarterly* 32, 3 (2001): 296-319; Colpitts, *Game in the Garden;* "Cougar Is Shot by Cloverdale Hunters," *Vancouver Daily Province,* 27 October 1911, 7; Robert Allison Hood, *By Shore and Trail in Stanley Park* (Toronto: McClelland and Stewart, 1929), 147.

87 Nigel Rothfels, *Savages and Beasts: The Birth of the Modern Zoo* (Baltimore: Johns Hopkins University Press, 2002), 7; John Berger, "Why Look at Animals?" in *About Looking* (New York: Pantheon, 1980), 24.

88 Board Minutes, 10 August 1904, 13 December 1905, 9 October 1907, Park Board, MCR 47-1, CVA.

89 "Animals at Zoo Have Survived Cold Snap," *Vancouver Daily Province,* 15 January 1907, 6.

90 "Pets Roasted Alive at Park Zoo at Night," *Vancouver Province,* 14 October 1905, 1; Board Minutes, 28 May 1913, 10 January 1917, 14 February 1917, Park Board, MCR 47-2, CVA; Annual Reports, 1920-21, Park Board, PDS 12, CVA.

Chapter 4: The City in the Park

1 Margaret W. Andrews, "Sanitary Conveniences and the Retreat of the Frontier: Vancouver, 1886-1926," *BC Studies* 87 (1990): 6; Engineering Report of Henry Badeley Smith, M.C.S.C., 1889, Vancouver Waterworks Company fonds, 509-B-6, file 1, City of Vancouver Archives

(CVA). For an excellent account of the construction of the Capilano pipeline, see Louis P. Cain, "Water and Sanitation Services in Vancouver: An Historical Perspective," *BC Studies* 30 (1976): 27-43.

2 "The Water Works," *Vancouver Daily News-Advertiser,* 29 August 1888, 8.

3 Engineering Report of Henry Badeley Smith, 1889; "The Water Works," 8.

4 Editorial, *Vancouver Daily News-Advertiser,* 29 August 1888, 4.

5 Cain, "Water and Sanitation Services in Vancouver," 32; Engineering Report of Henry Badeley Smith, 1889; "Big Excavation in Stanley Park," *Vancouver Province,* 20 July 1905, 11; "The Great Reservoir in Stanley Park," *Vancouver Province,* 11 November 1905, 24.

6 David Schuyler, *The New Urban Landscape: The Redefinition of City Form in Nineteenth-Century America* (Baltimore: Johns Hopkins Press, 1986), 102; Daniel M. Bluestone, "From Promenade to Park: The Gregarious Origins of Brooklyn's Park Movement," *American Quarterly* 39, 4 (1987): 542.

7 Editorial, *Vancouver Daily News-Advertiser,* 29 August 1888, 4.

8 Superintendent of Parks to A.D. Creer, Engineer, Vancouver Sewerage Board, 2 August 1917; Superintendent of Parks to J. Stables, Chairman of the Vancouver Sewerage Board, 6 October 1918, both in Board of Parks and Recreation fonds (Park Board), Correspondence, Stanley Park, 1911-1920, 49-A-5, file 9, CVA.

9 Robert Allison Hood, *By Shore and Trail in Stanley Park* (Toronto: McClelland and Stewart, 1929), 86. Hood tended to "naturalize" objects in the park in an attempt to blend them into the landscape. Elsewhere in his book, he makes a similar effort to justify the presence of the families at Brockton Point.

10 Board Minutes, 26 May 1944, 9 October 1945, 8 January 1946, Park Board, MCR 47-6, CVA.

11 Lilia D'Acres and Donald Luxton, *Lions Gate* (Burnaby: Talonbooks, 1999), 15; *Lions' Gate Bridge: Souvenir Book* (Vancouver: Lions' Gate Bridge Company, 1938), Spam 14387, University of British Columbia Special Collections (UBCSC).

12 D.G. Macdonell of Macdonell, Henderson and Jones, Solicitors, to the Chairman of the Board of Park Commissioners, 31 March 1908, Park Board, Correspondence, January–December 1908, 48-C-1, file 2, CVA; "Scenic Bridge Quarter Mile Long Will Span Narrows," *Vancouver Daily Province,* 7 April 1908, 14; First Assistant Engineer, the Scherzer Rolling Lift Bridge Co., to Board of Park Commissioners, 27 August 1909, Park Board, Correspondence, January–December 1909, 48-C-1, file 3, CVA.

13 D'Acres and Luxton, *Lions Gate,* 33; *Lions' Gate Bridge: Souvenir Book.*

14 "First Narrows Suspension Bridge – Vancouver B.C. 1934?" *Vancouver Daily Province,* 15 November 1924, 21.

15 David Louter, *Windshield Wilderness: Cars, Roads, and Nature in Washington's National Parks* (Seattle: University of Washington Press, 2006), 19.

16 D'Acres and Luxton, *Lions Gate,* 33; Board Minutes, 8 July 1926, Park Board, MCR 47-5, CVA; "Bridge Plans Are Submitted," *Vancouver Daily Province,* 8 September 1926, 7.

17 Bruce Macdonald, *Vancouver: A Visual History* (Vancouver: Talonbooks, 1992), 38-41; "Board of Trade Opposed to Bridging the Lions Gate," *Vancouver Daily Province,* 24 November 1926, 7; "First Narrows Bridge Proposal Joint Submission of the Vancouver Merchants' Exchange and the Shipping Federation of British Columbia" (5 April 1927), Spam 14383, UBCSC.

18 Daniel Francis, *L.D.: Mayor Louis Taylor and the Rise of Vancouver* (Vancouver: Arsenal, 2004), 139; Editorial, "Lions' Gate Bridge," *Vancouver Daily Province,* 1 October 1926, 6; A.H. Gordon, letter to the editor, *Vancouver Daily Province,* 14 April 1927, 4.

19   Editorial, "Lions' Gate Bridge," *Vancouver Daily Province,* 1 October 1926, 6; 1 October 1926, 6; A.H. Gordon, letter to the editor, 1 October 1926, 10; "Vancouverite," letter to the editor, 17 October 1926, 8 (magazine section); J.A. Wragg, letter to the editor, 26 October 1926, 19; Harold E. Escott, letter to the editor, 25 June 1927, 6.

20   F. Lefeaux, letter to the editor, *Vancouver Daily Province,* 31 October 1926, 12; "Citizen," letter to the editor, *Vancouver Daily Province,* 29 November 1926, 11.

21   A.S. Wootton, Park Engineer, to the Board of Park Commissioners, 9 September 1926; A.S. Wootton, Park Engineer, to the Board of Park Commissioners, 13 October 1926, both in Park Board, Correspondence, First Narrows Bridge, 49-C-7, file 14, CVA. In his analysis of the interwar origins of the Wilderness Society, Paul Sutter describes similar objections to highway expansion in US national parks. Paul S. Sutter, *Driven Wild: How the Fight against Automobiles Launched the Modern Wilderness Movement* (Seattle: University of Washington Press, 2002).

22   A.S. Wootton to Park Board, 9 September 1926.

23   "Report re Proposed Lions' Gate Bridge Submitted by W.S. Rawlings, Superintendent" (20 June 1927), Park Board, Correspondence, First Narrows Bridge, 49-C-7, file 14, CVA.

24   "Franchise for Bridge Given," *Vancouver Daily Province,* 27 May 1927, 1; *A by-law to author-ize the Council to submit a plebiscite to the ratepayers as to whether a roadway shall be constructed through Stanley Park connecting with a proposed bridge across the First Narrows in the Harbour of Vancouver,* 8 June 1927, City of Vancouver By-Laws, By-law no. 1845, CVA; *Lions' Gate Bridge* (Vancouver: Lions' Gate Bridge Committee, 1927), Spam 14384, UBCSC.

25   Record of Nominations and Elections, 1886-1949, 25 June 1927, MCR 4-2, CVA.

26   Macdonald, *Vancouver: A Visual History,* 40-41.

27   Ibid., 44-45; Jean Barman, *The West beyond the West: A History of British Columbia,* rev. ed. (Toronto: University of Toronto Press, 1996), 252.

28   Patricia E. Roy, "Vancouver: 'The Mecca of the Unemployed,' 1907-1929," in *Town and City: Aspects of Western Canadian Urban Development,* ed. Alan F.J. Artibise (Regina: Canadian Plains Research Center, 1981), 393; Todd McCallum, "Introduction," in Andrew Roddan, *Vancouver's Hoboes* (Vancouver: Subway Books, 2005), v; Francis, *L.D.: Mayor Louis Taylor,* 174.

29   Francis, *L.D.: Mayor Louis Taylor,* 109.

30   Eric Strikwerda explores similar relief work conditions for men in prairie cities during the 1930s in "'Married Men Should, I Feel, Be Treated Differently': Work, Relief, and Un-employed Men on the Urban Canadian Prairie, 1929-32," *Left History* 12, 1 (2007): 30-51.

31   For more on Canadian and American relief work in national and state parks, see Bill Waiser, *Park Prisoners: The Untold Story of Western Canada's National Parks, 1915-1946* (Calgary: Fifth House, 1995); and James Wright Steely, *Parks for Texas: Enduring Landscapes of the New Deal* (Austin: University of Texas Press, 1999). See also Board Minutes, 25 November 1914, 10 February 1915, 12 January 1921, 14 January 1932, Park Board, MCR 47-2, MCR 47-3, MCR 47-5, CVA.

32   D'Acres and Luxton, *Lions Gate,* 36; W.C. Ditmars to A.J.T. Taylor, 28 January 1931, Major Matthews Collection, First Narrows Bridge, Add. MSS. 54, 503-B-6, vol. 1, CVA.

33   "City Fights Lions Gate Bridge Measure," *Vancouver Daily Province,* 13 March 1931, 16; "Prospect Point Site for First Narrows Bridge," *Vancouver Daily Province,* 9 September 1932, 1; "'Secrecy' on the Lions' Gate Bridge," *Vancouver Sun,* 22 September 1932, 1.

34   "Lions Gate Bridge Is Fourth Stage of Development in Vancouver's Growth," *Vancouver Daily Province,* 12 August 1933, 7; C.W. Bertram, "Will Lions Gate Bridge Affect Vancouver Real Estate Values?" *Vancouver Sun,* 2 September 1933, 24.

35 George Duncan, letter to the editor, *Vancouver Daily Province*, 21 September 1933, 22; C.M. Campbell, letter to the editor, *Vancouver Daily Province*, 3 October 1933, 12.

36 "Lions' Gate Bridge Adds Millions To Vancouver's Payroll," *Vancouver Daily Province*, 19 August 1933, 2; "City Hears Proposal for First Narrows Span," *Vancouver Daily Province*, 13 April 1933, 1.

37 Michael Dawson, "Taking the 'D' out of 'Depression': The Promise of Tourism in British Columbia, 1935-1939," *BC Studies* 132 (2001-02): 33; "City Hears Proposal For First Narrows Span," 3.

38 "'In All the World No Park Like Stanley Park,'" *Vancouver Daily Province*, 18 August 1933, 7.

39 "The Future of the Harbor Entrance," *Vancouver Daily Province*, 20 September 1933, 15; William Elgie Bland, letter to the editor, *Vancouver Daily Province*, 26 September 1933, 3; "First Narrows Bridge to Improve Park," *Vancouver Sun*, 30 November 1933, 1.

40 "The Future of the Harbor Entrance," 15; George Duncan, letter to the editor, *Vancouver Daily Province*, 21 September 1933, 22.

41 "The Passer By," letter to the editor, *Vancouver Daily Province*, 28 September 1933, 14.

42 Board Minutes, 23 April 1931, 30 April 1931, 18 August 1933, 30 November 1933, Park Board, MCR 47-5, CVA; "Gradual Circuit," *Vancouver News-Herald*, 19 August 1933, 8.

43 "Two-to-One Vote for $6,000,000 Span across First Narrows," *Vancouver Sun*, 14 December 1933, 1; Record of Nominations and Elections, 1886-1949, 13 December 1933, MCR 4-2, CVA. The number of votes cast in the 1933 plebiscite was much larger than in 1927 because it followed the amalgamation of Vancouver, South Vancouver, and Point Grey. For more on the Vancouver City Hall project, see "Vancouver Gives Emphatic Mandate to British Group to Build $6,000,000 Span," *Vancouver News-Herald*, 14 December 1933, 1; and David Monteyne, "'From Canvas to Concrete in Fifty Years': The Construction of Vancouver City Hall, 1935-6," *BC Studies* 124 (1999-2000): 41-68.

44 "First Narrows Bridge Objections Swept Away; 'It's Time to Act,'" *Vancouver Sun*, 4 June 1934, 1; "Bennett Will Protect Public on New Bridge," *Vancouver Daily Province*, 7 June 1934, 1; "Lion's Gate Bridge OK'd at Ottawa," *Vancouver Daily Province*, 29 April 1936, 1; Vancouver Board of Trade, "Report of Special Committee regarding Proposal for the Construction of a Bridge across the First Narrows Burrard Inlet" (November 1933), Spam 14385, UBCSC.

45 D'Acres and Luxton, *Lions Gate*, 66; "Work Progressing on Span Roadway," *Vancouver Daily Province*, 12 July 1937, 17; "Overhead Passes at Bridge Urged," *Vancouver Daily Province*, 29 October 1938, 17; Board Minutes, 25 March 1937, 12 August 1937, 13 May 1938, Park Board, MCR 47-5, CVA; Annual Reports, 1937 and 1938, Park Board, PDS 12, CVA; "Mrs. Mary Sutton, 76, 'First' across Bridge," *Vancouver Sun*, 12 November 1938, 1.

46 *Lions Gate Bridge, Vancouver, Canada* (Vancouver: Vancouver Sun, 1939); Souvenir Folder of the Lion's Gate Bridge, 12 November 1938, Major Matthews Collection, First Narrows Bridge, Add. MSS. 54, 503-B-6, vol. 2, CVA; *Lions' Gate Bridge: Souvenir Book*, n.p.

47 Douglas Coupland, *Polaroids from the Dead* (Toronto: Harper Collins, 1996), 69, 75; *Lions Gate Bridge, Vancouver, Canada*, n.p.

48 Chairman of the Board of Park Commissioners to Colonel J. Duff Stuart, Senior Military Officer, Vancouver, B.C., 6 August 1914, Park Board, Correspondence, Requests and Complaints, 1913-1915, 48-C-5, file 8, CVA.

49 Peter N. Moogk, assisted by R.V. Stevenson, *Vancouver Defended: A History of the Men and Guns of the Lower Mainland Defences, 1859-1949* (Surrey, BC: Antonson, 1978), 32.

50 Margaret A. Ormsby, *British Columbia: A History* (1958; repr., Toronto: Macmillan, 1976), 377.

51 Moogk, *Vancouver Defended*, 31; Barman, *The West beyond the West*, 198.

52 Moogk, *Vancouver Defended*, 51; Board Minutes, 26 August 1914, Park Board, MCR 47-2, CVA.

53 Superintendent of the Parks to Col. J. Duff Stuart, 14 January 1915; Superintendent of the Park Board to Col. J. Duff Stuart, Staff headquarters, 29 November 1915 all in Park Board, Correspondence, Requests and Complaints, 1913-1915, 48-C-5, file 8, CVA; Superintendent of Parks to Major J.E. Ward, O.C. 6th Field Co. C.E., North Vancouver, B.C., 24 March 1916, Park Board Correspondence, Stanley Park, 1915-1919, 49-A-5, file 6, CVA; Board Minutes, 12 April 1916, Park Board, MCR 47-2, CVA; E. Davies, Secretary Treasurer of the Vancouver Engineering Works, Ltd., to the Superintendent of Parks, 1 October 1917, Park Board, Correspondence, Stanley Park, 1911-1920, 49-A-5, file 9, CVA.

54 Board Minutes, 13 January 1938, 28 January 1938, 11 February 1938, Park Board, MCR 47-5, CVA; Moogk, *Vancouver Defended*, 59; "To Shift Park Road for Defence Guns," *Vancouver Daily Province*, 19 January 1938, 3; "Start on Road for Gun Emplacements," *Vancouver Daily Province*, 12 February, 1938, 12; "Coastal Defence Guns to Command Harbor Approach," *Vancouver Sun*, 14 January 1938, 1.

55 During the summer of 1942, the 6-inch guns were exchanged for a pair of 4.7-inch guns from Yorke Island, Johnstone Strait. In the only direct attack on British Columbia during the Second World War, an enemy submarine had recently shelled a lighthouse at Estevan Point on the west coast of Vancouver Island, heightening fears that Yorke Island might be subject to a Japanese attack.

56 Board Minutes, 13 September 1940, Park Board, MCR 47-5, CVA; Board Minutes, 11 July 1941, 22 May 1942, 12 June 1942, 24 July 1942, 11 August 1942, 23 October 1942, 25 June 1943, Park Board, MCR 47-6, CVA.

57 Moogk, *Vancouver Defended*, 111; Board Minutes, 22 December 1944, 12 January 1945, Park Board, MCR 47-6, CVA.

58 Annual Reports, 1945, Park Board, PDS 12, CVA.

59 Annual Reports, 1948, Park Board, PDS 12, CVA.

Chapter 5: Restoring Nature

1 Richard M. Steele, *The Stanley Park Explorer* (North Vancouver: Whitecap Books, 1985), 139; E. Pauline Johnson, *Legends of Vancouver* (1911; repr., Toronto: Douglas and McIntyre, 1997), 113, 114; Catherine Mae MacLennan, *Rambling round Stanley Park* (Vancouver: Roy Wrigley, 1935), 13; Allen Roy Evans, "The Majestic Old Family That Rules Stanley Park," *Vancouver Province*, 12 January 1957, 8 (magazine section).

2 Board Minutes, 9 June 1943, Board of Parks and Recreation fonds (Park Board), MCR 47-6, City of Vancouver Archives (CVA); "Seven Sisters Shed Two Tons of Bark," *Vancouver Sun*, 18 March 1947, 9. Today, a plaque marks the place where the Seven Sisters once stood.

3 Paul S. Sutter, *Driven Wild: How the Fight against Automobiles Launched the Modern Wilderness Movement* (Seattle: University of Washington Press, 2002), 14.

4 Lorenz developed his theory during the 1960s in regard to the complexity of weather prediction. He posited that an infinite number of minute factors could produce an infinite number of meteorological outcomes. Therefore, the flap of a butterfly's wings in Asia could theoretically cause a hurricane in the Caribbean. Essentially, he argued that there were no predictable patterns in weather. His theory formed a foundation for the development of later chaos and complexity theories.

5 US Fleet Weather Central/Joint Typhoon Warning Center, *Annual Typhoon Report, 1962* (San Francisco, 1962), 29. A joint task force of the United States Navy and Air Force, the centre provides tropical cyclone warnings for American protectorates and military bases in the Asia-Pacific region.

6 Although the storm was commonly called a typhoon, it was actually an extratropical cyclone. The term "typhoon" refers to tropical cyclones that occur in the western Pacific.

7 US Fleet Weather Central/Joint Typhoon Warning Center, *Annual Typhoon Report, 1962* (San Francisco, 1962), 179-182, http://www.usno.navy.mil/NOOC/nmfc-ph/RSS/jtwc/atcr/1962atcr.pdf; Jerome Namias, "Large-Scale Air-Sea Interactions over the North Pacific from Summer 1962 through the Subsequent Winter," *Journal of Geophysical Research* 68, 22 (1963): 6171-86; Fred W. Decker, Owen P. Cramer, and Byron R. Harper, "The Columbus Day 'Big Blow' in Oregon," *Weatherwise* 15 (December 1962): 238-45; Robert E. Lynott and Owen P. Cramer, "Detailed Analysis of the 1962 Columbus Day Windstorm in Oregon and Washington," *Monthly Weather Review* 94, 2 (1966): 105-17.

8 Lynott and Cramer, "Detailed Analysis," 105; Arthur Daley, "Storm Damage," *New York Times,* 16 October 1962, 68; Decker, Cramer, and Harper, "The Columbus Day 'Big Blow,'" 241.

9 "Weather," *Vancouver Sun,* 11 October 1962, 3; "Storm Lashes B.C. Coast," *Vancouver Sun,* 12 October 1962, 1-3. The inadequate forecasting was merely a by-product of the state of weather prediction in Canada in the 1960s. The Meteorological Service of Canada had been in operation in some form since the 1840s and kept apace with Western European and American advances in weather prediction. British Columbia established its first forecast office in 1890. Although the Meteorological Service had grown into a more sophisticated network and started to use new radar technologies developed during the war, forecasting in 1962 had only recently started to apply computer technology for more accurate numerical predictions. Despite the insufficient warning regarding the first storm, Vancouver officials should have been more prepared for the second. For a comprehensive administrative history of the Meteorological Service of Canada and further accounts of developments in meteorological sciences, see Morley Thomas, *The Beginnings of Canadian Meteorology* (Toronto: ECW Press, 1991); Morley Thomas, *Forecasts for Flying: Meteorology in Canada, 1918-1939* (Toronto: ECW Press, 1996); Morley Thomas, *Metmen in Wartime: Meteorology in Canada, 1939-1945* (Toronto: ECW Press, 2001); and John D. Cox, *Storm Watchers: The Turbulent History of Weather Prediction from Franklin's Kite to El Niño* (Hoboken: John Wiley and Sons, 2002).

10 Environment Canada, Daily Data Report for October 1962, National Climate Data and Information Archive, http://climate.weatheroffice.gc.ca/climateData/bulkdata/; "Five Die as Killer Storm Hits City," *Vancouver Sun,* 13 October 1962, 1-3; "Storm Toll Tops $10 Million," *Vancouver Sun,* 15 October 1962, 1; "Put Wiring Underground Says Mayor in Wake of Storm," *Vancouver Sun,* 16 October 1962, 1. Despite the storm of the night before and warnings that a second one was approaching, City officials irresponsibly permitted traffic to travel along the connector to Lions Gate Bridge. Forty vehicles were trapped in the park while emergency service workers struggled to make their way through the debris.

11 "Tea House Operator, Wife Trapped While Gas Leaks," *Vancouver Sun,* 16 October 1962, 10; "New-Style Stanley Park," *Vancouver Province,* 15 December 1962, 4; "B.C. Storm Fatal to 6," *Toronto Globe and Mail,* 15 October 1962, 2; Raymond A. Green, "The Weather and Circulation of October 1962: A Warm Month with a Mid-Month Circulation Reversal," *Monthly Weather Review* 91, 1 (January 1963): 46.

12 Jack McCaugherty, "Axes Flash in Park After Frieda's Blow," *Vancouver Province,* 7 January 1963, 5; "Savage 50-Mile Gale Causes Heavy Losses in City and Valley," *Vancouver Daily Province,* 22 October 1934, 1; Annual Reports, 1934, Park Board, PDS 12, CVA. In 1934, as in 1962, newspaper reports and estimates of the number of downed trees were inaccurate and unreliable. The newspapers of 1934 reported that up to two thousand trees had fallen, but this was a rough guess since the Park Board kept no record of the damage.

13 Namias, "Large-Scale Air-Sea Interactions," 6180. ENSO commonly refers to "the active ocean component of a vast, Pacific basin-wide oscillation in air mass and ocean temperature." Mike Davis, *Late Victorian Holocausts: El Niño Famines and the Making of the Third World* (London: Verso, 2002), 17.

14 "Furious Winds Cause Damage in the Park and Money Is Needed," *Vancouver Province,* 30 December 1901, 4; Board Minutes, 8 January 1913, 22 December 1915, Park Board, MCR 47-1, MCR 47-2, CVA.

15 For more on nature as autonomous, see Thomas Heyd, ed., *Recognizing the Autonomy of Nature: Theory and Practice* (New York: Columbia University Press, 2005). Keekok Lee's essay, "Is Nature Autonomous?" in ibid., 54-74, very clearly lays out the theoretical foundations of the idea.

16 Frederick Turner, "The Invented Landscape," in *Beyond Preservation: Restoring and Inventing Landscapes,* ed. A. Dwight Baldwin Jr., Judith de Luce, and Carl Pletsch (Minneapolis: University of Minnesota Press, 1994), 51 (emphasis in original); William R. Jordan III, "'Sunflower Forest': Ecological Restoration as the Basis for a New Environmental Paradigm," in Baldwin, de Luce, and Pletsch, *Beyond Preservation,* 27.

17 Eric Katz, "The Big Lie: Human Restoration of Nature," in *Nature as Subject: Human Obligation and Natural Community,* ed. Eric Katz (Lanham, MD: Rowman and Littlefield, 1997), 390; Robert Elliot, *Faking Nature: The Ethics of Environmental Restoration* (London: Routledge, 1997), 76.

18 Marcus Hall, *Earth Repair: A Transatlantic History of Environmental Restoration* (Charlottesville: University of Virginia Press, 2005), 218, 6 (emphasis in original); Richard Grove, *Green Imperialism: Colonial Expansion, Tropical Island Edens and the Origins of Environmentalism* (Cambridge: Cambridge University Press, 1995), 3.

19 "Forestry in Stanley Park: Extracts from Superintendent's Annual Reports" (1919) Park Board, Correspondence, Stanley Park, 1920-1921, 49-B-5, files 2-6, CVA; Board Minutes, 10 November 1920, Park Board, MCR 47-4, CVA; Hamish Kimmins, *Balancing Act: Environmental Issues in Forestry,* 2nd ed. (Vancouver: UBC Press, 1992), 42.

20 Editorial, "Stanley Park! A Challenge! An Emergency!" *Vancouver Daily Province,* 6 February 1935, 1; "Vancouver Citizens All Say 'Save the Park,'" *Vancouver Daily Province,* 8 February 1935, 1-2; "Park Work Will Start on Monday," *Vancouver Daily Province,* 20 February 1935, 4; "Ottawa Urged to Assist in Park," *Vancouver Daily Province,* 22 February 1935, 3.

21 Board Minutes, 21 February 1935, Park Board, MCR 47-5, CVA; P.Z. Caverhill, Chief Forester of British Columbia, Department of Lands, Forest Branch, to Chairman of the Board of Park Commissioners, 13 February 1935, Dominion Unemployment Relief Commissioner, Department of Labour, Correspondence with British Columbia re Dominion-British Columbia Agreement, 1935, respecting improvements to Stanley Park, Vancouver, RG 27-H-1, file Y1-8-11, Library and Archives Canada (LAC).

22 T.G. Murphy, Minister of the Interior, to W.A. Gordon, Minister of Labour, 2 May 1935; Memorandum of Agreement entered into this sixth day of November, 1935 between the Dominion of Canada and the Vancouver Board of Park Commissioners, both in Dominion Unemployment Relief Commissioner, Department of Labour, Correspondence with British

Columbia re Dominion–British Columbia Agreement, 1935, respecting improvements to Stanley Park, Vancouver, RG 27-H-1, file Y1-8-11, LAC.

23 Board Minutes, 9 December 1901, Park Board, MCR 47-1, CVA; Seth R. Reice, *The Silver Lining: The Benefits of Natural Disasters* (Princeton: Princeton University Press, 2001), 15.

24 Hall, *Earth Repair,* 214.

25 Editorial, *Vancouver Sun,* 4 June 1936, 4.

26 Board Minutes, 19 November 1931, Park Board, MCR 47-5, CVA; Annual Reports, 1949 and 1952, Park Board, PDS 12, CVA.

27 Eddie Simons, "Behind-Scenes Workers Keep Park in Shape," *Vancouver News-Herald,* 9 April 1951, 13; "Stanley Park Virgin Forest; $9000 Keeps It 'Natural,'" *Vancouver Sun,* 14 March 1950, 7.

28 Board Minutes, 15 October 1962, Park Board, MCR 47-7, CVA; "Costs of Storm Will 'Break' City," *Vancouver Sun,* 15 October 1962, 2; "Put Wiring Underground, Says Mayor in Wake of Storm," *Vancouver Sun,* 16 October 1962, 1; "Storm Aid Asked in Winter Works," *Vancouver Sun,* 17 October 1962, 29.

29 "Logging Camp in Town? It Sure Looks Like One," *Vancouver Sun,* 20 October 1962, 25; Pat Carney, "New Trees Spring Up in Stanley Park," *Vancouver Province,* 23 February 1963, 16.

30 Robert A.J. McDonald, "'Holy Retreat' or 'Practical Breathing Spot'? Class Perceptions of Vancouver's Stanley Park, 1910-1913," *Canadian Historical Review* 54, 1 (1984): 127-53; Editorial, "A Park for Use," *Vancouver Sun,* 27 December 1962, 4; D. Morgan, letter to the editor, *Vancouver Province,* 14 October 1964, 4; "A Park Must Be Undisturbed," *Vancouver Times,* 30 October 1964, 4.

31 Hall, *Earth Repair,* 150; M.J. Bowden, "The Invention of American Tradition," *Journal of Historical Geography* 18 (1992): 4.

32 George Vancouver, *A Voyage of Discovery to the North Pacific Ocean and round the World, 1791-1795,* edited by W. Kaye Lamb (London: Hakluyt Society, 1984), 2:561.

33 Editorial, *Vancouver Daily News-Advertiser,* 13 June 1888, 2.

34 "Lover of Stanley Park Strongly Opposed to Lions' Gate Bridge," *Vancouver Province,* 17 October 1926, 8 (magazine section); Robert Allison Hood, *By Shore and Trail in Stanley Park* (Toronto: McClelland and Stewart, 1929), 16; C. Roscoe Brown, *Stanley Park and Its Environs* (n.p., 1937), PAM 1937-46, CVA; "Stanley Park's Wooded Wonderland Is 67 Years Old," *Vancouver Sun,* 28 September 1955, 25; Editorial, "Keep It Stanley Park," *Vancouver Province,* 17 July 1951, 4; Theodore Binnema and Melanie Niemi, "'Let the Line Be Drawn Now': Wilderness, Conservation, and the Exclusion of Aboriginal People from Banff National Park in Canada," *Environmental History* 11, 4 (2006): 724-50; Kathy S. Mason, *Natural Museums: U.S. National Parks, 1872-1916* (East Lansing: Michigan State University Press, 2004).

35 Hood, *By Shore and Trail in Stanley Park,* 112; MacLennan, *Rambling round Stanley Park,* 13; Evans, "The Majestic Old Family That Rules Stanley Park," 8; Claire Campbell, *Shaped by the West Wind: Nature and History in Georgian Bay* (Vancouver: UBC Press, 2005), 128 (emphasis in original).

36 Simon Schama, *Landscape and Memory* (New York: Alfred A. Knopf, 1995), 188; Michael Kammen, *Mystic Chords of Memory: The Transformation of Tradition in American Culture* (New York: Vintage, 1993), 44; Campbell, *Shaped by the West Wind,* 128; Maria Tippett, *Emily Carr: A Biography* (Toronto: Oxford University Press, 1979), 72-73; Emily Carr, *Growing Pains: The Autobiography of Emily Carr,* 2nd ed. (Toronto: Clarke, Irwin, 1966), 207-8, 253.

37 J. Keri Cronin, *Manufacturing National Park Nature: Photography, Ecology, and the Wilderness Industry of Jasper* (Vancouver: UBC Press, 2011), 8; UBC Library Digital Collections, University of British Columbia Archives, "Rosetti Studios – Stanley Park Collection," http://angel.library.ubc.ca.

38 Harold Kalman and Lorne Whitehead, "Conservation of the Hollow Tree in Vancouver's Stanley Park," *APT Bulletin: Journal of Preservation Technology* 42, 4 (2011): 4; "Stanley Park Hollow Tree Fitted for Steel Girdle," *Vancouver Sun,* 30 March 1965, 8; "Park Forest," *Vancouver Sun,* 1 June 1943, 4.

39 George H. Raley, *Our Totem Poles: A Souvenir of Vancouver* (Vancouver, 1937); B.A. McKelvie, *Legends of Stanley Park: Vancouver's Magnificent Playground* (n.p., 1941); John C. Goodfellow, *The Totem Poles in Stanley Park* (Vancouver: Art, Historical, and Scientific Association of Vancouver, c. 1920). For more information on the Aboriginal inhabitants, see Jean Barman, *Stanley Park's Secret: The Forgotten Families of Whoi Whoi, Kanaka Ranch and Brockton Point* (Vancouver: Harbour, 2005).

40 "Fifty Years a Park," *Vancouver News-Herald,* 30 October 1939, 4.

41 Annual Reports, 1947, Park Board, PDS 12, CVA.

42 Ibid.; Annual Reports, 1960, Park Board, PDS 12, CVA.

43 Editorial, "Sorry Zoo Conditions," *Vancouver News-Herald,* 23 March 1946, 4; Editorial, "Is Stanley Park Zoo Worth Keeping?" *Vancouver Province,* 8 July 1947, 4; Annual Reports, 1947.

44 "Zoo Stays in Park, So Baboon's Happier," *Vancouver Province,* 24 January 1950, 24; "Penguin Pool to Be Constructed in Park," *Vancouver Sun,* 24 July 1952, 18; Annual Reports, 1950, 1952, 1955, Park Board, PDS 12, CVA.

45 Annual Reports, 1946, 1954, 1955, 1956, Park Board, PDS 12, CVA.

46 Kay J. Anderson, *Vancouver's Chinatown: Racial Discourse in Canada, 1875-1980* (Montreal and Kingston: McGill-Queen's University Press, 1991), 200; Derek Hayes, *Historical Atlas of Vancouver and the Lower Fraser Valley* (Vancouver: Douglas and McIntyre, 2005), 154; Paul Tennant, "Vancouver Civic Politics, 1929-1980," *BC Studies* 46 (1980): 3-27.

47 "First Narrows Crossing Approaches Proposed New Ocean Parkway" (March 1960), PD 1044, CVA.

48 Board Minutes, 17 December 1962, 7 October 1963, Park Board, MCR 47-7, CVA; "New Park Road Opposed," *Vancouver Sun,* 8 October 1963, 13.

49 Board Minutes, 25 October 1965, Park Board, MCR 47-7, CVA; Philip A. Gaglardi to William Rathie, 18 July 1966; Mayor Thomas J. Campbell to Premier W.A.C. Bennett, 4 August 1967, City Council and Office of the City Clerk fonds, 16-G-6, file 14, file 15, CVA.

50 Board Minutes, 30 May 1967, Park Board, MCR 47-7, CVA; "Mayor Backs Span, Sunken Park Road," *Vancouver Sun,* 1 April 1967, 60; "Park Road Fought," 19 April 1967, 55.

51 "Ban on Cars in Stanley Park Urged," *Vancouver Province,* 16 February 1965, 2; "Park Causeway 'unforgivable,' Says Veteran of City Classrooms," *Vancouver Times,* 26 November 1964, 4 (magazine section); E.S. Woodward, letter to the editor, 16 November 1964, 4; Editorial, "Save the Park," 6 November 1964, 4; Elizabeth A. Lane, President of the Community Arts Council of Vancouver, to Philip A. Gaglardi, Minister of Highways, Province of British Columbia, 27 April 1965, City Council and Office of the City Clerk fonds, 16-G-6, file 13, CVA; "Park Plea Sent to Pearson," *Vancouver Sun,* 23 October 1964, 2.

52 "Puil Fears Effects of Tunnel," *Vancouver Province,* 8 February 1972, 6; E.A. Sandy Robertson, Vice Chairman, Board of Parks and Public Recreation, "A Second Crossing of Burrard Inlet at the First Narrows, Vancouver, B.C.: A Case for a Twin Span Bridge at Lions Gate and the Return of Stanley Park to Full Use – For All People for All Times" (11 August 1969), City Council and Office of the City Clerk fonds, 142-D-1, file 5, CVA.

53 Hayes, *Historical Atlas of Vancouver,* 158.

54 Frank Zelko, "Making Greenpeace: The Development of Direct Action Environmentalism in British Columbia," *BC Studies* 142-43 (2004): 225, 226-27.

55 Jeff Buttle, "Naturalists Oppose Park Plan," *Vancouver Sun,* 4 May 1989, B5; "Board Alters Course on Plan to Replace Stanley Park Trees," *Vancouver Sun,* 13 February 1990, B1; "They Vow a Fight for Park Trees," *Vancouver Province,* 11 September 1989, 5.

Conclusion: Reconciliation with Disturbance

1 "Park Still Feels Frieda's Punch," *Vancouver Sun,* 8 May 1968, 16.

2 Miro Cernetig, "One for the History Books," *Vancouver Sun,* 16 December 2006, A1, A8.

3 *Stanley Park Restoration: Meeting the Challenges, Progress Report* (Vancouver: Vancouver Parks and Recreation, 2007), 3-4 (emphasis added).

4 Stanley Park Ecology Society, *State of the Park: Report for the Ecological Integrity of Stanley Park* (Vancouver: Stanley Park Ecology Society, 2010), 125; Memo from the General Manager of Parks and Recreation Arboriculture Section to the Vancouver Board of Parks and Recreation, "Stanley Park Forest Management Plan Report" (23 March 2009).

5 Vancouver Board of Parks and Recreation, "Stanley Park Forest Management Plan" (March 2009), 5-10.

6 Richard West Sellars, *Preserving Nature in the National Parks: A History* (New Haven: Yale University Press, 1997), 288-89.

7 Al Sheehan, "Zoo Friends and Foes Square Off," *Vancouver Sun,* 2 June 1993, B1; Jeff Lee, "Controversial Zoo Expansion Approved Despite Opposition," *Vancouver Sun,* 7 July 1993, B1.

8 "Menagerie of Zoo Ideas to Go to Referendum," *Vancouver Sun,* 5 October 1993, A1; "Stanley Park Zoo Proposal Defeated," *Vancouver Sun,* 22 November 1993, B1; Bill Burns, "Retiring Polar Bear," *Beautiful British Columbia* 38, 3 (1996): 47.

9 Stanley Park Ecology Society, *State of the Park,* 21.

10 Carolyn Merchant, *Reinventing Eden: The Fate of Nature in Western Culture* (New York: Routledge, 2003), 216.

Bibliography

Archival Sources

British Columbia Archives (BCA)
Archibald McKinley fonds, E/C/M21
Colonial Correspondence, GR-1372
Department of Lands and Works, GR-1404
Indian Reserve Commission, 1876-1878, GR-0494
Joint Reserve Commission, GR-2982
Moody Family fonds, MS-0060
Pre-emption Notices, GR-0567
Stamp's Mill Burrard Inlet, MS-0120

City of Vancouver Archives (CVA)
Board of Parks and Recreation fonds (Park Board)
   Annual Reports, PDS 12
   Board Minutes, MCR 47
   Correspondence
   Public Documents, PDS 14
Brown, C. Roscoe. *Stanley Park and Its Environs.* N.p., 1937. PAM 1937-46
Canadian Pacific Railway Company fonds, Add. MSS. 42
City Council and Office of the City Clerk fonds
City Engineering Services fonds
   Vancouver Board of Works Minutes, 1886-1951, 116-D-4, MCR 36
City of Vancouver By-Laws
Corporation of Point Grey fonds
Deadman's Island Land Use Privy Council Records Collection Proceedings and Judgement,
   1905-1906, Add. MSS. 202
First Narrows Bridge, Add. MSS. 54
"First Narrows Crossing Approaches Proposed New Ocean Parkway." March 1960. PD 1044

George Henry Cowan fonds, Add. MSS. 800
Major Matthews Collection Topical Files
   Animals – Beaver, AM0054.013.06014
   George Eldon, AM0054.013.01347
   Henry Avison, AM0054.013.00126
   Theodore L. Ludgate, AM0054.013.02735
   William Hailstone, AM0054.013.01938
Major Matthews Collection Topical and Categorical Files
   Report of the Board of Works, 1888, AM0054.013.04360, Add. MSS. 54, 505-C-6,
     file 312
   Stanley Park, Trees, AM0054.013.04370
   William T. Cummings, 504-B-3, file 386
Maps Collection
Record of Nominations and Elections, 1886-1949, MCR 4
Vancouver City Council Minutes, MCR 1
Vancouver Waterworks Company fonds

Library and Archives Canada (LAC)
Dominion Unemployment Relief Commissioner, Department of Labour, RG 27-H-1
"Report of the British Columbia Reserve Commission with Census Reports," Department
   of Indian Affairs, RG 10, vol. 3645, file 793

University of British Columbia Special Collections (UBCSC)
"First Narrows Bridge Proposal Joint Submission of the Vancouver Merchants' Exchange
   and the Shipping Federation of British Columbia." 5 April 1927. Spam 14383
Hastings Sawmill Company fonds
Lions' Gate Bridge. Vancouver: Lions' Gate Bridge Committee, 1927. Spam 14384
Lions' Gate Bridge: Souvenir Book. Vancouver: Lions' Gate Bridge Company, 1938. Spam
   14387
Vancouver Board of Trade. "Report of Special Committee regarding Proposal for the
   Construction of a Bridge across the First Narrows Burrard Inlet." November 1933.
   Spam 14385

Vancouver Public Library Special Collections
Attorney General of Canada and City of Vancouver v. Alfred Gonzalves, 971.133 v22ca

Newspapers and Journals

New Westminster British Columbian
New York Times
Toronto Globe and Mail
Vancouver Daily News-Advertiser
Vancouver Historical Journal
Vancouver News-Herald
Vancouver Province
Vancouver Sun
Vancouver World
Victoria Daily-Colonist

Other Sources

Ames, Kenneth M., and Herbert D.G. Maschner. *Peoples of the Northwest Coast: Their Archaeology and Prehistory.* London: Thames and Hudson, 1999.

Anderson, Alexander Caulfield. *The Dominion at the West: A Brief Description of the Province of British Columbia, Its Climate and Resources.* Victoria: R. Wolfenden, 1872.

Anderson, Virginia DeJohn. *Creatures of Empire: How Domestic Animals Transformed Early America.* Oxford: Oxford University Press, 2004.

Andrews, Margaret W. "Sanitary Conveniences and the Retreat of the Frontier: Vancouver, 1886-1926." *BC Studies* 87 (1990): 3-22.

Armstrong, Christopher, and H.V. Nelles. *Monopoly's Moment: The Organization and Regulation of Canadian Utilities, 1830-1930.* Philadelphia: Temple University Press, 1986.

Armstrong, John E. *Vancouver Geology.* Vancouver: Geological Association of Canada, 1990.

Artibise, Alan F.J., ed. *Town and City: Aspects of Western Canadian Urban Development.* Regina: Canadian Plains Research Center, 1981.

Asdal, Kristin. "The Problematic Nature of Nature: The Post-Constructivist Challenge to Environmental History." *History and Theory* 42, 4 (2003): 60-74.

Backhouse, Constance. *Colour-Coded: A Legal History of Racism in Canada, 1900-1950.* Toronto: University of Toronto Press, 1999.

Bailey, Peter. *Leisure and Class in Victorian England: Rational Recreation and the Contest for Control, 1830-1885.* Toronto: University of Toronto Press, 1978.

Bain, David. "The Early Pleasure Grounds of Toronto." *Ontario History* 91, 2 (1999): 165-82.

–. "The Queen's Park and Its Avenues: Canada's First Public Park." *Ontario History* 95, 2 (2003): 192-215.

Baldwin, A. Dwight, Jr., Judith de Luce, and Carl Pletsch, eds. *Beyond Preservation: Restoring and Inventing Landscapes.* Minneapolis: University of Minnesota Press, 1994.

Barman, Jean. *The Remarkable Adventures of Portuguese Joe Silvey.* Madeira Park, BC: Harbour, 2004.

–. *Stanley Park's Secret: The Forgotten Families of Whoi Whoi, Kanaka Ranch and Brockton Point.* Vancouver: Harbour, 2005.

–. *The West beyond the West: A History of British Columbia.* Rev. ed. Toronto: University of Toronto Press, 1996.

Bella, Leslie. *Parks for Profit.* Montreal: Harvest House, 1987.

Beveridge, Charles E. *Frederick Law Olmsted: Designing the American Landscape.* New York: Rizzoli, 1995.

Binnema, Theodore, and Melanie Niemi. "'Let the Line Be Drawn Now': Wilderness, Conservation, and the Exclusion of Aboriginal People from Banff National Park in Canada." *Environmental History* 11, 4 (2006): 724-50.

Birch, Thomas H. "The Incarceration of Wilderness: Wilderness Areas as Prisons." *Environmental Ethics* 12 (1990): 3-26.

Bluestone, Daniel M. "From Promenade to Park: The Gregarious Origins of Brooklyn's Park Movement." *American Quarterly* 39, 4 (1987): 529-50.

Blunden, Roy H. "Vancouver's Downtown (Coal) Peninsula: Urban Geology." B.Sc. thesis, University of British Columbia, 1971.

Bouchier, Nancy B., and Ken Cruikshank. "The War on the Squatters, 1920-1940: Hamilton's Boathouse Community and the Re-Creation of Recreation on Burlington Bay." *Labour/Le Travail* 51 (2003): 9-46.

Bowden, M.J. "The Invention of American Tradition." *Journal of Historical Geography* 18 (1992): 3-26.

Boyd, Robert. *The Coming of the Spirit of Pestilence: Introduced Infectious Diseases and Population Decline among Northwest Coast Indians, 1774-1874.* Vancouver: UBC Press, 1999.

–, ed. *Indians, Fire, and the Land in the Pacific Northwest.* Corvallis: Oregon University Press, 1999.

Brennan, William. "Visions of a City Beautiful: The Origin and Impact of the Mawson Plans for Regina." *Saskatchewan History* 46 (1994): 19-33.

British Columbia. *Proclamations and Ordinances, 1858-1864.* Victoria and New Westminster, 1858-64.

British Columbia Ministry of Tourism, Sport and the Arts, Archaeology Branch. "Stanley Park, Resource Management Report." 2006.

Bunting, Robert. *The Pacific Raincoast: Environment and Culture in an American Eden.* Lawrence: University Press of Kansas, 1997.

Burnham, Philip. *Indian Country, God's Country: Native Americans and the National Parks.* Washington, DC: Island Press, 2000.

Burns, Bob, and Mike Schintz. *Guardians of the Wild: A History of the Warden Service of Canada's National Parks.* Calgary: University of Calgary Press, 2000.

Cail, Robert E. *Land, Many, and the Law: The Disposal of Crown Lands in British Columbia, 1871-1913.* Vancouver: UBC Press, 1974.

Cain, Louis P. "Water and Sanitation Services in Vancouver: An Historical Perspective." *BC Studies* 30 (1976): 27-43.

Campbell, Claire. *Shaped by the West Wind: Nature and History in Georgian Bay.* Vancouver: UBC Press, 2005.

Canada, Secretary of State. *Correspondence and Papers in Reference to Stanley Park and Deadman's Island, British Columbia.* Ottawa: S.E. Dawson, 1899.

Carlson, Keith Thor, ed. *A Stó:lō–Coast Salish Historical Atlas.* Vancouver: Douglas and McIntyre, 2001.

Carr, Ethan. *Wilderness by Design: Landscape Architecture and the National Park Service.* Lincoln: University of Nebraska Press, 1998.

Castonguay, Stéphane. "Naturalizing Federalism: Outbreaks and the Centralization of Entomological Research in Canada, 1884-1914." *Canadian Historical Review* 84, 1 (2004): 1-34.

Catton, Theodore. *Inhabited Wilderness: Indians, Eskimos, and National Parks in Alaska.* Albuquerque: University of New Mexico Press, 1997.

–. *National Park, City Playground: Mount Rainier in the Twentieth Century.* Seattle: University of Washington Press, 2006.

Chadwick, George F. *The Park and the Town: Public Landscape in the 19th and 20th Centuries.* London: London Architectural Press, 1966.

Cioc, Marc, and Char Miller. "Alfred Crosby." *Environmental History* 14, 3 (2009): 559-68.

Clague, John, and Bob Turner. *Vancouver, City on the Edge: Living with a Dynamic Geological Landscape.* Vancouver: Tricouni, 2003.

Coates, Colin M. *The Metamorphoses of Landscape and Community in Early Quebec.* Montreal and Kingston: McGill-Queen's University Press, 2000.

Colpitts, George. *Game in the Garden: A Human History of Wildlife in Western Canada to 1940.* Vancouver: UBC Press, 2002.

Cook, George M. "'Spray, Spray, Spray!' Insecticides and the Making of Applied Ento-
mology in Canada, 1871-1914." *Scientia Canadensis* 22-23, 51 (1998-99): 7-50.
Coupland, Douglas. *Polaroids from the Dead.* Toronto: Harper Collins, 1996.
Cox, John D. *Storm Watchers: The Turbulent History of Weather Prediction from Franklin's
Kite to El Niño.* Hoboken: John Wiley and Sons, 2002.
Cranz, Galen. *The Politics of Park Design: A History of Urban Parks in America.* Cambridge,
MA: MIT Press, 1982.
Cronon, William. *Changes in the Land: Indians, Colonists, and the Ecology of New England.*
New York: Hill and Wang, 1983.
–. *Nature's Metropolis: Chicago and the Great West.* New York: W.W. Norton, 1991.
–, ed. *Uncommon Ground: Rethinking the Human Place in Nature.* New York: W.W. Norton,
1995.
Crosby, Alfred. *The Columbian Exchange: Biological and Cultural Consequences of 1492.*
Westport, CT: Greenwood, 1973.
–. *Ecological Imperialism: The Biological Expansion of Europe, 900-1900.* Cambridge: Cam-
bridge University Press, 1986.
–. *Germs, Seeds and Animals: Studies in Ecological History.* Armonk, NY: M.E. Sharpe, 1994.
–. "The Past and Present of Environmental History." *American Historical Review* 100 (1995):
1177-89.
Cruikshank, Ken, and Nancy B. Bouchier. "Blighted Areas and Obnoxious Industries:
Constructing Environmental Inequality on an Industrial Waterfront, Hamilton,
Ontario, 1890-1960." *Environmental History* 9, 3 (2004): 464-96.
Curtis, Bruce. "The Playground in Nineteenth-Century Ontario: Theory and Practise."
Material History Bulletin 22 (1985): 21-29.
D'Acres, Lilia, and Donald Luxton. *Lions Gate.* Burnaby: Talonbooks, 1999.
Dagenais, Michèle. "Entre tradition et modernité: Espaces et temps de loisirs à Montréal
et Toronto au xxe siècle." *Canadian Historical Review* 82, 2 (2001): 307-30.
Daniels, John D. "The Indian Population of North America in 1492." *William and Mary
Quarterly* 49, 2 (1992): 298-320.
Davis, Mike. *City of Quartz: Excavating the Future in Los Angeles.* New York: Vintage, 1992.
–. *Dead Cities and Other Tales.* New York: New Press, 2002.
–. *Ecology of Fear: Los Angeles and the Imagination of Disaster.* New York: Metropolitan
Books, 1998.
–. *Late Victorian Holocausts: El Niño Famines and the Making of the Third World.* London:
Verso, 2002.
Davis, Mike, Kelly Mayhew, and Jim Miller. *Under the Perfect Sun: The San Diego Tourists
Never See.* New York: New Press, 2005.
Dawson, Michael. *Selling British Columbia: Tourism and Consumer Culture, 1890-1970.*
Vancouver: UBC Press, 2004.
–. "Taking the 'D' out of 'Depression': The Promise of Tourism in British Columbia,
1935-1939." *BC Studies* 132 (2001-02): 31-56.
Decker, Fred W., Owen P. Cramer, and Byron R. Harper. "The Columbus Day 'Big Blow'
in Oregon." *Weatherwise* 15 (December 1962): 238-45.
Deur, Douglas, and Nancy J. Turner, eds. *Keeping It Living: Traditions of Plant Use and
Cultivation on the Northwest Coast of North America.* Vancouver: UBC Press, 2005.
Diamond, Jared. *Guns, Germs, and Steel: The Fates of Human Societies.* New York: W.W.
Norton, 1999.

Dick, Lyle. "Commemorative Integrity and Cultural Landscapes: Two National Historic
    Sites in British Columbia." *Association for Preservation Technology Bulletin* 31, 4 (2000):
    29-36.
Dunlap, Thomas. *Nature and the English Diaspora: Environment and History of the United
    States, Canada, Australia and New Zealand.* Cambridge: Cambridge University Press,
    1999.
Elliot, Robert. *Faking Nature: The Ethics of Environmental Restoration.* London: Routledge,
    1997.
Entomological Branch. "Forest Insect Investigations in British Columbia." *Agricultural
    Gazette of Canada* 1, 9 (1914): 698-99.
Environment Canada. Daily Data Report for October 1962. National Climate Data and
    Information Archive. http://www.climate.weatheroffice.ec.gc.ca/.
Evenden, Matthew. *Fish versus Power: An Environmental History of the Fraser River.* New
    York: Cambridge, 2004.
Fisher, Robin, and Hugh Johnston, eds. *From Maps to Metaphors: The Pacific World of
    George Vancouver.* Vancouver: UBC Press, 1993.
Fladmark, Knut. *A Paleoecological Model for Northwest Coast Prehistory.* National Museum
    of Man Mercury Series, Archaeological Survey of Canada, no. 43. Ottawa: National
    Museum of Man, 1975.
Flores, Dan. "Place: An Argument for Bioregional History." *Environmental History Review*
    18, 4 (1994): 1-18.
Foster, Janet. *Working for Wildlife: The Beginning of Preservation in Canada.* Toronto: Uni-
    versity of Toronto Press, 1998.
Francis, Daniel. *L.D.: Mayor Louis Taylor and the Rise of Vancouver.* Vancouver: Arsenal, 2004.
Gaffield, Chad, and Pam Gaffield. *Consuming Canada: Readings in Environmental History.*
    Toronto: Copp Clark, 1995.
Galois, R.M. "The Indian Rights Association, Native Protest Activity and the 'Land
    Question' in British Columbia, 1903-1916." *Native Studies Review* 8, 2 (1992): 1-34.
Germic, S.A. *American Green Class: Crisis and the Deployment of Nature in Central Park,
    Yosemite, and Yellowstone.* Lanham, MD: Lexington Books, 2001.
Glacken, Clarence. *Traces on the Rhodian Shore: Nature and Culture in Western Thought from
    Ancient Times to the End of the Eighteenth Century.* Berkeley: University of California
    Press, 1967.
Glazenbrook, George P. de T. *A History of Transportation in Canada.* Toronto: Ryerson
    Press, 1938.
Goodfellow, John C. *The Totem Poles in Stanley Park.* Vancouver: Art, Historical, and
    Scientific Association of Vancouver, c. 1920.
Gottleib, Robert. *Forcing the Spring: The Transformation of the American Environmental
    Movement.* Washington, DC: Island Press, 1993.
Graf, W.L., ed. *Geomorphic Systems of North America.* Vol. 2. Boulder, CO: Geological
    Society of America, 1987.
Grant, Paul, and Laurie Dickson. *The Stanley Park Companion.* Winlaw, BC: Bluefield
    Books, 2003.
Gray, Stephen. "The Government Timber Business: Forest Policy and Administration in
    British Columbia, 1912-1928." *BC Studies* 81 (1989): 24-49.
Green, Raymond A. "The Weather and Circulation of October 1962: A Warm Month with
    a Mid-Month Circulation Reversal." *Monthly Weather Review* 91, 1 (January 1963):
    41-46.

Griffiths, Tom, and Libby Robin, eds. *Ecology and Empire: Environmental History of Settler Societies.* Seattle: University of Washington Press, 1997.

Grove, Richard. *Green Imperialism: Colonial Expansion, Tropical Island Edens and the Origins of Environmentalism.* Cambridge: Cambridge University Press, 1995.

Hak, Gordon. *Turning Trees into Dollars: The British Columbia Coastal Lumber Industry, 1858-1913.* Toronto: University of Toronto Press, 2000.

Hall, Marcus. *Earth Repair: A Transatlantic History of Environmental Restoration.* Charlottesville: University of Virginia Press, 2005.

Hardy, Stephen. "Parks for the People: Reforming the Boston Park System, 1870-1915." *Journal of Sport History* 7 (1980): 5-24.

Harley, J. Brian. "Rereading the Maps of the Columbian Encounter." *Annals of the Association of American Geographers* 82, 3 (1992): 522-36.

Harris, Douglas C. *Fish, Law and Colonialism: The Legal Capture of Salmon in British Columbia.* Toronto: University of Toronto Press, 2001.

Harris, R. Cole. *Making Native Space: Colonialism, Resistance, and Reserves in British Columbia.* Vancouver: UBC Press, 2002.

–, ed. *The Resettlement of British Columbia: Essays on Colonialism and Geographical Change.* Vancouver: UBC Press, 1997.

Hayes, Derek. *Historical Atlas of Vancouver and the Lower Fraser Valley.* Vancouver: Douglas and McIntyre, 2005.

Hays, Samuel P. *Beauty, Health, and Permanence: Environmental Politics in the United States, 1955-1985.* Cambridge: Cambridge University Press, 1987.

–. *Conservation and the Gospel of Efficiency: The Progressive Conservation Movement.* Cambridge, MA: Harvard University Press, 1959.

Hazlitt, William Carew. *British Columbia and Vancouver Island; Comprising a Historical Sketch of the British Settlements in the North-West Coast of America.* London: G. Routledge, 1858.

Hebda, Richard J. "British Columbia Vegetation and Climate History with Focus on 6 KA BP." *Géographie Physique et Quaternaire* 49 (1995): 55-79.

Henderson's British Columbia Gazetteer and Directory and Mining Companies for 1899-1900. Vol. 6. Vancouver: Henderson, 1900.

Hermer, Joe. *Regulating Eden: The Nature of Order in North American Parks.* Toronto: University of Toronto Press, 2002.

Heyd, Thomas, ed. *Recognizing the Autonomy of Nature: Theory and Practice.* New York: Columbia University Press, 2005.

Hill-Tout, Charles. *The Salish People: The Local Contribution of Charles Hill-Tout.* Vol. 2, *The Squamish and the Lillooet.* Edited by Ralph Maud. Vancouver: Talonbooks, 1978.

Hood, Robert Allison. *By Shore and Trail in Stanley Park.* Toronto: McClelland and Stewart, 1929.

Hooke, Roger. "On the History of Humans as Geomorphic Agents." *Geology* 28, 9 (2000): 843-46.

Howay, F.W. "Early Settlement on Burrard Inlet." *British Columbia Historical Quarterly* 1, 2 (1937): 101-43.

–. "Early Shipping in Burrard Inlet, 1863-1870." *British Columbia Historical Quarterly* 1, 1 (1937): 3-20.

Jacoby, Karl. *Crimes against Nature: Squatters, Poachers, Thieves, and the Hidden History of American Conservation.* Berkeley: University of California Press, 2001.

Jane, Cecil, trans. *A Spanish Voyage to Vancouver and the Northwest Coast of America Being the Narrative of the Voyage Made in the Year 1792 by the Schooners "Sutil" and "Mexicana" to Explore the Strait of Fuca.* New York: AMS Press, 1971.

Jasen, Patricia. *Wild Things: Nature, Culture, and Tourism in Ontario, 1790-1914.* Toronto: University of Toronto Press, 1995.

Johnson, E. Pauline. *Legends of Vancouver.* 1911. Reprint, Toronto: Douglas and McIntyre, 1997.

Kalman, Harold, and Lorne Whitehead. "Conservation of the Hollow Tree in Vancouver's Stanley Park." *APT Bulletin: Journal of Preservation Technology* 42, 2 (2011): 3-11.

Kammen, Michael. *Mystic Chords of Memory: The Transformation of Tradition in American Culture.* New York: Vintage, 1993.

Katz, Eric, ed. *Nature as Subject: Human Obligation and Natural Community.* Lanham, MD: Rowman and Littlefield, 1997.

Keeling, Arn. "Sink or Swim: Water Pollution and Environmental Politics in Vancouver, 1889-1975." *BC Studies* 142-43 (2004): 69-101.

–. "Urban Waste Sinks as a Natural Resource: The Case of the Fraser River." *Urban History Review* 34, 1 (2005): 58-70.

Keller, Robert H., and Michael F. Turek. *American Indians and National Parks.* Tucson: University of Arizona Press, 1998.

Kelman, Ari. *A River and Its City: The Nature of Landscape in New Orleans.* Berkeley: University of California Press, 2003.

Kheraj, Sean. "Demonstration Wildlife: Negotiating the Animal Landscape of Vancouver's Stanley Park, 1888-1996." *Environment and History* 18, 4 (2012): 1-31.

–. "Improving Nature: Remaking Stanley Park's Forest, 1888-1931." *BC Studies* 158 (2008): 63-90.

–. "Restoring Nature: Ecology, Memory, and the Storm History of Vancouver's Stanley Park." *Canadian Historical Review* 88, 4 (2007): 577-612.

Killan, Gerald. *Protected Places: A History of Ontario's Provincial Park System.* Toronto: Dundurn Press, 1993.

Kimmins, Hamish. *Balancing Act: Environmental Issues in Forestry.* 2nd ed. Vancouver: UBC Press, 1992.

Krajina, V.J. "Biogeoclimatic Zones and Classification of British Columbia." *Ecology of Western North America* 1 (1965): 1-17.

Krech, Shepard. *The Ecological Indian: Myth and History.* New York: W.W. Norton, 1999.

Lears, T.J. Jackson. *No Place of Grace: Antimodernism and the Transformation of American Culture, 1880-1920.* New York: Pantheon, 1981.

Leier, Mark. *Red Flags and Red Tape: The Making of a Labour Bureaucracy.* Toronto: University of Toronto Press, 1995.

Lions Gate Bridge, Vancouver, Canada. Vancouver: Vancouver Sun, 1939.

Loo, Tina. "Making Modern Wilderness: Conserving Wildlife in Twentieth-Century Canada." *Canadian Historical Review* 82, 1 (2001): 91-120.

–. "Of Moose and Men: Hunting for Masculinities in British Columbia." *Western Historical Quarterly* 32, 3 (2001): 296-319.

–. *States of Nature: Conserving Canada's Wildlife in the Twentieth Century.* Vancouver: UBC Press, 2006.

Lord, John Keast. *The Naturalist in Vancouver Island and British Columbia.* Vol. 2. London: R. Bentley, 1866.

Louter, David. *Windshield Wilderness: Cars, Roads, and Nature in Washington's National Parks.* Seattle: University of Washington Press, 2006.

Lynott, Robert E., and Owen P. Cramer. "Detailed Analysis of the 1962 Columbus Day Windstorm in Oregon and Washington." *Monthly Weather Review* 94, 2 (1966): 105-17.

Macdonald, Bruce. *Vancouver: A Visual History.* Vancouver: Talonbooks, 1992.

MacDonald, Norbert. *Distant Neighbours: A Comparative History of Seattle and Vancouver.* Lincoln: University of Nebraska Press, 1987.

MacEachern, Alan. "In Search of Eastern Beauty: Creating National Parks in Atlantic Canada, 1935-1970." PhD diss., Queen's University, 1997.

–. *Natural Selections: National Parks in Atlantic Canada, 1935-1970.* Montreal and Kingston: McGill-Queen's University Press, 2001.

Macfie, Matthew. *Vancouver Island and British Columbia: Their History, Resources, and Prospects.* London: Longman, Roberts and Green, 1865.

MacLaren, I.S. "Cultured Wilderness in Jasper National Park." *Journal of Canadian Studies* 34, 3 (1999): 7-58.

MacLennan, Catherine Mae. *Rambling round Stanley Park.* Vancouver: Roy Wrigley, 1935.

Mason, Kathy S. *Natural Museums: U.S. National Parks, 1872-1916.* East Lansing: Michigan State University Press, 2004.

Mather, Susan. "One of Many Homes: Stories of Dispossession from 'Stanley Park.'" Master's thesis, Simon Fraser University, 1998.

Matson, R.G. *The Glenrose Cannery Site.* National Museum of Man Mercury Series, Archaeological Survey of Canada, no. 52 Ottawa: National Museums of Canada, 1976.

Matson, R.G., and G. Coupland. *The Prehistory of the Northwest Coast.* San Diego: Academic Press, 1995.

Matson, R.G., Gary Coupland, and Quentin Mackie, eds. *Emerging from the Mist: Studies in Northwest Coast Culture History.* Vancouver: UBC Press, 2003.

Matthewes, R.W. "A Palynological Study of Postglacial Vegetation Changes in the University Research Forest, Southwestern British Columbia." *Canadian Journal of Botany* 51 (1973): 2085-103.

Matthewes, R.W., and G.E. Rouse. "Palynology and Paleoecology of Postglacial Sediments from the Lower Fraser River Canyon of British Columbia." *Canadian Journal of Earth Science* 12 (1975): 745-56.

Matthews, J.S. *Conversations with Khatsalano, 1932-1954.* Vancouver: City Archives, 1955.

–. *Early Vancouver: Narratives of Pioneers of Vancouver.* Vol. 1. 1932. Reprint, Vancouver: City of Vancouver Archives, 2011.

–. *Early Vancouver: Narratives of Pioneers of Vancouver.* Vol. 2. 1933. Reprint, Vancouver: City of Vancouver Archives, 2011.

–. *Early Vancouver: Narratives of Pioneers of Vancouver.* Vol. 3. 1935. Reprint, Vancouver: City of Vancouver Archives, 2011.

–. *Early Vancouver: Narratives of Pioneers of Vancouver.* Vol. 4. 1944. Reprint, Vancouver: City of Vancouver Archives, 2011.

–. *Early Vancouver: Narratives of Pioneers of Vancouver.* Vol. 5. 1945. Reprint, Vancouver: City of Vancouver Archives, 2011.

–. *Early Vancouver: Narratives of Pioneers of Vancouver.* Vol. 7. 1956. Reprint, Vancouver: City of Vancouver Archives, 2011.

Mawani, Renisa. "Genealogies of the Land: Aboriginality, Law, and Territory in Vancouver's Stanley Park." *Social and Legal Studies* 14, 3 (2005): 315-39.

–. "Imperial Legacies (Post) Colonial Identities: Law, Space and the Making of Stanley Park, 1859-2001." *Law Text Culture* 7 (2003): 98-141.

Mawson, Thomas H. *Civic Art: Studies in Town Planning, Parks, Boulevards and Open Spaces.* London: B.T. Batsford, 1911.

–. *The Life and Work of an English Landscape Architect: An Autobiography by Thomas H. Mawson.* New York: Charles Scribner's Sons, 1927.

McClelland, Linda Flint. *Building the National Parks: Historic Landscape Design and Construction.* Baltimore: Johns Hopkins University Press, 1998.

McDonald, Robert A.J. "'Holy Retreat' or 'Practical Breathing Spot'? Class Perceptions of Vancouver's Stanley Park, 1910-1913." *Canadian Historical Review* 45, 2 (1984): 127-53.

–. "Lumber Society on the Industrial Frontier: Burrard Inlet, 1863-1886." *Labour/Le Travail* 33 (1994): 69-96.

–. *Making Vancouver: Class, Status and Social Boundaries, 1863-1913.* Vancouver: UBC Press, 1996.

McKee, W.C. "The History of the Vancouver Park System, 1886-1929." Master's thesis, University of Victoria, 1976.

McKelvie, B.A. *Legends of Stanley Park: Vancouver's Magnificent Playground.* N.p., 1941.

McLeod, Anne Burnaby, and Pixie McGeachie, eds. *Land of Promise: Robert Burnaby's Letters from Colonial British Columbia, 1858-1863.* Burnaby: City of Burnaby, 2002.

McNeill, J.R. "Observations on the Nature and Culture of Environmental History." *History and Theory* 42, 4 (2003): 5-43.

–. *Something New under the Sun: An Environmental History of the Twentieth-Century World.* New York: Norton, 2000.

McShane, Clay. *Down the Asphalt Path: The Automobile and the American City.* New York: Columbia University Press, 1994.

–. "Transforming the Use of Urban Space: A Look at the Revolution in Street Pavements, 1880-1924." *Journal of Urban History* 5, 3 (1979): 279-307.

McShane, Clay, and Joel Tarr. "The Decline of the Urban Horse." *Journal of Transport History* 24 (2003): 177-99.

Melosi, Martin V. *Effluent America: Cities, Industry, Energy, and the Environment.* Pittsburgh: University of Pittsburgh Press, 2001.

–. *Garbage in the Cities: Refuse, Reform, and the Environment, 1880-1980.* College Station: Texas A&M University Press, 1981.

–. *The Sanitary City: Urban Infrastructure in America from Colonial Times to the Present.* Baltimore: Johns Hopkins University Press, 2000.

Melville, Elinor. *A Plague of Sheep: Environmental Consequences of the Conquest of Mexico.* Cambridge: Cambridge University Press, 1994.

Menzies, Archibald. *Menzies' Journal of Vancouver's Voyage, April to October 1792.* Victoria: W.H. Cullin, 1923.

Merchant, Carolyn. *Reinventing Eden: The Fate of Nature in Western Culture.* New York: Routledge, 2003.

–. "The Theoretical Structure of Ecological Revolutions." *Environmental Review* 11, 4 (1987): 265-74.

Metcalfe, Alan. "The Evolution of Organized Physical Recreation in Montreal, 1840-1895." *Histoire sociale/Social History* 11, 21 (1978): 144-66.

Montes, G.E. "San Diego's City Park, 1868-1902: An Early Debate on Environment and Profit." *Journal of San Diego History* 23 (1977): 40-59.

Monteyne, David. "'From Canvas to Concrete in Fifty Years': The Construction of Vancouver City Hall, 1935-6." *BC Studies* 124 (1999-2000): 41-68.

Moogk, Peter N., assisted by R.V. Stevenson. *Vancouver Defended: A History of the Men and Guns of the Lower Mainland Defences, 1859-1949.* Surrey, BC: Antonson, 1978.

Morton, James. *The Enterprising Mr. Moody, the Bumptious Captain Stamp: The Lives and Colourful Times of Vancouver's Lumber Pioneers.* North Vancouver: J.J. Douglas, 1977.

Murray, A.L. "Frederick Law Olmsted and the Design of Mount Royal Park." *Journal of the Society of Architectural Historians* 26 (1967): 163-71.

Namias, Jerome. "Large-Scale Air-Sea Interactions over the North Pacific from Summer 1962 through the Subsequent Winter." *Journal of Geophysical Research* 68, 22 (1963): 6171-86.

Nash, Roderick. "The State of Environmental History." In *The State of Environmental History,* ed. Herbert J. Bass, 249-60. Chicago: Quadrangle Books, 1970.

–. *Wilderness and the American Mind.* 4th ed. New Haven: Yale University Press, 2001.

Nelles, H.V. "How Did Calgary Get Its River Parks?" *Urban History Review* 34, 1 (2005): 28-45.

–. *The Politics of Development: Forests, Mines and Hydro-Electric Power in Ontario, 1849-1941.* Toronto: Macmillan of Canada, 1974.

Nelson, J.G., and R.C. Scace, eds. *The Canadian National Parks Today and Tomorrow.* Calgary: National and Provincial Parks Association of Canada and the University of Calgary, 1969.

Newell, Dianne. *Tangled Webs of History: Indians and the Law in Canada's Pacific Coast Fisheries.* Toronto: University of Toronto Press, 1993.

Oelschlaeger, Max. *The Idea of Wilderness, from Prehistory to the Age of Ecology.* New Haven: Yale University Press, 1991.

Olmsted, Frederick Law. *Public Parks and the Enlargement of Towns.* 1870. Reprint, New York: Arno Press, 1970.

Ormsby, Margaret A. *British Columbia: A History.* 1958. Reprint, Toronto: Macmillan of Canada, 1976.

Owram, Doug. *Promise of Eden: The Canadian Expansionist Movement and the Idea of the West, 1856-1900.* Toronto: University of Toronto Press, 1980.

Parkinson, Alison, ed. *Wilderness on the Doorstep: Discovering Nature in Stanley Park.* Surrey, BC: Harbour, 2006.

Partnow, Patricia H. "Ursine Urges and Urban Ungulates: Anchorage Asserts Its Alaskaness." *Western Folklore* 58, 1 (1999): 33-56.

Pyne, Stephen J. *Fire in America: A Cultural History of Wildland and Rural Fire.* Princeton: Princeton University Press, 1982.

Pyne, Stephen J., Patricia L. Andrews, and Richard D. Laven. *Introduction to Wildland Fire.* 2nd ed. New York: Wiley and Sons, 1996.

Rajala, Richard A. *Clearcutting the Pacific Rain Forest: Production, Science, and Regulation.* Vancouver: UBC Press, 1988.

–. *Feds, Forests, and Fire: A Century of Canadian Forestry Innovation.* Ottawa: Canada Science and Technology Museum, 2005.

Raley, George H. *Our Totem Poles: A Souvenir of Vancouver.* Vancouver, 1937.

Reice, Seth R. *The Silver Lining: The Benefits of Natural Disasters.* Princeton: Princeton University Press, 2001.

Reichwein, Pearlann. "'Hands Off Our National Parks': The Alpine Club of Canada and Hydro-Development Controversies in the Canadian Rockies, 1922-1930." *Journal of the Canadian Historical Association* 6 (1995): 129-55.

Rickard, T.A. "Gilbert Malcolm Sproat." *British Columbia Historical Quarterly* 1, 1 (1937): 21-32.

Robertson, Angus Everett. "The Pursuit of Power, Profit and Privacy: Study of Vancouver's West End Elite, 1886-1914." Master's thesis, University of British Columbia, 1977.

Roddan, Andrew. *Vancouver's Hoboes*. Vancouver: Subway Books, 2005.

Roddick, J.A. Capsule Geology of the Vancouver Area and Teacher's Field-Trip Guide. Vancouver: Geological Survey of Canada, 2001.

Rogers, G.C. "An Assessment of the Megathrust Earthquake Potential of the Cascadia Subduction Zone." *Canadian Journal of Earth Sciences* 25 (1988): 844-52.

Roper, Laura Wood. *FLO: A Biography of Frederick Law Olmsted*. Baltimore: Johns Hopkins University Press, 1973.

Rosenzweig, Roy. "Middle-Class Parks and Working-Class Play: The Struggle over Recreational Space in Worcester, Massachusetts, 1870-1910." *Radical History Review* 21 (1979): 31-46.

Rosenzweig, Roy, and Elizabeth Blackmar. *The Park and the People: A History of Central Park*. Ithaca: Cornell University Press, 1992.

Rothman, Hal. *Neon Metropolis: How Las Vegas Started the Twenty-First Century.* New York: Routledge, 2003.

–. *The New Urban Park: Golden Gate National Recreation Area and Civic Environmentalism.* Lawrence: University of Kansas Press, 2004.

Roy, Susan. *These Mysterious People: Shaping History and Archaeology in a Northwest Coast Community.* Montreal and Kingston: McGill-Queen's University Press, 2010.

Runte, Alfred. *National Parks: The American Experience.* 3rd ed. Lincoln: University of Nebraska Press, 1997.

–. *Yosemite: The Embattled Wilderness.* Lincoln: University of Nebraska Press, 1990.

Russell, Edmund. "Evolutionary History: Prospectus for a New Field." *Environmental History* 8, 2 (2003): 204-28.

Sandlos, John. "Federal Spaces, Local Conflicts: National Parks and the Exclusionary Politics of the Conservation Movement in Ontario, 1900-1935." *Journal of the Canadian Historical Association* 16 (2005): 293-318.

–. "From the Outside Looking In: Aesthetics, Politics, and Wildlife Conservation in the Canadian North." *Environmental History* 6, 1 (2001): 6-31.

–. *Hunters at the Margin: Native People and Wildlife Conservation in the Northwest Territories.* Vancouver: UBC Press, 2007.

–. "Northern Wildlife, Northern People: Native Hunters and Wildlife Conservation in the Northwest Territories, 1894-1970." PhD diss., York University, 2004.

Schama, Simon. *Landscape and Memory.* New York: Alfred A. Knopf, 1995.

Schatzki, Theodore. "Nature and Technology in History." *History and Theory* 42, 4 (2003): 82-93.

Schmidt, Andrew J. "Pleasure and Recreation for the People: Planning St. Paul's Como Park." *Minnesota History* 58, 1 (2002): 40-58.

Schrodt, Barbara. "Control of Sports Facilities in Early Vancouver: The Brockton Point Athletic Association at Stanley Park, 1880 to 1913." *Canadian Journal of History of Sport* 23, 2 (1992): 26-53.

Schuyler, David. *The New Urban Landscape: The Redefinition of City Form in Nineteenth-Century America*. Baltimore: Johns Hopkins Press, 1986.

Sellars, Richard West. *Preserving Nature in the National Parks: A History*. New Haven: Yale University Press, 1997.

Selwood, John, John C. Lehr, and Mary Cavett. "'The Most Lovely and Picturesque City in All of Canada': The Origins of Winnipeg's Public Park System." *Manitoba History* 31 (1996): 21-29.

Smith, Adam. *An Inquiry into the Nature and Causes of the Wealth of Nations*. 1776. Reprint, London: W. Pickering, 1995.

Spence, Mark David. *Dispossessing the Wilderness: Indian Removal and the Making of the National Parks*. Oxford: Oxford University Press, 1999.

Spirn, Anne Whiston. *The Granite Garden: Urban Nature and Human Design*. New York: Basic Books, 1984.

Sproat, Gilbert Malcolm. *British Columbia; Information for Emigrants*. London: W. Clowes, 1873.

–. *Scenes and Studies of Savage Life*. London: Smith, Elder, 1868.

Spry, Irene. "The Great Transformation: The Disappearance of the Commons in Western Canada." In *Man and Nature on the Prairies*. Canadian Plains Studies 6, ed. Richard Allen, 21-45. Regina: Canadian Plains Research Center, 1976.

Steele, Mike. *Stanley Park: The Year-Round Playground*. Surrey, BC: Heritage House, 1993.

Steele, Richard M. *The Stanley Park Explorer*. North Vancouver: Whitecap Books, 1985.

Steely, James Wright. *Parks for Texas: Enduring Landscapes of the New Deal*. Austin: University of Texas Press, 1999.

Steinberg, Ted. *Acts of God: The Unnatural History of Natural Disaster in America*. New York: Oxford University Press, 2000.

–. *Down to Earth: Nature's Role in American History*. New York: Oxford University Press, 2002.

Styrd, Arnold H., and Vicki Feddemma. *Sacred Cedar: The Cultural and Archaeological Significance of Culturally Modified Trees: A Report of the Pacific Salmon Forests Project*. Vancouver: David Suzuki Foundation, 1998.

Sutter, Paul S. *Driven Wild: How the Fight against Automobiles Launched the Modern Wilderness Movement*. Seattle: University of Washington Press, 2002.

Szczygiel, Bonj. "'City Beautiful' Revisited: An Analysis of Nineteenth-Century Civic Improvement Efforts." *Journal of Urban History* 29, 2 (2003): 107-32.

Tarr, Joel A. *The Search for the Ultimate Sink: Urban Pollution in Historical Perspective*. Akron, OH: University of Akron Press, 1996.

Taylor, Joseph E. *Making Salmon: An Environmental History of the Northwest Fisheries Crisis*. Seattle: University of Washington Press, 1999.

Tennant, Paul. "Vancouver Civic Politics, 1929-1980." *BC Studies* 46 (1980): 3-27.

Thomas, Morley. *The Beginnings of Canadian Meteorology*. Toronto: ECW Press, 1991.

–. *Forecasts for Flying: Meteorology in Canada, 1918-1939*. Toronto: ECW Press, 1996.

–. *Metmen in Wartime: Meteorology in Canada, 1939-1945*. Toronto: ECW Press, 2001.

Turner, R.J.W., J. Page, M. Klassen, H. Quo Vadis, and A. Jensen. *Vancouver Rocks*. Geological Survey of Canada, Miscellaneous Report no. 68. N.p.: Geological Survey of Canada, 2000.

US Fleet Weather Central/Joint Typhoon Warning Center. *Annual Typhoon Report, 1962*. San Francisco, 1962. http://www.usno.navy.mil/NOOC/nmfc-ph/RSS/jtwc/atcr/1962atcr.pdf.

Van Nus, Walter. "The Fate of City Beautiful Thought in Canada, 1893-1930." *Canadian Historical Association, Historical Papers* 54 (1975): 191-210.

Vancouver, George. *A Voyage of Discovery to the North Pacific Ocean and round the World, 1791-1795.* Vol. 2. Edited by W. Kaye Lamb. London: Hakluyt Society, 1984.

Waiser, Bill. *Park Prisoners: The Untold Story of Western Canada's National Parks, 1915-1946.* Calgary: Fifth House, 1995.

Walker, Richard. *Country in the City: The Greening of the San Francisco Bay Area.* Seattle: University of Washington Press, 2009.

Warecki, George M. *Protecting Ontario's Wilderness: A History of Changing Ideas and Preservation Politics, 1927-1973.* New York: Peter Lang, 2000.

Warren, Louis S. *The Hunter's Game: Poachers and Conservationists in Twentieth-Century America.* New Haven: Yale University Press, 1997.

White, Richard. *The Organic Machine: The Remaking of the Columbia River.* New York: Hill and Wang, 1995.

Whorton, James C. "Insecticide Spray Residues and Public Health, 1865-1938." *Bulletin of the History of Medicine* 45, 3 (1971): 219-41.

Williams, Michael. *Americans and Their Forests: A Historical Geography.* New York: Cambridge University Press, 1989.

Wilson, William H. *The City Beautiful Movement.* Baltimore: Johns Hopkins University Press, 1989.

–. "Reginald H. Thomson: Planning for Strathcona Park, 1912-1915." *Planning Perspectives* 17 (2002): 373-87.

Woodcock, George. "Savage and Domestic: The Parks of Vancouver." *Journal of Garden History* 3, 3 (1983): 26-53.

Worster, Donald. *Dust Bowl: The Southern Plains in the 1930s.* New York: Oxford University Press, 1979.

–, ed. *The Ends of the Earth: Perspectives on Modern Environmental History.* Cambridge: Cambridge University Press, 1988.

–. *Nature's Economy: A History of Ecological Ideas.* Cambridge: Cambridge University Press, 1994.

–. *Rivers of Empire: Water, Aridity, and the Growth of the American West.* New York: Pantheon Books, 1985.

–. *The Wealth of Nature: Environmental History and Ecological Imagination.* New York: Oxford University Press, 1993.

Wynn, Graeme, and Timothy Oke, eds. *Vancouver and Its Region.* Vancouver: UBC Press, 1992.

Young, Terence. *Building San Francisco's Parks, 1850-1930.* Baltimore: Johns Hopkins University Press, 2004.

Zaitzevsky, Cynthia. *Frederick Law Olmsted and the Boston Park System.* Cambridge: Belknap Press, 1982.

Index

Note: "(f)" after a page number indicates a figure; "(m)" after a page number indicates a map.

Jamie Linton, *What Is Water? The History of a Modern Abstraction*

Dean Bavington, *Managed Annihilation: An Unnatural History of the Newfoundland Cod Collapse*

Shannon Stunden Bower, *Wet Prairie: People, Land, and Water in Agricultural Manitoba*

J. Keri Cronin, *Manufacturing National Park Nature: Photography, Ecology, and the Wilderness Industry of Jasper*

Jocelyn Thorpe, *Temagami's Tangled Wild: Race, Gender, and the Making of Canadian Nature*

Darcy Ingram, *Wildlife, Conservation, and Conflict in Quebec, 1840-1914*

Caroline Desbiens, *Power from the North: Territory, Identity, and the Culture of Hydroelectricity in Quebec*

Printed and bound in Canada by Friesens
Set in Goudy Sans and Garamond by Artegraphica Design Co. Ltd.
Copy editor: Deborah Kerr
Proofreader: Shirarose Wilensky
Cartographer: Eric Leinberger
Indexer: Cheryl Lemmens